# Understanding Indian Place Names In Southern New England

Frank Waabu O'Brien, Ph.D.

Library of Congress Cataloging-in-Publication Data

O'Brien, Francis Joseph, Jr. (Frank Waabu O'Brien)
Understanding Indian Place Names In Southern New England
     p. cm.
     Includes bibliographical references.
     1. Eastern Algonquian Indian Languages. 2. American Indian
     Place Names, southern
     New England—etymology
     I. The Massachusett-Narragansett Language Revival Project.

ISBN 13: 978-0-9820467-6-0

Bäuu Press
PO Box 4445
Boulder, Colorado

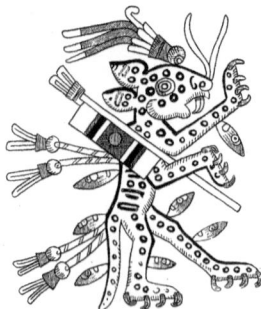

Printed in the United States of America
All Rights Reserved

# To the memory of

⚔

## *Peeyaûtam*

Algonquian Couple, *They Are Sitting At Meate,* 1500-1599, Theodor de Bry
This Algonquian couple sits together on a mat, sharing food from a bowl, much as a native man and woman might have done in sanctifying their marriage, according to the account written by Samson Occom.

Front Cover:  Colonial Map of the State of Rhode Island and Providence Plantations.  In Rider, S. S. (1904).  The Lands of Rhode Island and Massachusetts as They were known to Counounicus and Miantunnomu When Roger Williams Came in 1636.  Providence, RI: S. S. Rider.  Courtesy of the Rhode Island Historical Society.

# Understanding Indian Place Names in Southern New England

‡

Massachusett-Narragansett Revival Program
A project for the reconstruction of the extinct American Indian
Languages of
Southeastern New England

---

Dr. Frank Waabu O'Brien
Aquidneck Indian Council

## WUNNOHTEAONK

☼

## MAY PEACE BE IN YOUR HEARTS

This project was funded [in part] by the National Historical Publications and Records Commission (National Archives and Records Administration), The Rhode Island Council [Committee] for the Humanities/National Endowment for the Humanities, The Rhode Island Foundation, The Rhode Island Indian Council, and the Aquidneck Indian Council.

# TABLE OF CONTENTS

# LIST OF ILLUSTRATIONS

# FOREWORD

The author is an autodidact in some fields including those subjects traditionally taught in secondary public schools in the United States. Since early 1990s I have added to my list Algonquian Studies (southern New England). I am trained formally in philosophy, social science, and applied mathematics. My Ph.D. dissertation at Columbia was on the language of Black Americans.

As a Native American educator, I bring a different perspective to American Indian toponymy in lower New England. Toponymy is the scientific study of place names, their origins, meanings, use, etc. It is the topic of this book. It is a difficult area of research for Indian names of southern New England. Not much progress has been made since the 19th century in the interpretation of the numerous Indian names that populate our States, maps, cities and towns, institutions, waterways, thoroughfares, and so much more.

The most frequently consulted secondary source reference for Indian toponyms in New England is the book, *Indian Place Names of New England*, 1962, Prof. John H. Huden. A few professional linguists criticize this work. In particular, they question the reliability and validity of some of Prof. Hudens' Algonquian translations. I suspect this is due in part to the inherent nature of the task—extracting "signal" from a sea of linguistic "noise" (i.e., interfering or corrupting factors that mask or disguise a true reading of meaning—the signal). Since few other toponymic linguists put forth alternative interpretations, it seems reasonable to conclude that local Indian place name analysis is partly a voyage through turbulent chaos. Alas, some fields of inquiry do not readily admit of tidy, clean "closed-form" solutions! Serious efforts are required to filter the noise and recover the signal structure of these aboriginal tongues so poorly documented in the written records.

The modern-day Algonquian linguist desires Indian place name translations that can be justified by appeal to the theoretical framework of Proto-Algonquian analysis (the interpretation of "Connecticut" is an oft-quoted example). Ideally, the source of the name to analyze should be a 17th century full-blooded fluent Algonquian speaker, and the translator/recorder should be highly proficient like Rev. John Eliot, who provided the first Bible translation in America. But rarely is this information available. Hence, the Babel, which leaves many frustrated and unhappy.

Since I published the first edition (2003) of my research on American Indian place names in Rhode Island on the Internet, over 80,000 "hits" have been registered on the Rhode Island genealogy website. This indicates a high degree of interest in the footprints that the ancient peoples have left in this region.

7

It is with the hope of adding some useful information in this field that I have agreed to disseminate this decade-long work through the Bäuu Institute Press in Colorado. I thank Dr. Peter N. Jones, Editor, for his continued support.

In this volume we attempt to provide a methodology for interpreting regional American Indian place names that challenge translation. The audience is the layperson and scholar interested in our shared experience of early American civilization. The book will also appeal to those who like word puzzles and decoding verbal material, especially for things they see on a daily basis.

*Understanding Indian Place Names in Southern New England* consists of two major chapters. First, an updated summary is presented of the database of Indian place names in Rhode Island. This is supplemented by the Dictionary which provides a glossary of the most common vocabulary words and phrases that make up place name terminology, and a longer listing of the corrupted spellings of those elements seen in the modern names on maps &c throughout southern New England.

Related books by the author (Moondancer or O'Brien) are listed in the References section. Those works pertain to the history, language and culture of American Indians in southern New England. In particular we recommend the comprehensive book, *A Cultural History of the Native Peoples of Southern New England* (Moondancer & Strong Woman), Bäuu Press, 2007.


Frank Waabu O'Brien
Newport, Rhode Island
2010

They want to dry the tears that drowned the sun

They want laughter to return to their hearts

They want to go home -- to Mother and Grandmother

They want to hear their ancestral voices 'round the fire

...[T]he Indian aimed at extreme precision. His words were so constructed as to be thoroughly self-defining and immediately intelligible to the hearer.

...J. H. Trumbull, "On the Best Method of Studying the North American Languages," 1869-1870, p. 78.

# Introduction

## American Indian Place Names in Rhode Island: Past and Present

The revised and updated database of American Indian Place Names in Rhode Island is a continuation of the Massachusett-Narragansett Language Revival Program. This ongoing research effort is coordinated under the aegis of the Aquidneck Indian Council in Newport, RI, and documented in the publications held by the U.S. Library of Congress.

The first chapter of this volume details the Native American historical contributions to the landscape of the State of Rhode Island and Providence Plantations. The Federal Government, under the agency of the Geographic Names Information System (GNIS) is responsible by law for standardizing all geographic name usage for the United States Government. This complex system currently possesses about 5,665 names of "features" wholly or partially in Rhode Island. Of this population, the author counted about 187 names that are, or believed to be, of American Indian origin (primarily the Narragansett language, with contributions from Wampanoag, the Niantic dialect and Nipmuck).

Extending a records search back to Colonial times (circa 1636) offered the possibility of cataloguing an historical database. Approximately 534 names of Indian origin were traceable back to the now extinct languages, synthesized from various and sundry sources (listed in the Sources & References). This number is a better estimate of the Native American contributions to the historical and geographical landscape of Rhode Island[1]. When variant spellings are accounted for in the records, about 1,600 individual entries are documented.

The structure of the place-names listing is straightforward. The text is presented in tabular format, consisting of three columns with headers Names, Historical and Geographical Information, and Translation. On the left side is given the Native American place name; each variant spelling is included separately with a reference back to a primary entry which contains information in each column. The middle column is important. Approximately 400 of the entries in this column were abstracted from Dr. Usher Parson's 1861 book, since this source provides more elaborate data that any other single source. But it must be remembered that, while Parsons is cited nearly verbatim, his historical reference point is up to only the year 1861, and some information listed may not apply to the year 2003 and beyond. It was included because of its historical significance to the place name literature. Moreover, Parson's linguistic data

---

[1] Based on these data, it is significant to note that only 1/3 of the Indian place names in our recorded State history have survived to the present day in official government data bases. It seems that 2/3 have failed the test of time, and the dynamic forces of historical and political evolution.

must be discounted almost entirely since Algonquian linguistics was not a mature science in his day. The right hand column provides linguistic translation(s) for a given place name. I have drawn heavily from the standard comprehensive work of Prof. Huden, with a modest contribution by the author.

The degree of orthographic corruption in some place names offers a real challenge to the linguist. Alternative translations for some names may seem peculiar, but the name "noise" sometimes permits only an approximation to the true language roots and the translation. This issue is described in more detail below.

Map 1 shows the general region of discussion. The American Indian tribes of southern New England spoke similar[1] languages/dialects comprising a uniform subset of the Eastern Algonquian Language Family (Goddard, 1978). These oral languages were highly structured, complicated and only imperfectly recorded before they passed into Silence[2]. Map 2 focuses on the Wampanoag (Pokanoket) region of Narragansett and Mount Hope Bays with some Indian place names interpreted. The Rhode Island map on the front cover is too big to reproduce legibly on one page. When viewed on the Internet each map can be magnified for enhanced readability.

*Understanding Indian Place Names in Southern New England* is an extension of the contributions of Dr. James Hammond Trumbull (1881/1974) and Prof. John C. Huden (1962). Huden (pp. 300 ff.) provided a 68-page alphabetical glossary (by English) of Algonquian "roots" to aid in the interpretation of corrupted or arbitrary spellings (phonemes) seen in New England place names. Trumbull, the 19th century Algonquian philologist *par excellence*, previously published a similar compact listing (by Algonquian) for common language terms classified as "land names," "water names," and "adjectivals" for the Indian place names in Connecticut and parts of Rhode Island that he studied.

Such interpretive guides allow one to decipher or follow translations of some corrupted regional Indian place names by fuzzy linguistic decomposition (etymological analysis). Moreover, one is able to detect certain patterns in the misheard sounds of the Indian names which vary by dialect (see END NOTE, below). For example, the consonant sounds *m* or *p* were typically missed if they preceded a sibilant or mute sound like *sh*—thus *Mashapaug* becomes corrupted to the modern spelling "Shepaug". Likewise the initial letter n was often misheard (i.e., dropped) as in "Ashaway" for *Nashaue*. Thus, dropped initial consonants or syllables is one phenomenon to attend to carefully in place name analysis. Other such systematic errors are replete in southern language.

---

1        The differences between "similar" languages—especially far removed in distance—prompts a neologism, "simerent" (<u>sim</u>ilar + diff<u>erent</u>) languages.

2        The Guinness Book of World Records lists an Algonquian language, Ojibwe, as the most complicated language world-wide to learn.

# Map 1.
## Ancient Tribal Territories In Southern New England

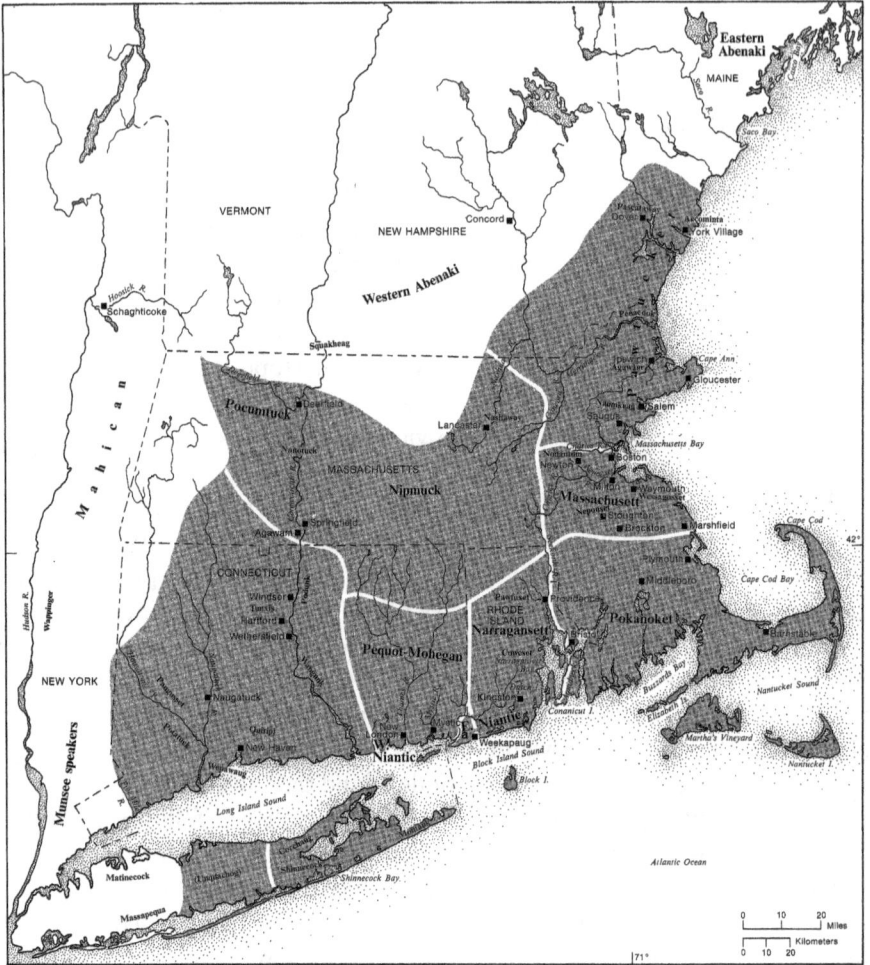

      The broad white lines in the grey region show tribal territories (ancestral homelands). A black square indicates a modern non Indian town. A large bold-type name refers to an Indian Nation (e.g., **Massachusett**), the smaller bold-type names indicate tribal subdivisions (e.g., **Neponset**), and present day State boundaries are indicated by dashed lines. State names are capitalized (e.g., MASSACHUSETTS), and geographical features are italicized (e.g., *Atlantic Ocean*). Source: Bruce G. Trigger (Volume Editor), Handbook of North American Indians, vol. 15 (Northeast), 1978. Washington, DC: The Smithsonian Institution (Page 160). Used with permission. NOTE: "Wampanoag" is modern term for historic "Pokanoket".

12

# Map 2.
## Map of Indian Localities about Narragansett and Mount Hope Bays.

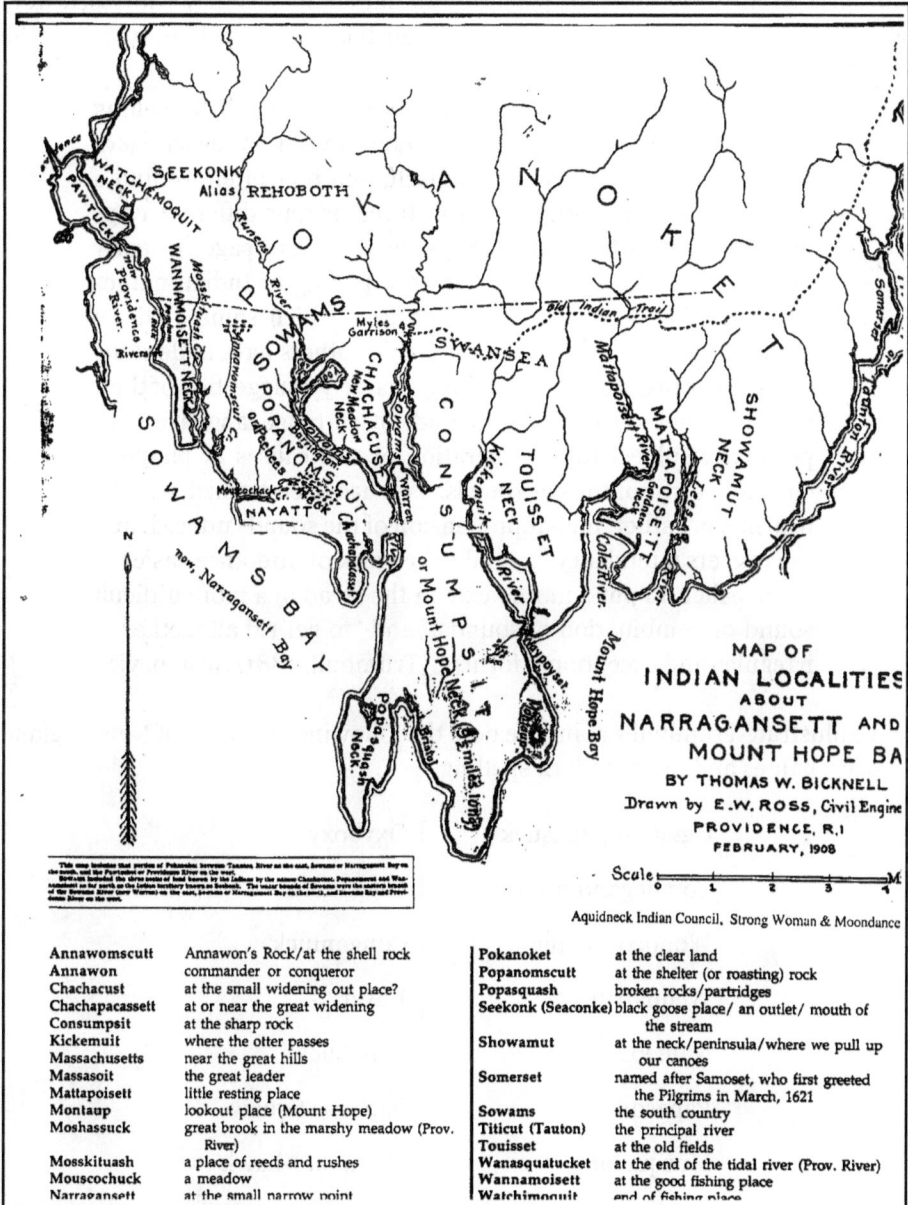

MAP OF
### INDIAN LOCALITIES
ABOUT
### NARRAGANSETT AND
### MOUNT HOPE BA
BY THOMAS W. BICKNELL
Drawn by E.W. ROSS, Civil Engine
PROVIDENCE, R.I
FEBRUARY, 1908

Aquidneck Indian Council, Strong Woman & Moondance

| | | | |
|---|---|---|---|
| Annawomscutt | Annawon's Rock/at the shell rock | Pokanoket | at the clear land |
| Annawon | commander or conqueror | Popanomscutt | at the shelter (or roasting) rock |
| Chachacust | at the small widening out place? | Popasquash | broken rocks/partridges |
| Chachapacassett | at or near the great widening | Seekonk (Seaconke) | black goose place/ an outlet/ mouth of the stream |
| Consumpsit | at the sharp rock | | |
| Kickemuit | where the otter passes | Showamut | at the neck/peninsula/where we pull up our canoes |
| Massachusetts | near the great hills | | |
| Massasoit | the great leader | Somerset | named after Samoset, who first greeted the Pilgrims in March, 1621 |
| Mattapoisett | little resting place | | |
| Montaup | lookout place (Mount Hope) | Sowams | the south country |
| Moshassuck | great brook in the marshy meadow (Prov. River) | Titicut (Tauton) | the principal river |
| | | Touisset | at the old fields |
| Mosskituash | a place of reeds and rushes | Wanasquatucket | at the end of the tidal river (Prov. River) |
| Mouscochuck | a meadow | Wannamoisett | at the good fishing place |
| Narragansett | at the small narrow point | Watchimoquit | end of fishing place |

Source: Bicknell, Thomas W. (1908). Sowams. New Haven, CT: Associated Publishers of American Records. [Courtesy of the Rhode Island Historical Society Library].

13

New England American Indian toponyms.  Figures 1 through 5, below, exemplify intuitively these principles of corruption.

On another level, the poorly educated Colonists who were charged with interpreting and recording for posterity the Indian names they witnessed were also struggling with the erratic 17th cent. English language spelling system of the day.

> Remembering how unsettled and capricious English spelling in the seventeenth century was, how absolutely every clerk and recorder was a law unto himself, and how often we find a common English word spelled in three or four different ways by the same writer and perhaps on the same page, in early Colonial records,—uniformity in the spelling of Indian names was not to be expected. The variations which some of these names present are almost innumerable. Others have undergone complete transformation, retaining scarcely a suggestion of their original sounds. The strange sounds of a strange language were peculiarly subject to the operation of two causes of phonetic change,—error of the ear (otosis, as it has been termed,) a mis-hearing, or rather, mis-apprehension of the sounds uttered; and the universal tendency "to make the work of utterance easier to the speaker, to put a more facile in the stead of a more difficult sound or combination of sounds," and "to get rid altogether of irregular and exceptional forms." (Trumbull, 1881/1974, p. vi).

To illustrate Trumbull's point, we note the following examples of New England place names and their modern spellings:

| | |
|---|---|
| Oggusse-paugsuck | Oxyboxy |
| Tomheganompskut | Higganum |
| Wonococomaug | Congamuck |
| Wequapaugset | Boxet |
| Nameock | May Luck |
| Papasquash | Papoose Squaw |
| Musquetaug | Musqueto-hawk |

The translator works with right-hand column material and tries to return the left-hand column arrangement in order to reproduce the original meaning.

Over 125 years ago Dr. Trumbull summarized well the general difficulty in translating regional place names derived from the complex oral Algonquian American Indian languages of southern New England:

> Two hundred years ago, when the Mohegan and Narragansett and Massachusetts were living languages, the meanings of most of these names could have been easily enough ascertained had one cared to undertake the task: but now, comparatively few can be analyzed or interpreted, with certainty. (Trumbull, 1881, p. v)

Years earlier Trumbull's (1870, p. 45) investigations led him to single out Rhode Island and Connecticut as exhibiting exceptional corruption related to the haphazard manner in which Indian place names were recorded in early deeds and conveyances[1].

---

1      Trumbull (1870, p. 46) mentions several names of Anglo-Colonial translators whose work can be relied upon for accuracy in CT & MA—Rev. John Eliot, Experience Mayhew, and Thomas Stanton. From other sources we can add the names of Ezra Stiles (CT) and perhaps Daniel Gookin and J. Cotton (MA) as well as Roger Williams, author of A Key into the Language of America.

# The Dictionary

The second chapter of the book provides an Algonquian alphabetical glossary of (a) Algonquian vocabulary words and (b) common variant spellings (called "fragments") of the roots and combining elements culled by analysis of various sources. Included with each entry is a reference to the original Algonquian source term (roots and combining elements) taken from the author's brief Algonquian dictionary (Moondancer & Strong Woman, 1996/2001) and other sources (primarily Trumbull's 1903 Natick Dictionary). Appendix II—in the rear of the book—may be consulted for a condensed summary of common misspelled terms (similar to Trumbull's 1881 classification)[1].

It is unreasonable to believe that every conceivable permutation of the spurious spellings have been captured in the Dictionary. A one-to-one match cannot always be assumed.

The compilation, encompassing several southern New England dialects, attempts to incorporate the common misapprehension, spelling, and recording errors cited above. In the Dictionary some past and present place name examples are provided to exemplify the analysis of fragments or corrupted spellings derived from the original Algonquian languages and dialects of the region (Rhode Island, Massachusetts and parts of Connecticut).

For example, the following entry in the Dictionary under A for fragment *agun-* tells us three things:

| Algonquian | English |
|---|---|
| agun- (see *agwe*) | Under, underneath, below (e.g., *Aguntaug* = "under a tree" or "big tree place") |
| | |
| NOTES on Dictionary entries: (a) the author has attempted to be careful in indicating the placement of hyphens for the fragments to specify the place order (beginning-middle-end of place name—cf. Figures 1-4). In most instances, the general case as in -om- (i.e., the fragment om can possibly occur anywhere in name) is probably the safest assumption except in certain cases where location is obvious. (b) some fragments have several spelling permutations sometimes with multiple meanings; not all are listed as separate entries in the Dictionary, so be patient in your search. (c) some entries have not been seen per se in published sources but may appear in a document as either a variant spelling or new name. (d) for language/dialect/ location see Huden (1962). | |

---

[1] Differences in intertribal dialect were not merely phonetic, as neighboring tribes had different words for the same river, animals &c. "Every tribe, almost every village had its peculiarities of speech. Names etymologically identical might have widely different meanings in two languages or even two nations speaking substantially the same language." (Trumbull, 1870, p. 50). Specialized Algonquian vocabularies (by southern New England dialect) for animal, fish, water & tree names, etc., may be found in the author's work, American Indian Studies in the Extinct Languages of Southeastern New England. See the website: http://www.docstoc.com/docs/3237496/ American-Indian-Studies-in-the-Extinct-Languages-of-Southeastern-New-England.

The Indian place name for a brook called *Aguntaug* (from the Rhode Island Narragansett-language) has been interpreted by Huden to mean either "under a tree" or "big tree place." That is, its' meaning is not evident on first reading. The linguistic "noise" needs to be filtered. Thirdly, if "under a tree" is the most likely meaning then we see that the translation was derived in part from Algonquian *agwe* (or *agwu, ogwu*—var. spellings)[1] meaning "under, underneath, below". Looking further along in the dictionary under -*taug*- informs us that fragment taug is possibly derived from the Algonquian root for "wood, tree" (*tugkh* in the Indian Bible with variant spellings). Hence, *Aguntaug* may possibly mean "under a tree" in corrupted form by this line of reasoning. Incidentally, *agwonk* means "under/below a tree" (*agwu* + *unk*) as given by J. Eliot in The Indian Bible. However, "under a tree" does not seem to fit the published description of *Aguntaug*—a brook, near an island called Mincamekek, in Cedar-swamp near or in a great pond. Therefore, there may be alternative true meanings of the fragment agun- seen in place names of this region. Such is the experience for a number of word bits and pieces in southern New England Indian toponyms.

Huden's second interpretation of *Aguntaug* is "big tree place" which might be written in Narragansett as, *Mangunckuck* (or *Mangunckag* ?). Linguistically, it could have degenerated into *Aguntaug* or *Aguntang* (a var. spelling) if syllables were elided. That interpretation seems to fit better the feature-description. This example emphasizes the need for extra-linguistic investigation in the toponymic interpretive process.

A deed or other document containing the oldest spelling(s) and describing the toponym in better detail may provide additional evidence in support of contending translations—or suggest a better one[2]. It is important to iterate that one is not likely to be able to translate many Indian place names in southern New England simply by linguistic analysis of the poorly spelled roots and combining elements. Trumbull's caveat remains true today despite significant scientific advances in Algonquian language studies since the 19th century and beyond.

As an aside, many lay people the author has corresponded with seem to think that linguistic analysis is all that is required for a translation. We have stressed the point that this is the last step in the toponymic interpretive process It seems the best one can do in the interpretation of mangled Indian place

---

1       The most important historical linguistic references for Algonquian place names in present-day Rhode Island and Massachusetts is The Indian Bible (J. Eliot, 1663/1685) and his The Indian Grammar (1666) written in and about the Natick dialect of the Massachusett (formerly Massachusee) language of the Eastern Algonquian Language family—see Goddard in "Eastern Algonquian Languages". The Trumbull 1903 Natick Dictionary is derived from Eliot's trans. of the Bible. A Key into the Language of America (1643) by Roger Williams presents a modest vocabulary for Narragansett (parts of Rhode Island), a language closely related to the Massachusett language that Eliot used. J. Cotton (1830) wrote a vocabulary for another dialect of Massachusett, and Prince and Speck (1904) for Mohegan-Pequot (Connecticut). The best modern linguistic summary of the Massachusett language is in Goddard and Bragdon, 1988. All Indian languages and their dialects in southern New England are extinct (See Goddard, 1978 & 1996).
2       Dr. Ives Goddard did just this in a 1990 letter to the editor of the New York Times where he challenged a long-standing translation of a famous Massachusetts place name in the lands of the Nipmuck.

names in southern New England is to "bound" the translation with one or more plausible hypotheses based on as much information as possible (geographical, historical, linguistic). The majority of the place names contain varying kinds and degrees of orthographic "noise" due to the corrupted spellings (ranging from mild to wild) in comparison to "ground truth" provided by the 17th cent. The Indian Bible of the missionary Rev. John Eliot and his Indian interpreters, or the works of Roger Williams (1643), J. Cotton (1830), Wm. Woods' brief "Nomenclator" (1634), Trumbull's 1903 Natick Dictionary, the author's brief Massachusett-Narragansett dictionary (1996/2001) and other noted sources. And the best the author can do is to make available as much information as possible with which to untangle the mangles. In some cases of high corruption, we might arrive at a general sense of the original meaning based on our best educated guess with little possibility of confirmation since no one speaks these languages fluently anymore.

The fragments list in the Dictionary summarizes the author's collection over a ten year period. About 2,000 vocabulary terms and associated fragments have been compiled, derived from various sources. The fragments glossary is pertinent primarily in the interpretation of Rhode Island, and some Massachusetts and Connecticut toponyms although the reader may be helped in deciphering existing place names in other regions comprising Algonquian Indian place names[1]. It is believed that some unknown number of regional Indian place names—or their variant spellings—have not been published in standard sources such as Trumbull or Huden. The Dictionary may be of service in the interpretation of new local names that surface from time to time in Colonial records, old deeds or maps or historical journals or newspapers, manuscripts, letters, and other records and documents.

More detailed information on differences in regional dialects, strategies of interpretation, and important technical Algonquian word-formation grammatical features such as "glides[2]," "reduced vowels," "obviation," "reduplication," and "accommodating t" *inter alia,* can be found in Huden (1962), Trumbull's works, the authors' Narragansett-language *Indian Grammar Dictionary* (Appendix, 2001) & *Grammatical Studies* (2009), Afable & Beeler (1996), Gahan (1959 & 1961), and Goddard and Bragdon's Massachusett-language linguistic treatise (1988).

Trumbull (1881, reprinted 1974, and reviewed by Goddard, 1977) has written the best work on the translation of Indian place names in southern New England. He interweaves feature description, historical events, and comparative linguistic analysis in his toponymic interpretations. Trumbull's 1870 classic

---

1      Little effort was expended in categorizing misspellings for various dialects of Connecticut Indian place names since Trumbull's place name book (1881/1974) is quite satisfactory on the whole.

2      Glides and "reduced vowels" are very important in distinguishing roots and combining elements. They are interspersed vowels or consonants or syllables, the most common ones being in modern place names—a, e, i, l, m, n, o, p, q, qua, quo, r, t, u, w, y. Colonial grammarians like John Eliot explained their role in speech as for "euphony"; i.e., gliding or connecting the primitive elements to aid pronunciation.

work, *Comp. Indian Geographic Names*, is also a useful source for detailed explanations of the meanings and shades of meanings in place name elements. Both works are available on the Internet.  Also, see Kennicutt's (1909, 1911) two books for Massachusetts place names.  These works, which also reside on the Internet (Google Books), are good in citing data from deeds and historical events, important information in toponymic interpretation[1]. Prof. Wm. Bright (2004) presents a national survey of Indian place names and  includes more recent source material.

---

1       For an interesting mix of geography, history,  and linguistics in a place name analysis, see Goddard and Love's work, "Oregon, the Beautiful."

# Examples

To illustrate the translation process Figure 1 shows the analysis for the Rhode Island place name, Aquidneck, based on the Narragansett language. Aquidneck Island is a large island adjacent to the mainland, located in Narragansett Bay (Map 1). As far as we know, the Narragansett word for "island" was not published by Roger Williams, the primary source for this Indian language. But Eliot's Massachusett–language Indian Bible translated a close resemblance as *ahquednet* meaning "on (some kind) of island"[1]. The present-day name "Aquidneck" is very high "signal"—its meaning is readily apparent by linguistic analysis and supported by corroborating evidence (an uncommon occurrence in place names of Rhode Island). Knowledge of both the Massachusett language and the closely related Narragansett tells us that the word Aquidneck contains two only slightly corrupted elements consisting of a noun + a "locative": aquidn– and –eck. The first element, spelled several ways in historical documents, is based on a noun written *ahquedne*, known to mean "some kind of island". The second element –eck is a locative (a grammatical feature specifying location). It is recognizable from R. Williams' presentation of elementary Narragansett where he spelled it as "-ick" (and variant spellings) which has the correlative spelling –et in the Massachusett language recorded by Eliot[2]. This ubiquitous locative or location suffix—always written at the end of the name—is roughly a preposition meaning "in, at, on, near, etc." and commonly transferred as "place of". Combining the two gives us the correct translation, Aquidneck = "on some kind of island".

To demonstrate further the translation process, consider the following three place-name-charts. Let's illustrate first with the name for the Massachusetts town Mattapoisett, meaning (in the author's own interpretation) "little resting place" (a verb + an adjective + a locative). That is, a resting place on the end of a portage for a long canoe trip between two rivers or other waterways. See Map 2 for location. This word has a little "noise". The first step involves dividing up the given word into Algonquian language elements that might correspond to the basic meanings of the toponym. Now, using knowledge of the Wampanoag language called Massachusett, we recognize that the word-part "mattapo" probably comes from *mattappu* = "he sits down" (or) "he rests" (Moondancer & Strong Woman, 1996/2001). Next we decide that the terminal fragment "isett" is probably two Algonquian elements (is-ett) that come from diminutive marker, *es-* = "little" and the locative explained above, -et. Thus, putting it all together, we assemble the primary root elements, mattappu-es-et. In the final step (pronunciation), we contract the elements to obtain something like, mattappuset = "he rests + little + at, near" or just "a little resting place,"

1      This translation was given by the Narragansetts in the 17ᵗʰ cent. A place name translation provided by local Indians to a competent translator, and transcribed by an accurate recorder, is a highly valued (but rare) piece of interpretive evidence.
2      A brief linguistic summary of Narragansett is given in the work, Grammatical Studies in the Narragansett Language (O'Brien, 2009).

freely translated into English.   This is probably how Wampanoag Indians called this place, which in the ears and hands of the English, was perceived and recorded as "Mattapoisett" (among other spellings).  Figure 2 summarizes what we just said. Thus, the modern place name Mattapoisett is fairly close to the original Algonquian and not much seems to be lost in the translation. Historical information also supports the translation. This is not always the case, especially for the Rhode Island Indian place names.

The next example (Fig. 3) gives another chart-analysis for the place in Massachusetts called Swampscott, with derived meaning "at the red rock", or "red rock place" (a noun + an adjective + a locative)[1]. The analysis for Swampscott demonstrates that many, many old Indian place names in southern New England were corrupted (sometimes beyond recognition) by the Europeans. To illustrate this problem, one well-known 19th cent. Algonquian translator has said of the place names in Rhode Island, that one-half of them defy analysis altogether (cited Huden, p. ix).  As stated above, different assumptions about the correct Algonquian roots and combining elements lead to different conclusions about the correct translation or multiple translations.

# Figure 1.
# Place Name Analysis for Aquidneck

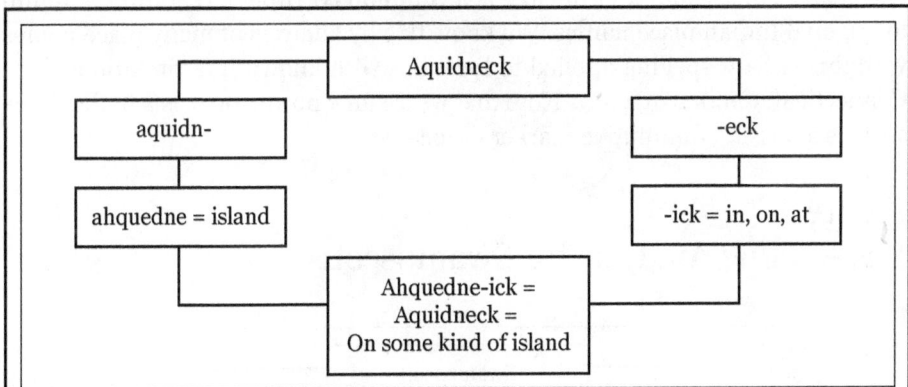

NOTE: Two words for "island" were translated in the Eliot Bible which are seen in place names: ahquedne & munnoh (see Goddard, 2002); munnoh seems to imply any dry place or refuge like an island (perhaps derived from m'nunnu = "dry place"). Ahquedne may imply a floating or suspended mass, and is related to other Algonquian languages for "canoe". Trumbull (1870) hypothesizes that ahquedne was used for islands (perhaps large ones) close to or spoken of in reference to the mainland. See Goddard's fuller explanation in Appendix I which shows how a master linguist analyzes local place names.

---

1        "Red" in Algonquian is actually documented as a type of transitive verb ("It is red," inanimate form or "He/she is red," animate form), but for purposes of simplicity we classify it as a noun modifier (adjective).  Likewise we streamline the translations in order to convey the esse
ntial meaning which results in some loss of generality.

## Figure 2.
## Place Name Analysis for Mattapoisett

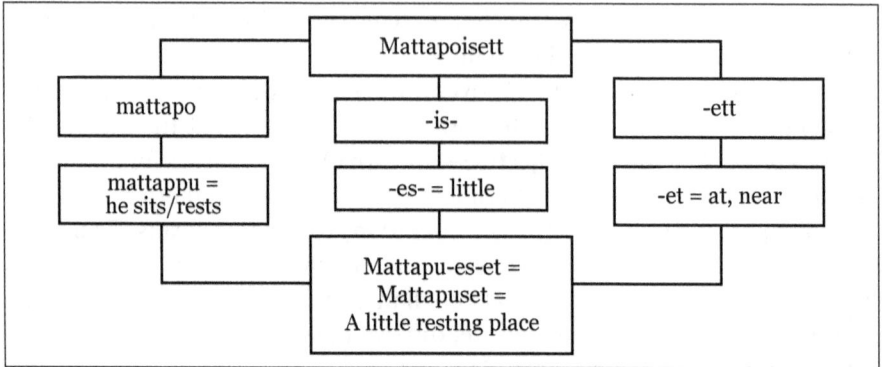

| Mattapoisett | | |
|---|---|---|
| mattapo | -is- | -ett |
| mattappu = he sits/rests | -es- = little | -et = at, near |
| | Mattapu-es-et = Mattapuset = A little resting place | |

Lastly, Fig. 4 demonstrates a fair amount of noise for the Rhode Island place name Canopaug. The fragment cano- is most likely corrupted from the Narragansett verb qunni = "it is long." The interpretation Canopaug = "long pond" is less certain than that of Aquidneck, but the translation seems reasonable since cano- and the like is a common corruptive rendition of qunni in regional Indian place names. We know this by analysis of many place names with this variant spelling applied to locations with known interpretations (e.g., Connecticut, Canonicut, etc.). Note that we assume no elision exists in the name such as a missing diminutive marker or locative.

## Figure 3.
## Place Name Analysis for Swampscott

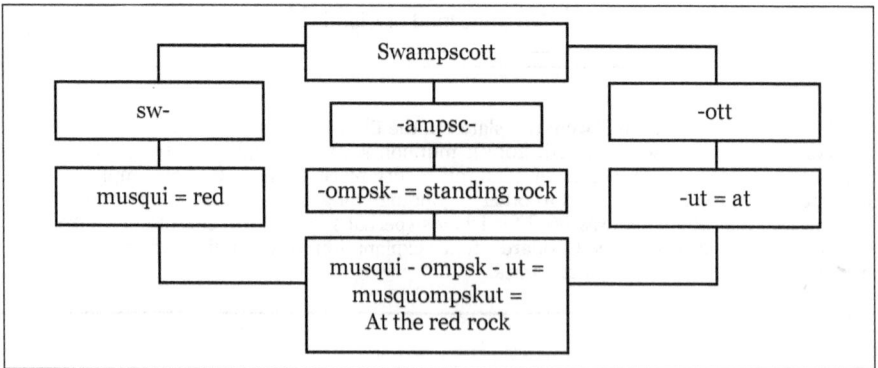

| Swampscott | | |
|---|---|---|
| sw- | -ampsc- | -ott |
| musqui = red | -ompsk- = standing rock | -ut = at |
| | musqui - ompsk - ut = musquompskut = At the red rock | |

# Figure 4.
# Place Name Analysis For Canopaug

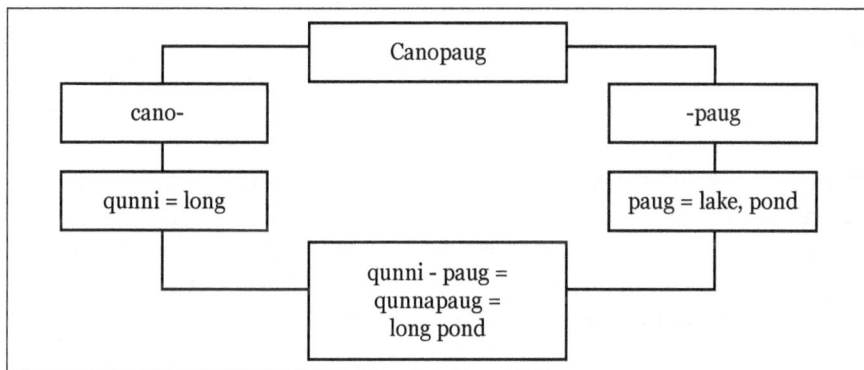

```
                    ┌──────────────────┐
         ┌──────────┤    Canopaug      ├──────────┐
         │          └──────────────────┘          │
┌────────┴─────────┐                    ┌──────────┴───────┐
│      cano-       │                    │      -paug       │
└────────┬─────────┘                    └──────────┬───────┘
┌────────┴─────────┐                    ┌──────────┴───────┐
│  qunni = long    │                    │ paug = lake, pond│
└────────┬─────────┘                    └──────────┬───────┘
         │        ┌──────────────────┐             │
         └────────┤   qunni - paug = ├─────────────┘
                  │   qunnapaug =    │
                  │   long pond      │
                  └──────────────────┘
```

❖

      The four examples presented led to a single translation. In the author's summary of over 500 historic Indian place names in Rhode Island a majority are translated with multiple interpretations. For example, the place Escoheag (with several variant spellings)—believed to be possibly a reduction of the original Indian name Neastoquoheaganuck—is recorded with 6 different meanings. The high degree of orthographic corruption in that name cannot be reduced to a single defensible linguistic construction corresponding to evidence derived from the Eliot Indian Bible or Trumbull's Dictionary, the most extensive historical linguistic documentation we have for the lost regional American Indian languages, or other pertinent extra-linguistic data.

# More Examples

In Figure 5 is a list of about 25 southern New England place names which provides additional examples of place names analysis. The reader may find it helpful to use the author's chart-method to trace the process. Most samples are relatively "moderate signal". Those names will give the reader practice in using the glossary that follows in the next part of the book. They will also provide an intuitive insight into the structure of place names. Most place names of this region consist of a noun + an adjective/verb with or without a locative, dimunitive, and pluralization stem. In addition, an Indian place name is quite literal in its descriptive simplicity, summarizing a referenced landmark, or reference to a geographical feature (either exact or proximate in location), historical event, animal habitat, important person, and place of importance for survival or daily life (see Afable & Beeler, 1996, and Gahan, for more details)[1].

The place name selections given below are based on proximity of the name with the hypothesized original Algonquian language elements (some roots are combined; i.e., not reduced to primitive form). This simplifies the etymological derivation for the beginning student. In the left hand column of Figure 5 is given the Indian name of a geographic land and water name, animal habitat, etc., and what is believed to be the original name from the Algonquian language roots and other combining forms (different tribal languages/dialects are mixed in). On the right side is the translation. For example, the place now called Nepaug, which seems to mean either "good or fresh pond" (adjective + noun), may have come originally from Algonquian *wunni-paug* or *nunni-paug*. Analysis shows that the name may consist possibly of one of two Algonquian elements (*wunni* = good or *nunni* = fresh) and paug = pond. Obviously the initial fragment "ne-" has been corrupted under this hypothesis rendering the interpretation of *Nepaug* as ambiguous. This was noted earlier with respect to initial consonants.

The meanings we assign are based purely on a literal meaning of the Algonquian word elements, and are not the most elegant or full-bodied translations one finds, for instance, in the reference book by Trumbull (1881/1974). The hyphens used in the Algonquian terms show the basic root-elements of the place names.

For the Algonquian place names in Figure 5, look up in Dictionary the Algonquian fragments for each toponym, and verify the essential meaning(s) of each root and combining element. Appendix II gives many more names throughout southern new England with which to practice. This exercise will

---

1    Bear in mind that some small number of local Indian place names represent personal names of the Sachem (or Chief) who lived in or ruled the territory so named (e.g., Moosup River, Hyannis, Uncasville). Although every personal name can in principle be translated into English, such names attached to a toponymic feature will not correspond to the meaning of the place name (see Trumbull, 1870, p. 37)

warm up the toponymic analyst in the difficult and often frustrating task of translating southern New England American Indian toponyms.

# Figure 5.
## Place Name Analysis Practice

| Algonquian | English |
| --- | --- |
| Aquapauksit = ukque-paug-es-it | at the end of the small pond |
| Chappaquiddick = cheppi-ahquidne-ick | separated island land |
| Connecticut = quinni-tuk-ut | on the long tidal river |
| Kenunckpacook = qunnunkque-paug-aûke | high pond place |
| Kittemaug = kehte-âmaug | great (principal) fishing place |
| Kuttuck (now Titicut) = kehte-tuk-ut | principal river place |
| Massapaug = massa-paug | large pond |
| Mashantucket = mishuntugk-et = missi-tugk-et | where there are many trees |
| Massachusetts = massa-wadchu-ash-et | at or near the great hills |
| Massaco = massa-sauk | the great outlet |
| Mistik = missi-tuk | great tidal river |
| Nepaug = wunni-paug or nunni-paug | good pond or fresh pond |
| Norwalk = naïag | a point of land |
| Ohomowauke = oohomaus- aûke | owl's abode |
| Oxecoset = oggusse-koua-ash-et | small pine (fir) trees place ? |
| Pachaug = pachau-aûke | a turning place |

| | |
|---|---|
| Pocasset = pohq-es-et | little opening place (i.e., where the stream or straits widen or the narrows open out) |
| Qunnapaug = quinni-paug | a long pond |
| Quononoquott (now Canonicut = Jamestown) = quinni- aûke-et | at the long place (or) Narragansett Sachem Canonicus' abode |
| Saugatuck = sauki-tuk | tidal river outlet |
| Tomheganomset = tomheg 'n-ompsk-ut | at the ax (tomahawk) rock |
| Wachuset = wadchu-es-et | little hill/mountain place |
| Watchoog = wadchu-aûke | hill country |
| | |

NOTE: As we can see so far, the vast majority of regional Indian place names denote land or country, waterway, fishing-place, hill and mountain, stone and rock, natural or man-made enclosure, and island. To these elemental features are added modifiers of size, number, quality and locatives, and of course, intertribal dialectical (phonetic & semantic) variations.

Now we will test your knowledge of fragment analysis. Try to decipher the following words with the aid of the Dictionary. Suggested translations given in footnote.[1]

- Mississippi (not a New England name)    • Wequapaug
- Misquamicut        • Chepatchet        • Woonsocket

    As mentioned, the last step in translation typically involves contracting or abbreviating the primary root elements and combining elements[2]. Algonquian languages are described as being polysynthetic, meaning that many simple elements or roots are combined into a single word, phrase or sentence usually involving final contraction or abbreviation of the primary forms. For example, to say "a white man" we pick our primary elements from the Massachusett language: wompesu = "(he is) white" (animate objects) + wosketomp = "(he is) a man (young warrior?)". The final word is womposketomp = "(he is) a white man". Can you see what was changed in the primary terms? The ability to form the right word through polysynthetic analysis requires knowledge of the correct grammatical rule (many exist). These rules (and southern New England Indian languages in general) continue to challenge the best minds in linguistics.

1    +Mississippi = big river; Wequapaug = at the end of the pond; Misquamicut = red-fish (salmon) place; Chepatchet = boundary place; Woonsocket = place of steep descent.

2    Rev. John Eliot first described this grammatical feature in his 1666 Grammar on Natick-Massachusett.

# END NOTE
## Dialectical Differences In Speech

Many Algonquian language dialects existed among the tribes shown in Map 1 (see Goddard, 1978). Phonetics (the study of such differences) is a detailed subset of Algonquian linguistics, and we cannot cover all the details. To give a flavor for these differences we quote an old-fashioned source—Dr. J.H. Trumbull. His terms (sonant, guttural, surd mute, liquids, semi-vowel, nasal, lisp, spirant) can be looked up to clarify when the context is not helpful. Technical material can be found in the multi-volume Smithsonian encyclopedia (Trigger, 1978 & Goddard, 1996). "Algonkin" and "Algonquian" are the same terms.

> In and about the borders of Connecticut four or five distinct Algonkin dialects were spoken, and each of these had its local idioms. In the speech of the Pequot-Mohegans, in the south-east, sonants and gutturals abounded. In the Narragansett and Niantic dialects, the surd mutes, *k, t, p,* were more common than the sonants, *g, d, b,* and nasals than gutturals. The Nipmucks, of the north-east, substituted *l* for the Niantic and Mohegan *n,* and generally made the final *k* of place-names sonant (*aug, og, for auk, ock,* etc.). The tribes of the Connecticut valley preferred liquids and semi-vowels to nasals, and some of their local idioms were characterized by an occasional lisp, an original sibilant becoming a spirant *t,* sometimes passing to a soft lingual mute, *t.* In the dialects of the Quiripi (or Quinnipiac) Indians, near the Sound, from New Haven to the western bounds of the colony, the preference for liquid sounds was more strongly marked; *r* took the place of the eastern *n* or *l,* and there was a tendency to drop or soften final consonants.
> (Trumbull, 1881, pp. v-vi).

# American Indian Place Names In Rhode Island:  Past and Present (rev. ed)

| Name | Historical & Geographical Information | Translation |
|---|---|---|
| | | |
| **A** | | |
| **Absalona** | hill. Two to three miles east of Chepachet [in Glocester]. | Indian man named Absalom? |
| **A'Wumps, A'Waumps** | Pond, Providence County, Burriville.  See **Alum** for Nipmuck name. | The fox (Quinebaug[1] tribe Indian Chief or Sachem) |
| **Absalone** | See **Absalona** | |
| **Absalonomiscut** | a TRACT of land on the west side of Johnston. The Seven Mile line ran parallel with Mooshassuck and Providence river, at Fox point. Johnston, west of this line, was called Absalonomiscut. See city records. | Place of the fish trap; where fish are caught in a weir |
| **Achagomiconset** | See **Ashagomiconset** | |
| **Achetonsick** | See **Assapumsic** | |
| **Acoaxet** | Ancient Wampanoag village | See **Acokesit** |
| **Acokesit** | RIVER. Judge Brayton thinks it is Acoaxet [in Little Compton]. | At fishing promontory; at the place of young pines?; place of small fields? |
| **Acontaug** | See **Aguntaug** | |
| **Acquababpogue** | See **Aquabapaug** | |
| **Acquebapaug** | See **Aquabapaug** | |
| **Acquedneck** | See **Aquidneck** | |
| **Acquednecke** | See **Aquidneck** | |
| **Acquedneessucks** | See **Aquednesuk** | |
| **Acquedneseth** | See **Quidnesit** | |
| **Acqueebapaguck** | See **Aquabapaug** | |

| Acqueednuck | River (a branch of the Paw-tuxet), Washington County, Coventry | Place beyond the hill |
|---|---|---|
| Acquidneck | See **Aquidneck** | |
| Acquidnesit, Ac-quidneset | See **Quidnesit** | |
| Agawan | Hunt Club Golf Course, Providence County, East Providence | Low land; overflowed by water; place to unload canoes |
| Aguntang | See **Aguntaug** | |
| Aguntaug | BROOK [in Westerly], near an island called Mincamekek, in Cedar-swamp near or in a great pond two miles due East from Westerly bridge, called Puscomattas pond, or Borden's pond. [Potter, page 65] Runs to the S. bend of Pawcatuck river, and thence to the North bend, at Ashawa [in Ashaway]. | Under tree; big tree place |
| Aguspemokick | See **Aquopimokuk** | |
| Akoaxet | RIVER, in Little Compton, about five miles S. E. from Seconnet. | At fishing promontory; at the place of young or small pines?; place of small fields? |
| Alum, Allum, Al-lumps | Now Wallum Lake. See **A'Wumps** for Pequot name | Dog (Lake); a favorite haunt for dogs |
| Amataconet | Providence County, Lincoln | Observation place?; meeting place? |
| Anackatuseck | River, Kent County ? | Place where brooks join? |
| Anackatusicke | See **Anackatuseck** | |
| Anaquacut, Anaquacutt | See **Annaquacutt** | |

| Anaquatucket | RIVER. Orkatucket. S. and S. West of Wickford, and within one mile of it. The road to Boston Neck and Tower Hill crosses it a mile S. from Wickford. | At the end of the river; at end of the tidal current; over-flowing river? |
|---|---|---|
| Anawan, Annawan², Anawon | See **Anawanscut** | He commands |
| Anawanscut | See **Annawanscut** | |
| Annaquacutt | POND, and FARM of 446 acres; sold for the benefit of Col. Angell's regiment. R. I. schedules, June 1791. In Tiverton. | At the end of the river |
| Annaquatucket | See **Anaquatucket** | |
| Annawamscutt | See **Annawanscut** | |
| Annawanscut | CREEK, in Barrington [Bristol per GNIS database], near the brick-kilns, and leads from them into the bay, a little N. of Nayatt point. | Rock summit?; end of the rocks; ruler's hill?; commander's rock |
| Annawomscutt | See **Annawanscut** | |
| Annoccotuckett | See **Anaquatucket** | |
| Annocotuckett | See **Anaquatucket** | |
| Annogatucket | See **Anaquatucket** | |
| Annogotucket | See **Anaquatucket** | |
| Anowanscut | See **Annawanscut** | |
| Anshanduck | See **Antashantuck** | |
| Antaghantic | NECK. Three miles west of Providence tide water shore, and about the west side of Neutaconcanut hill, near the river. [Land titles, Vol. 2, page 324.] | Turning backwards river (oxbows) |
| Antashantuc | See **Antashantuck** | |

| | | |
|---|---|---|
| **Antashantuck** | Neck and Pond, Providence County, Providence | Well forested place |
| **Antushantuck** | See **Antashantuck** | |
| **Apehungansett** | See **Apponaug** or **Ponaganset**? | |
| **Apehungunset** | See **Apponaug** | |
| **Aponack** | See **Apponaug** | |
| **Aponaganset** | See **Apponaug** | |
| **Aponahock** | See **Apponaug** | |
| **Aponake, Aponakee** | See **Apponaug** | |
| **Aponaugh** | See **Apponaug** | |
| **Aponihoak** | See **Apponaug** | |
| **Apponagansett** | See **Apponaug** | |
| **Apponaug** | VILLAGE, named from a small river, so called, running into the head of Greenwich Bay, at Coweset [in Warwick]. The meaning of the word is shell-fish. Opponenauhock, now Apponaug. It was a great place of resort to the Indians, as appears by banks of clam-shell dust left by them. | Where he roasts oysters |
| **Apponog** | See **Apponaug** | |
| **Aqethnec, Aquethnek** | See **Aquidneck** | |
| **Aquabapaug** | POND, near the head of Pawcatuck river, near and below Chipchug. S. W. from S. Kingstown depot, one mile. Probably Worden's Pond. The name means muddy water. | At the head of the pond; the pond before (another pond or land tract?) |
| **Aquantaug** | Brook, Washington County, Westerly | Under the trees; big trees |
| **Aquebapaug** | See **Aquabapaug** | |

31

| | | |
|---|---|---|
| **Aquebinocket** | | Round Island (Bicknell, 1920) |
| **Aquedenesick** | See **Aquidnesuk** | |
| **Aquedneck** | See **Aquidneck** | |
| **Aquedneset** | See **Aquidnesuk** | |
| **Aquednesset** | See **Aquidnesuk** | |
| **Aquednet** | Washington County, Coventry | At the island |
| **Aquednick** | See **Aquidneck** | |
| **Aquedoneck** | See **Aquidneck** | |
| **Aqueedennuck, Aqueedenuck** | See **Aqueednuck** | |
| **Aqueednuck** | Kent County, Coventry | Place beyond (or at the end of) the hill |
| **Aquethnick** | See **Aquidneck** | |
| **Aquetneck** | See **Aquidneck** | |
| **Aquetnet** | See **Aquidneck** | |
| **Aquiday** | See **Aquidneck** | |
| **Aquidesit** | See **Quidnesit** | |
| **Aquidneck**[3] | Island, Newport County, Narrgansett Bay | On (some kind of) island; at the island |
| **Aquidnesset** | See **Quidnesit** | |
| **Aquidnesuk, Aquidnesuc** | ISLAND, now Small or Dutch Island [in Narragansett Bay], near Potter's factory, at S. Kingstown ferry. It was occupied by the Dutch sent from N. Y. as a fur trading place, before the Pilgrims landed at Plymouth, or about 1616. | At the small island |
| **Aquidnic** | See **Aquidneck** | |

| Aquidy | or Aquidnic, NEWPORT [in Narragansett Bay], or rather Rhode Island, sometimes written Aquethnick, the middle syllable guttural. The word means longest island. It was deeded to Coddington by Canonicus and Miantinomy. | At the island (See **Aquidneck**) |
|---|---|---|
| Aquitamosit | See **Aquitawoset** | |
| Aquitawoset | a TRACT of land purchased by Atherton, N. and N. E. of Wickford. Same as Aquidnesit or Quidnesit. It is the shore between Potowomut and Cocumscusset or Wickford. | At the small island |
| Aquitawosit | See **Aquitawoset** | |
| Aquitoweset | See **Aquitawoset** | |
| Aquntaug | See **Aguntaug** | |
| Aquopimokuk, Aquopimekuk | ISLAND, now GOULD'S Island[4], off Newport [in Nar-ragansett Bay], once owned by Sachem Koskotop, who sold[5] it to Gould. It is the most northern isle off Newport Bay, being nearly a mile N. W. from the Alms-house at Coaster's Harbor . | At the short narrow straits which separate the island from the mainland |
| Aquopimoquk | See **Aquopimokuk** | |
| Asa | Pond, Kingston and Swamp & Brook, Pawtucket | Stone or stoney |
| Asamequin | See **Osamequin** | |
| Asapumsick | See **Assapumsik** | |
| Ascoamacot | See **Misquamacut** | |
| Ascoamacott, Ascoamicutt | See **Misquamacut** | |
| As-coc-a-nox-suck | See **Akoaxet?** | |
| Ascomackock | See **Misquamacut** | |
| Ascomacut | SAME as Misquamacut, Westerly | See **Misquamacut** |

| | | |
|---|---|---|
| **Ascomicut** | See **Misquamacut** | |
| **Ashagomiconset** | LAND through which Agun-taug brook runs before it enters the S. bend of Pawca-tuck river. This Ashagomicon-set land and two ponds form a line that runs through the middle of Westerly. | Where there are green meadows [for pas-ture] |
| **Ashamu** | Dance Building, Providence | Water spring? |
| **Ashanduck** | See **Antashantuck** | |
| **Ashanteaug** | Rocks, Washington County | Where lobsters are |
| **Ashawa** | or wake or wague, RIVER, runs to Potter's bridge and Ashawa village [in Ashaway]. It enters Pawcatuck river near its N. bend. From this junc-tion the State line of Connect-icut runs due N., and below, this river forms the State line to the ocean. | Land in the middle; land between |
| **Ashawag** | See **Ashawa** | |
| **Ashawake** | See **Ashawa** | |
| **Ashawaug** | See **Ashawa** | |
| **Ashawawague** | See Ashawa | |
| **Ashawawake** | See **Ashawa** | |
| **Ashaway** | River and Village, Washing-ton County, Ashaway | See **Ashawa** |
| **Ashawogue** | See **Ashawa** | |
| **Ashawoque** | See **Ashawa** | |
| **Ashumequin** | See **Osamequin** | |
| **Ashunaiunk** | RIVER, in Richmond, proba-bly Beaver river. It rises north of Ten Rod road, enters the N. side of Richmond at Reynold's factory, passes parallel with the Usquebaug, E. side of Shannock hill, to near Clarke's mill. | Rock point; stony point; stony stream? |

| | | |
|---|---|---|
| **Ashwauge** | See **Ashawa** | |
| **Askomackock** | See **Misquamacut** | |
| **Askomicutt** | See **Misquamacut** | |
| **Aspanansuck** | Washington County, Exeter | High place; brook near the high hill? |
| **Aspatnansuck** | or Hakewamepinke, the residence of Wawaloam, wife of Miantinomy. Potter, page 248. Supposed to be at Exeter hill, on Ten Rod road. | End of dry field; edge of the bank |
| **Aspotucket** | Providence County [corruption of **Pawtucket** ?] | At the fishnet cove; at the high place; at the falls? |
| **Assanapset** | Brook, Providence County, Providence | Where the nest was held down by rocks; at the small rocky stream (see **Assapumsik?**) |
| **Assapumpseat** | See **Assapumsik** | |
| **Assapumpset** | See **Assapumsik** | |
| **Assapumset** | See **Assapumsik** | |
| **Assapumsic** | See **Assapumsik** | |
| **Assapumsik** | BROOK, or spring, East from the great Elm in Johnston [Providence ?—GNIS database]. Only a few rods distant N. E. is an Indian retreat, in a ledge of rocks. | Place where wild hemp is gathered to make cords or nets; great meadow; stoney crossing place |
| **Assopumsett** | See **Assapumsik** | |
| **Astomacut** | See **Misquamacut** | |
| **Asuhmequin** | See **Osamequin** | |
| **Asumequin** | See **Osamequin** | |
| **Aswauge** | See **Ashawa** | |
| **Awashunks** | See **Awoshonks** | |

| | | |
|---|---|---|
| **Awoshonks** | SWAMP, S. [& Park] end of Little Compton, a mile or two N. E,. from Seconnet point. The Indian queen named Awoshonks resided near it. | Woman who rules (Sakonnet Tribe Sachem) |
| **Azoiquoneset[6]** | or Nonequasset, ISLAND [in Narragansett Bay]. Fox island, two miles S. E. from Wickford. It means Spruce Pitch island. | Spruce-pitch small-island place |
| **Azorquonseut** | See **Azoiquoneset** | |
| **Azoruonesut** | See **Azoiquoneset** | |

(Footnotes)

1      Quinebaug = "Long Pond".

2      Annawan was a Wampanoag Captain during King Philip's War (1675-6).

3      See Goddard (2002) for linguistic derivation of translation;region comprises the three towns of Portsmouth, Middletown and Newport, and presently called "Rhode Island". A number of spelling variants exist.

4      Occasionaly written Gold's Island in older records?

5      A clear misunderstanding of Native American ways regarding "buying," "selling" land.

6      See Sonanoxet for other names referring to Fox Island.

| Name | Historical & Geographical Information | Translation |
|---|---|---|
| | | |
| **B** | | |
| **Bapetaushat** | TRACT. N. W. corner of Charlestown, adjoining Machaquamaganset. [See Potter's History, 249.] | Hollow place; cave hiding place |
| **Bapetaushaut** | See **Bapetaushat** | |
| **Basskutoquoge** | See **Bassoqutoquaug** | |
| **Bassokutoquage** | See **Bassoqutoquaug** | |
| **Bassoquto-quaug, Basso-qutoquog** | a SACHEMDOM; or Bassku-toquoge [in Exeter]. [Potter, page 63, and Land Evidence, Vol. 1st, page 33.] This was sachemdom under Koskotop, who sold Aquopimekuk island to Gould. | Where trees were split; river branch place |

| Boxet | POND, near Tippecan pond, West Greenwich. Same as Wixerboxet | Small pond |

| Name | Historical & Geographical Information | Translation |
| --- | --- | --- |
| **C** | | |
| **Cacauwonch** | Kent County | The beginning place |
| **Cachanaquoant** | See **Cajanaquond** | |
| **Cachauaquan** | See **Cajanaquond** | |
| **Cacumgunsett** | Kent County | Whetstone quarry; place of high rocks |
| **Cacumquussuck** | See **Cocumscusset** | |
| **Cajacet** | POINT, or shore on Canonicut island [in Jamestown], near the north end and facing Portsmouth. [See Benedict Arnold's will.]. | See **Conanicut** |
| **Cajanaquant** | See **Cajanaquond** | |
| **Cajanaquond** | Narragansett Sachem or Chief | See **Narragansett Tribe** |
| **Cajaset** | See **Cajacet** | |
| **Cajocet** | See **Cajacet** | |
| **Cajoot** | MINE, of Blacklead, or Carburet of iron, at the foot of Tower Hill in S. Kingstown [at Narragansett Pier]. | Fir-tree place? |
| **Canada** | Pond, Dam, Providence | Village; group of houses (Mohawk language) |
| **Canangogum** | Northwestern Providence County, Burriville | The fence or boundary; highland? |

| | | |
|---|---|---|
| **Caneunsquisset** | TRACT. North Kingstown, between Wickford and Exeter. It makes the west side of N. Kingstown, and adjoins Cocumscusset, or Wickford. | High place; high rocky cliff |
| **Cannonicus**[1] | See **Canonicus** | |
| **Canob** | Pond | See **Canopaug** |
| **Canonchet** | Brook, Carolina | See **Canonchet** |
| **Canonchet**[2] | MILL SITE, S. W. of Fenner's hill one mile [& Farm Park and Memorial, Narragansett). The name was lately given in honor of Canonchet | He is ruler, overseer, protector (Narragansett Sachem & warrior, son of Miantonomi) |
| **Canonicus** | Spring | Of the long place? (Narragansett Sachem or Chief).  See **Canonicut** |
| **Canonicut**[3], **Cananicut** | or Quonotamaquot ISLAND [& Point, Park, Light], between S. Kingstown Ferry and Newport. It is Jamestown. | The especially long place |
| **Canopaug** | BROOK and SWAMP [and VILLAGE], in [North] Scituate, on the east side, sometimes spelled in deeds Quonopaug. The brook rises from the swamp and runs westerly to Moshwansicut river. | A long pond |
| **Capanagansitt** | Providence County, Warwick | Place of the enclosed (or plugged-up) well; closed up meadow? |
| **Cap-an-gan-sitt** | See **Capanagansitt** | |
| **Cappacommock** | SWAMP, three or four miles north from the Pequod shore [in Charlestown]. It signifies hiding-place, to which the squaws and children retired on the approach of boats, Another like it is Owlshead, called Ohomowauke swamp. | Refuge or hiding place |
| **Cappacomuck** | See **Cappacommock** | |

| | | |
|---|---|---|
| **Cassuckquunsh** | Narragansett Sachem or Chief | See **Narragansett Tribe** |
| **Casuckqunce** | See **Cassuckquunsh** | |
| **Caucan** | See **Caucaujawatchuck** | |
| **Caucauja-watchuck** | Providence County, Cranston | Sharp mountain peak; sharp mountain? Very long hill? |
| **Caucaunjawach** | See **Caucaujawatchuck** | |
| **Caucaumsqus-sick, Caucaum-squttock** | | See **Cocumscusset** |
| **Caucumsquissic** | See **Cocumscusset** | |
| **Caucumsqusuk** | See **Cocumscusset** | |
| **Caujaniquante** | See **Cajanaquond** | |
| **Caunaunacus** | See **Canonicus** | |
| **Causumset, Causumsett** | See **Cawsumsett** | |
| **Cawaude** | Kent County | Pine place |
| **Cawcawmsqus-sick** | See **Cocumscusset** | |
| **Cawncawnja-watchuk** | Providence County | Very long hill |
| **Cawsumsett** | Bristol (see **Cowsumpsit**) | Sharp rock place; whetstone rock place |
| **Cepasnetuxet** | See **Copassanatuxet** | |
| **Chabatawece** | See **Chibacoweda** | |
| **Chachacust** | NECK, meadow in Barrington. It is near Warren. [Gen. Fessenden.] | Where stream divides and opens; torrent rocks place |
| **Chachapacaset, Chachapacasett** | See **Chackapaucasset** | |
| **Chackacust** | See **Chachapaucasett** | |
| **Chackapacauset** | See **Chackapaucasset** | |

| | | |
|---|---|---|
| **Chackapaucasset** | or Chackapacauset, now called Rumstick point or neck, S. of Warren, in Barrington, [Gen. Fessenden.] Rumstick was applied to a portion of it as early as 1697 by whom and wherefore is not known. | Where the steam divides and opens up; at the great widening out place |
| **Chagum** | Pond, Newport County | A black bird [bobolink?; redwinged blackbird?] |
| **Chaipuachack** | See **Chippachooag** | |
| **Chanananonum** | See **Chanangongum** | |
| **Chanangongum** | LAND, in Nipmuck. [See Trumbull's History, page 346, vol. 1.] | Great reed place; great paint place |
| **Chapomeset** | See **Chopmist** | |
| **Chapom-pamiskock** | Providence County, Scituate? Same as Chompist? | Big fishing place near boundary rock? |
| **Chapumishcook[4]** | Northern part of Scituate | See **Chapom-pamiskock** ? |
| **Chaubatick** | Ancient Narragansett Village, Providence | At the forked river; river which bounds |
| **Chechechnessett** | See **Checkechnusset** | |
| **Checkechnusset** | Brook, Washington County | At the boundary; brook at the place of separation |
| **Cheepauke** | Providence County? | A place apart; an isolated island |
| **Cheetoskeunke** | Kent County | At the principal wading-place [ford, or bridge?] |
| **Chemagaze** | See **Chemanguz** | |
| **Chemangase** | See **Chemanguz** | |
| **Chemanguz** | POND, or Chemunganoc. Same as Watchaug. Poquient brook runs from it in a N., W, direction. It is in nearly the centre of Charlestown. | Small canoe?; small waterway?; big brant goose? |

| | | |
|---|---|---|
| **Chemaunguz** | See **Chemanguz** | |
| **Chemunaganoc** | See **Chemunganock** | |
| **Chemunaganock** | See **Chemunganock** | |
| **Chemunganoc** | See **Chemunganock** | |
| **Chemunganock** | HILL, in Charlestown, probably near Chemunganset Pond; which is the same as Watchaug Pond. It is in the centre of Charlestown. | At the abode of the brant goose; big stink place (rotting vegetation); place where we put down paddles; big ash-tree place |
| **Chemunganset** | See **Chemunganock** | |
| **Chepacchewag** | See **Chippachooag** | |
| **Chepachague** | Washington County | Principal turning place |
| **Chepachet** | RIVER and VILLAGE, or Chepatset. Fifteen miles N. W. of Providence, on Branch river (in Glouster). It means Devil's Bag. A bag or wallet was found here, probably dropped by some hunter, and as no one could tell who, an Indian said it was the Devil. Hence Chepuck, devil; chack, bag; now converted into Chepachet. | Place of separation (where stream divides); boundary place |
| **Chepachewag**[5] | See **Chippachooag** | |
| **Chepachuach** | See **Chepachague** | |
| **Chepachuack** | See **Chepachague** | |
| **Chepatset** | Providence County, Burriville | Boundary place |
| **Chepinoxet** | ISLAND, off Cowesit shore [in Narragansett Bay], near Baker's station and the summer residence of John Whipple. It means Devil's Island[6]. | Little place of departed spirits |
| **Chepiwanoxet** | Island & Village, Kent County, East Greenwich | At the small separated place |

41

| | | |
|---|---|---|
| **Cheppuxet** | See **Chippuxet** | |
| **Chepuckset** | See **Chippuxet** | |
| **Chepuxet** | See **Chippuxet** | |
| **Chesawane** | See **Chisawannock** | |
| **Chesewanne** | See **Chisawannock** | |
| **Chesewannock** | See **Chisawannock** | |
| **Chesewanock** | See **Chisawannock** | |
| **Chibachuesa** | See **Chibacoweda** | |
| **Chibachuwesa** | See **Chibacoweda** | |
| **Chibachuwese** | See **Chibacoweda** | |
| **Chibachuweset** | See **Chibacoweda** | |
| **Chibacoweda**[7] | ISLAND, Chibachuweset or Chippacurset, Prudence Island in the [Narragansett], bay, below Warwick neck point. It was presented by sachem Canonicut, to Roger Williams; or rather sold to Williams and Gov. John Winthrop, for twenty fathom wampum and two coats. | Little place separated by a passage (from Prudence Island[8]) |
| **Chickamug** | Washington County, Westerly | Fish trap; fish weir; a fishing place; principal fishing place |
| **Chickasheen** | Brook, Washington County, Kingston | Big spring; fish weir; high water; cedars |
| **Chipachuack** | or agne, LAND, is the S. E. corner of Hall's purchase of two miles, near and including S. Kingstown depot. | Where stream divides; place of separation |
| **Chipachuagne** | See **Chipachuack** | |
| **Chipacoweda** | See **Chibacoweda** | |
| **Chipchug** | POND, Duck pond. Probably either Sherman's or Teft's pond, in South Kingstown | Place apart; boundary place (see **Chipachuack**) |

| | | |
|---|---|---|
| **Chiponaug** | Kent County, Warwick | Separated or isolated point?; place of large oysters?; principal resting place |
| **Chippachooag** | Washington County, West Greenwich | Place of separation; where the stream divides (see **Chipa-chuack** |
| **Chippach-uachack** | See **Chippachooag** | |
| **Chippachuat** | See **Chepachague** | |
| **Chippacurset** | See **Chippecurset** | |
| **Chippanogset** | see **Chepinoxet** | |
| **Chippechuock** | See **Chipachuack** | |
| **Chippecurset** | ISLAND, Prudence same as Chipacoweda. | See **Chibacoweda** |
| **Chippuachack** | See **Chippachooag** | |
| **Chippuxet** | RIVER, or Chepachuack, or Chepacchewag, called also Wawoskepog. [See Potter, page 225,] deed of Nicholas Gardiner Jr., to John Thomas, state records. This river runs near S. Kingstown Depot, be-tween it and the hill or village of S. Kingstown. | Principal turning place (See **Chipach-uack**) |
| **Chipuxet** | See **Chippuxet** | |
| **Chisawamicke** | See **Chisawannock** | |

| | | |
|---|---|---|
| **Chisawannock**[9] | ISLAND, or Chesawane. Hog or Perry island [in Narragansett Bay]. Mouth of Bristol harbor, and west of Bristol Ferry about half a mile. Owned by the children of the late Capt. Raymond Perry. There was a contest, for the ownership of this island, -between Plymouth and Rhode Island. | Principal fishing place; muddy bottom |
| **Chisweanocke** | See **Chisawannock** | |
| **Chockalaug** | RIVER, rises in the south side of Douglas, and runs towards the centre of Burrillville [in Providence], at Wood's mill and Harris factory. | Fox place |
| **Chockalog** | See **Chockalaug** | |
| **Chomowauke** | See **Ohomawauke** | |
| **Chopequonset** | FARM or POINT, a mile S. of Pawtuxet, owned by the heirs of the late Nicholas Brown, Esq. | Isolated plantation; separated fields; fields at boundary place |
| **Chopmist** | HILL, north-west corner of Scituate [in Clayville], running three to four miles N. and S. | Boundary or dividing place; principal crossroads |
| **Coaksett** | See **Cokesit** or **Acoaxet?** | |
| **Coaxet** | Ancient Wampanoag village, Newport County | See **Cokesit** |
| **Cockampoag** | See **Cocumpaug** | |
| **Cocumcosuck** | See **Cocumscusset** | |
| **Cocumcussoc** | See **Cocumscusset** | |
| **Cocumcussuc** | See **Cocumscusset** | |

| | | |
|---|---|---|
| **Cocumpaug** | POND, or Cockampoag, on old map, two miles north from General Staunton's in Charlestown, about one mile long. In 1794, it was proposed in the legislature to divert the Pawcatuck river into the sea, by opening a channel from Champlin's bridge in a South East direction, to Cocumpaug pond, two and a half miles and through this to Fort neck, by Meadow Brook, and there at Fort neck enter Pauwangan-set-pond, at the N. E. corner of Champlin's farm, near the highway, one and a half miles E. of Gen. Staunton's The pond is in the centre of Charlestown, and one mile N. E. from Wotchaugh pond. | Long (fishing?) pond |
| **Cocumscusset** | BROOK, or Cawcawmsqus-sick, is now called Stoney Brook. It is the south bound-ary of Quidnesit, and a little north of Wickford. It gives name to the harbor of Wick-ford, and to the land where the Updike and Congdon house stands. The first English house erected in Narragansett, was here, by Richard Smith, who kept an Indian trading house; as did also Roger Williams, many of whose letters date here. It was here that the Mas-sachusetts troops marched from, and back to, in the Swamp battle. It was the mart of Indian trade of Narragan-sett shores two hundred years ago. | At the place where there are small sharp-ening stones; sharp stones in a cove; high cliff? |
| **Cocumussoc** | See **Cocumscusset** | |

45

| Coesit | See **Cowesit** | |
|---|---|---|
| Coessett | See **Cowesit** | |
| Cogamagooant | See **Cajanaquond** | |
| Cogamaquoant | See **Cajanaquond** | |
| Coginaquon | See **Cajanaquond** | |
| Coginaquond, Coginaquand | See **Cajanaquond** | |
| Coheassuck | Kent County | Pine tree place?; brook near the pines? |
| Cohoes | Shopping center, Providence | Small pine tree |
| Cojonoquant | See **Cajanaquond** | |
| Cojoot | See **Cajoot** | |
| Cokesit | TRACT, in Little Compton, near Dartmouth. It seems there were two Indian places of worship in the town in 1700; one in Seconnet, and the other northward and eastward at Cokesit | Pine place |
| Comnuc | See **Cumnuck** | |
| Conamicut | See **Canonicut** | |
| Conanicus | See **Canonicus** | |
| Conanicut | See **Canonicut** | |
| Conaquetoque | Island, Washington County | Place of the long stream |
| Conconchewa-chet | LAND. | See **Caucauja-watchuck** |
| Conectacutt | See **Connecticut** | |
| Conimicut[10] | Point Beach, Bristol | See **Connimicut** |
| Connannicutt | See **Canonicut** | |

| | | |
|---|---|---|
| **Connaug** | POND, Westconnang. See Stevens's map. S. E. corner of Foster. Westconnaug purchase was south part of Foster, Scituate and Cranston; which lies to the S. West of the North branch of the Pawtuxet river, See plat of it in H. L. Bowen's office. | Long place |
| **Connecticot** | See **Connecticut** | |
| **Connecticut**[11] | Common name on many geographical references | On the long tidal river |
| **Connimicut** | POINT, Warwick, opposite Nayatt. (See Stephen's map); also a map by Des Barres, 1776. | Name of Sachem Canonicus' granddaughter? [Quenimiquet or Quinimikit] |
| **Connitic** | See **Connecticut** | |
| **Conob** | PONDS a few rods east of Brand's Iron Works, west side of Richmond [in Hope Valley]. | Long rock |
| **Conochet** | See **Canonchet** | |
| **Conockonoquit**[12] | ISLAND, is Rose Island, off Newport [in Narragansett Bay], about one mile S. W. from the almshouse. Sold by Canonicus (formerly called Maussup[13],) to Peleg Sanford, 1675. | Long point place |
| **Conockonquit** | See **Conockonoquit** | |
| **Cononicut** | See **Canonicut** | |
| **Consamassett, Consamasset** | TRACT, a part of Moshantatuck or Pawtuxet river [in Cranston] | Place of sharp rocks?; place of long fish (eels) |
| **Consamset** | See **Causumset** | |
| **Conskuet** | Island, Newport County | At the long rock or reef; at the long outlet; the long pouring out place |
| **Consumpsit** | Rock, Bristol County (see **Cowsumpsit**) | Sharpening rock; whetstones; sharp rock |

| | | |
|---|---|---|
| **Coojoot** | See **Cajoot** | |
| **Coonempus** | Road, Newport County, Block Island | Long reef; long gravelly place |
| **Cooneymus** | See **Coonempus** | |
| **Coonimus** | Swamp, Block Island | See **Coonempus** |
| **Copassanatuxet** | LAND. Cepasnetuxet, or Occupassuatuxet. Henry Green farm. It lies on the north side of Gov. Francis's farm, and is of the same breadth, extending from the bay westward. It is the northern boundary line of Warwick | Cove on small tidewater river or inlet |
| **Copassanatuxett** | See **Copassanatuxet** | |
| **Copassnetuxit** | See **Copassanatuxet** | |
| **Copessnatuxit** | See **Copassanatuxet** | |
| **Copessuatuxit** | See **Copassanatuxet** | |
| **Cowaude** | Kent County, Warwick | Pine Place |
| **Cowekesit** | See **Cowesit** | |
| **Cowekesuck** | See **Cowesit** | |
| **Coweset[14], Cowesett[15], Cowessett[16]** | See **Cowesit** | |
| **Cowesit, Coweeset, Cowweeset, Cowweesit, Cowweset, Cowwesit** | LANDS, or kesit or suck. The shore between Apponaug and Greenwich village [in Warwick], including farms from the bay westward to Crompton mills and beyond. Sold to R. I. government, 1639, by Tacommanan and his son Wasewkil, and grandson Namowish. | Pine place |
| **Cowsumpsit** | Ancient Wampanoag village in Bristol and nearby | Place of sharp rocks |
| **Cummock** | Island, Kingston | See **Cumnuck** |
| **Cumnuck** | Island, Washington County, South Kingston | Shut-in place |

| Cushena | Little Compton | Wet land; near where the tide runs out |
|---|---|---|
| **Cushenah** | See **Cushena** | |
| **Cussucquunsh** | Narragansett Sachem or Chief, alias Pessicus and Maussup | See **Narragansett Tribe** |

(Footnotes)
1        Alternate spellings in LaFantasie, vol. 1.
2        Also known as *Nananawtûnu* ("he is ruler, overseer, protector"),  Nanuntenoo or Quananshett among other spellings.
3        Named for Canonicus [1565-1647, the eldest of four sons of Tashtassuck, the first of the recorded chiefs/Sachems of the Narragansett tribe of Indians.  He lived on Conanicut Island (see Quononicut for term less corrupted).  See **Narragansett Tribe.**
4        From *An Historical Sketch of The Town of Scituate, R.I.,* 1877.
5        Rider (page 144) believes this is same as Chipachuack.
6        "Devil" is a good illustration of layperson's misunderstanding of regional Indian languages. The root *chepi* means "separation" (including physical death).  This meaning is illustrated by Roger Williams (1643), where he records: *chepeck* = "the dead"; *Chepassôtam* = "the dead Sachim".
7        Now called Patience Island.
8        See **Wappewassick**.
9        Now called Hog Island.
10       Includes other places in East Greenwich and Bristol.
11       Alternate spellings in LaFantasie, vol. 1.
12       Now called Rose Island.
13       Perhaps not correct (see **Pessicus**); Mausup is believed to have been the brother of Miantonomi, whereas Miantonomi was the nephew of Canonicus. See **Narragansett.**
14       Ancient Nipmuck village in northern RI, west of Blackstone River.
15       Includes a Post office, East Greenwich.
16       Includes Shopping Center in Crompton.

| Name | Historical & Geographical Information | Translation |
|---|---|---|
|  |  |  |
| **D** | | |
| **Dusamequin** | See **Osamequin** | |

| Name | Historical & Geographical Information | Translation |
|---|---|---|
|  |  |  |
| **E** | | |
| **Eackhonk** | RIVER, in the edge of Connecticut, and runs into the Ashwague river. | This is the end of the fishing place; as far as the migratory fish go; a dry or large tree |

| Eascoheague | See **Easterig** | |
|---|---|---|
| **Easterig, Eastcrig** | HILL, or Eascoheague, S. West part of West Greenwich [in Voluntown]. The post office there is so named. The signification of the word is, 'origin of three rivers.' It is a great place for shooting game. | This is as far as the spear-fishing goes; fork in the river where we spear-fish; three forks in the river; source of three rivers; red land; a meadow |
| **Escoheag** | See **Easterig** | |
| **Escoheague** | See **Easterig** | |
| **Espowet** | CREEK, or Sapowet, makes in from the river. It is near Dr. West's house and the bay, in the S. W. part of Tiverton. | At the large cove |

| Name | Historical & Geographical Information | Translation |
|---|---|---|
| | | |
| **G** | | |
| **Genesee, Genessee** | Brook, Woods and Swamp, Kingston | Beautiful valley or there it has fine banks |
| **Gideon** | Alias of Quequaquenuit, Narragansett Sachem or Chief | See **Narragansett Tribe** |

| Name | Historical & Geographical Information | Translation |
|---|---|---|
| | | |
| **H** | | |
| **Hakewamepinke** | Exeter | See **Aspatnansuck** |

50

| | | |
|---|---|---|
| **Hassanamesit** | TRACT in Grafton, one of the principal towns of the Nipmuck Indians, whose south line extended probably into Rhode Island. | Small stones place; place of much gravel |
| **Homoganset** | HUNTING GROUND, Nonequasset, or quksett, or Kesikamuck. The neck of land between Wickford and Anaquatucket river. | At the fishing place; at low tide there are fresh springs; hunting grounds |
| **Horseneck**[1] | Beach, East Greenwich | At the stone (cave) place |
| **Hummock** | Point, Newport County, Portsmouth/Fall River | Fishing place?; enclosed place? |
| **Hummocks** | Newport County, Portsmouth/Fall River | Little fishing place?; enclosed place? |
| **Huron**[2] | Little Huron Pond, Crompton | French word "hure" meaning rough or ruffian per http://www.tolatsga.org/hur.html |
| **Hyens, Hyemps** | See **A'Wumps** | |

(Footnotes)
1        Shows the process of corruption through Anglicization.
2        A confederacy of American Indian peoples formerly occupying the country between Georgian Bay and Lake Ontario.

| Name | Historical & Geographical Information | Translation |
|---|---|---|
| | | |
| **I** | | |
| **Iagoo**[1] | Pond, Washington County | Boaster; story teller |
| **Iams** | See **A'Wumps** | |
| **Indian**[2] | Not a Native American word; of unknown origin, attributed to Christopher Columbus in 15th century | |

(Footnotes)
1        A corruption of name from W.W. Longfellow's poem, *Song of Hiawatha*.
2        Places so named in RI include Hill, Ridge, Neck, Cedar Swamp, Lake, Shores, Rock, Cemetery, Run, Reservoir &c in Carolina, Block Island, Narragansett Pier, North Scituate and Slocum.

| Name | Historical & Geographical Information | Translation |
|------|------|------|
| | | |
| **K** | | |
| **Kachanquant** | See **Cajanaquond** | |
| **Kedinker** | See **Kedinket** | |
| **Kedinket** | Island, Washington County, Ashaway | A ship; on the ship; it resembles a little ship |
| **Keech** | Hill, Georgiaville | See **Keeck** ? |
| **Keeck** | Pond, Providence County, Geogiaville | Kettle pond |
| **Keekamuett** | See **Kickamuit** | |
| **Keekamuit** | See **Kickamuit** | |
| **Keekkamuit** | See **Kickamuit** | |
| **Kekamenset** | See **Kickamuit** | |
| **Kekamewett** | See **Kickamuit** | |
| **Kekamuett** | See **Kickamuit** | |
| **Kesickamuck** | Washington County, Wickford | Stony fishing place; stone we stand on when fishing |
| **Kesikomuck** | See **Kesickamuck** | |
| **Kickamuit** | SPRING at the extreme N. E. part of Bristol, a few rods from the Warren line. In Narragansett dialect, springs were called Watchkecum; clear spring, Mishamuit. On the other side of the bay springs were called Dashmuit, Ashimuit; but Kickamuit means clear spring. | See alternative entry |
| **Kickamuit**[1] | RIVER, means a back river. It is in the north part of Warren. It was also applied, says Judge Brayton, to Apponaug mill stream, entering the N. W. corner of Greenwich bay, | Where the otter passes; at the large spring |
| **Kickemuet** | See **Kickamuit** | |

| | | |
|---|---|---|
| **Kickemuit** | See **Kickamuit** | |
| **Kickomuet** | See **Kickamuit** | |
| **Kikemuit** | See **Kickamuit** | |
| **King Philip, King Phillip** | Rock, Seat, Chair, House, Inn, Road & others throughout region | English (royal) name given to the Wampanoag Grand Sachem Pometacomet (or Pometacom or Metacom, or Metacomet, or Wawesawanit[2]), son of Massasoit and after whom is named "The King Philips' War" (1675-6). |
| **Kitachanniqut** | Kent County | Principal long place; principal long beach |
| **Kitacka muck nut** | See **Kittackamucket** | |
| **Kitackamuckqut** | See **Kittackamucket** | |
| **Kitackamuckqutt** | See **Kittackamucket** | |
| **Kitackquamuckopett** | See **Kittackamucket** | |
| **Kitamuckqut** | See **Kittackamucket** | |
| **Kitickamuckqutt** | See **Kittackamucket** | |
| **Kittacka mucket** | See **Kittackamucket** | |
| **Kittackamucket** | or Muckqut, COVE, on R[hode?]. Island, Narrgansett Bay[3] | On the mainland opposite |
| **Kittackquam uckquiet** | See **Kittackamucket** | |
| **Kittackquamuck opelle[4]** | See **Kittackamucket** | |
| **Kitts** | Corner & School, Crompton and Pond, Kingston | Cormorants[5]? |

(Footnotes)
1        About 16 different spelling exist for this place (Huden, page 81).

| | |
|---|---|
| 2 | Little spirit that circles and circles (like a fox) |
| 3 | Rider (Map, ff. page 58) shows this located in Portsmouth. |
| 4 | A single word—**Kittackquamuckopelle**. |
| 5 | Any dark-colored web-footed water birds that have a long neck, hooked bill, and distensible throat pouch. |

| Name | Historical & Geographical Information | Translation |
|---|---|---|
| | | |
| **L** | | |
| **Locasquiset** | See **Louisquissett** | |
| **Loisquisset** | See **Louisquissett** | |
| **Loquasquiscit** | See **Louisquissett** | |
| **Loquasquocit** | See **Louisquissett** | |
| **Loquasqusuck** | See **Louisquissett** | |
| **Loquassuck** | See **Louisquissett** | |
| **Loqusqusset** | See **Louisquissett** | |
| **Louisquissett**[1] | RIVER, or Loqusqusset, TRACT of land through which the turnpike runs at the Lime quarries, in Smithfield on which Jenks lives and the late Elisha Olney. | At the meeting place |

(Footnotes)

1      Also Golf Course in Providence. Name of ancient Wampanoag village near Pawtucket and spelled Loquasquscut in Swanton; more than 20 spellings recorded for this place (Huden, page 85).

| Name | Historical & Geographical Information | Translation |
|---|---|---|
| | | |
| **M** | | |
| | Washington County, Charlestown | Place of big beach wells (hollow logs that fill up with fresh water at low tide) |
| **Machepacon-aponsuck** | See **Machepaconapunsuck** | |

| | | |
|---|---|---|
| **Machepacon-apunsuck** | Washington County, Coventry | Big enclosure near falls in the brook?; big bank near brook falls |
| **Machipscat** | Kent County | A "bad" (i.e., stony) path; rough place |
| **Maddock** | Alumni Building, Providence | Bad land place |
| **Mae-baquamagauset[1]** | Little Compton | ? |
| **Mamaniskak** | Washington County, Westerly | Near the joined rocks |
| **Mamantapit** | TRACT, or wading river or place, being another boundary of the same line of Willet's purchase last mentioned, and near the junction of Cumberland and Attleboro', in their northern line. [See deed in Bliss' History.] | Customarily he walks in the water here; wading-place |
| **Mamaquag** | See **Mammaquaug** | |
| **Mammaquaug** | BROOK, running south from Hopkinton to the Pawcatuck river in N, W. corner of the town of Westerly. There is a small fish thus called. | Small fish (smelts) |
| **Mananiskak** | Washington County, Westerly | Near the joined rocks |
| **Manchuck** | See **Manshuck** | |
| **Manipsconasset** | ROCK, near Pawtuxet bridge, Warwick | Place of split rock island |
| **Manisses** | Block Island, or Monasses, It means Island of little God. | Little island; little god place |
| **Manquock** | See **Misquamacut** | |
| **Manshuck** | near the "Olney's Land". [See page 29, Vol. 1. Registry of Deeds of Providence.] It is near Olney's lane, N. E. of Constitution hill, Providence. | Place of split rock island |
| **Masantatack** | See **Mashatatack** | |
| **Mascachaug** | See **Mascachowage** | |
| **Mascachowage** | Brook, Providence County, West Greenwich | Place of long rushes (cat tails?) |

| | | |
|---|---|---|
| **Mascachuge** | See **Mascachowage** | |
| **Mascachusett** | Greenwich, Kent County ? | Near place of flags or rushes (See **Mascachowage**) |
| **Mascacowage** | See **Mascakonage** | |
| **Mascakonage** | BROOK, or RIVER, and is applied to a tract of land called Wyaxcumscut, being a tract bought by Richard Smith, Gov. Winthrop and Major Allerton. It lies N. W. of Wickford, was bought from Coquinaquon sachem and son of Miantonomia. | Place of long rushes (cat tails?) (See **Mascakonage**) |
| **Maschaug** | Pond, Watch Hill | See **Massachaug** |
| **Mashantatuck** | Knightsville, Cranston | See **Mashentuck** |
| **Mashanticut** | See **Mashentuck** | |
| **Mashantotat** | Near North side of Pawtuxet River | See **Mashantatuck ?** |
| **Mashapaug** | POND, two miles S. W. from Providence bridge [in Providence, per GNIS database]. There is also a Mashapaug pond in Old Warwick, sometimes called Pomamganset. | A large pond |
| **Mashapaug** | BROOK runs S. from the pond. | See **Mashapaug** above |
| | TRACT, N. W. corner of Charlestown to Pawcatuck river, including, probably, Poquyent brook, [See page 249, Potter,] and having Nisquitianxsett between it and the ocean, and Wecapaug on the west side and Seepooke on the east side. | Place of big rocks in the pool |
| **Mashatatack** | Brook, Providence County | Well forested place |
| **Mashattaneeseck** | Hill, Washington County | Brook near great hill; great hill near brook |

| | | |
|---|---|---|
| **Mashentuck** | Town, Providence | Many trees; well forested place |
| **Mashepok** | See **Mashapaug** | |
| **Mashipaug** | See **Mashapaug** | |
| **Mashonaug** | ISLAND, in Pauwanget pond, Charlestown, and near the east end of it. Three small islands, called Browning isles, are represented on an old map, in said pond. | Nettles?; dug-out canoe place?; place reached by boat? |
| **Mashovsakit** | See **Niswosakit** | |
| **Mashpaug** | Ponds, Washington County | Great ponds |
| **Mashpoag** | Pond, Cranston | See **Mashapaug** |
| **Maskaeowage** | See **Mascakonage** | |
| **Maskataquatt** | Providence County | Place of rushes; grassy place |
| **Maskechusett** | Brook & Hill, Kent County | At the grassy place; place of flags |
| **Maskechusic** | POINT, at the mouth of Hunt's river. | See Maskechusett |
| **Maskerchugg** | River, East Greenwich | See **Masquachug** |
| **Maskituash** | Bristol County, Barrington | Hay-marsh; grassy places |
| **Masquachow-awaug** | Washington County | Place where rushes grow?; salmon fishing place? |
| **Masquachug** | BROOK, Muddy brook, or Maskachaug or Mascachusett, on old map [in Warwick ]. It is applied also to a hill, half way between Greenwich and Potowomut [in East Greenwich]. Potter says at the mouth of Hunt's river. | See **Mascachusett** |
| **Massachaug** | Pond, Watch Hill, Westerly | Land near the great hill; land where rushes grow (See **Mascachowage)** |

| | | |
|---|---|---|
| **Massachuset, Massachusett[2]** | See **Massachusetts** | |
| **Massachusetts** | Many locations | At or near the great hills |
| **Massanegto-caneh** | TRACT, on the east side of Blackstone river, in the north part of Cumberland. [See deed of Wamsitta to Thomas Willet, in Bliss' History of Re-hoboth, page 51,] where this is the name of the boundary sold to Willet. | Place of source of the great stream; union of great streams |
| **Massapaug** | See **Mashapaug** | |
| **Massapoag** | See **Mashapaug** | |
| **Massasoit** | Spring, Camp, Avenue, etc., Bristol County, Bristol | Great Commander or Leader (Grand Sachem of Wampanoag people in 17th century) |
| **Massathusets** | See **Massachusetts** | |
| **Massatucket** | See **Massatuxet** | |
| **Massatusitts** | See **Massachusetts** | |
| **Massatuxet** | BROOK, between Westerly and Watch Hill. | At the great brook |
| **Massaugatucket** | River, Washington County | At the great outlet of the tidal river |
| **Masscomscott** | Unknown (see Bartlett, Vol. I) | Place of large rock ? |
| **Masshattaneesec** | Hill, Washington County | Brook at the great hill |
| **Masswascutt** | Land between the rivers, Moshassuck and Wanas-quatucket Rivers (Providence River) in Providence (Bartlett, Vol. I) | Great meadow (or green) place; great hill (or stone) place? |
| **Mastuxet** | See **Massatuxet** | |
| **Matacompemis-cok** | Washington County, Westerly | Place (far away) up country |
| **Matanuck** | Post office, Kingston | See **Matunuck** |

| Matateconit | See **Mattetakonitt** | |
|---|---|---|
| **Matatucket** | River, Washington County, North Kingston | Poorly forested; at the worthless river? |
| **Matony, Matomy** | HILL, runs S. E. by East some miles and the turnpike crosses it near its south end, three miles S. E. of Chepachet [in Burriville]. | Lookout place; observation height |
| **Mattachusetts, Mattachusett** | See **Massachusetts** | |
| **Mattantuck, Matantuck** | Narragansett Sachem or Chief (alias "The Old Queen" or "Magnus") | See **Narragansett Tribe** |
| **Mattapoiset, Mattapoisett** | See **Mattapoysett** | |
| **Mattapoysett** | RIVER, means crying chief, - in Swanzy. Gardner's neck, so called, is bounded by it. | Little resting place |
| **Mattato** | HILL, in N. W. part of Providence county, probably in Burrillville. [See deed signed by Daniel Mathewson, 1719, vol. 4, page 28, Prov. Records.] | Bad hill ? |
| **Mattatuxet** | See **Mattatuxot** | |
| **Mattatuxot** | River, Washington County, Wickford | At the worthless little river?; poorly wooded place? |
| **Mattetakonitt** | Providence County, North Providence | At the great spring; distant spring |

| | | |
|---|---|---|
| **Mattoonuc** | NECK, and RIVER or BROOK, N. W. part of Point Judith, the river runs into Point Judith pond [in South Kingston]; it crosses the road east of Judge Peckham's a little west of Wakefield. The name was given by M. C. Perry to his country place on the Hudson. Near this brook is the birth-place of the two Com. Perrys | Lookout hill place |
| **Matunuc** | Lake, Kingston | See **Matunuck** |
| **Matunuck** | Village, Washington County, South Kingston | High or observation place (see **Mattoonuc**) |
| **Maushapog** | See **Mashapaug** | |
| **Maushapogue** | Ancient Narragansett village, Providence County | See **Mashapaug** |
| **Maussup** | See **Moosup** | |
| **Mausup** | See **Moosup** | |
| **Mawsup** | See **Mausup** | |
| **Meantonomeah** | See **Miantonomi** | |
| **Mecksa** | Narragansett Sachem or Chief | See **Narragansett Tribe** |
| **Mesanagtaconeh** | See **Massanegtocaneh** | |
| **Meshantic** | Brook and State Park, Providence | Woody place; canoe-tree? |
| **Meshanticut** | City, Brook and State Park, &c in Providence, East Greenwich | At place of many big trees; well forested place (same as **Meshantic** ?) |
| **Metacom** | [Avenue, Bristol] & seat of King Philip, N. E. side of Mount Hope bay [on grounds of Haffenreffer Museum, Brown University in Bristol], at its base, and on land of the late Hon. James De Wolf. | At a faraway place?; Of the Massasoits' house? (see **King Philip** & **Pometacomet**)) |

| | | |
|---|---|---|
| **Metacomet**[3] | Brook, Country Club, Providence | Of the Massasoits' house? (see **King Philip**, **Metacom** & **Pometacomet**) |
| **Metacurset**[4] | TRACT, contiguous to the last or Mascakonage; deeded by said sachem [Coquinaquont]. | ? |
| **Metapoiset** | See **Mattapoysett** | |
| **Metatoxet** | River, Washington County, Wickford | Well wooded stream place |
| **Metatuxet** | See **Metatoxet** | |
| **Metaubscot** | See **Mettaubscut** | |
| **Metonomy** | See **Tommany/ Miantonomi** | |
| **Mettaubscut** | an Indian village, once stood west from Cowesett shore, between Apponaug and East Greenwich. [See letter of Roger Williams.] | Black rocks place (or cliff) |
| **Mettobscot** | See **Mettaubscut** | |
| **Miantenomi** | See **Miantonomi** | |
| **Miantomi** | See **Miantonomi** | |
| **Miantonomi**[5], **Miantonomy**, **Miantunnomues**, **Miantunnomus**, **Miantunomu** | Hill, Park & Avenue, Newport County, Newport & Hill, Prudence Island | He wages war (Narragansett Sachem or Chief) |
| **Miantonomia** | See **Miantonomi** | |
| **Miantunnomu** | See **Miantonomi** | |
| **Micksa** | See **Mecksa** | |
| **Minabauge** | See **Minnabaug** | |

61

| | | |
|---|---|---|
| **Minacommuck** | ISLAND, in Westerly, near the west end of Cedar Swamp, and near a large pond called Pascommattos, marked as Borden or Chapman pond. It is about two miles due east from Westerly village. A brook leads from the Pas-comattas pond to the most southerly bend of Pawca-tuck river, called Aquantaug brook, and its course is through Ashagomiconset. | Berry farm or fields; fields in low lands; plantation in a deep place |
| **Minacomuc** | See **Minacommuck** | |
| **Mincamekek** | See **Minacommuck** ? | |
| **Minebauge** | See **Minnabaug** | |
| **Minnabaug** | POND, of great length on the Charlestown beach. Marked in maps as Babcock's pond. [Potter, page 65.] | Berry (or deep) pond |
| **Miscoe** | Lake, Providence County, Franklin | Great Hill?; small rock?; peeble? |
| **Mishannok** | See **Mishannoke** | |
| **Mishannoke** | Hill, Washington County, Richmond | Large squirrel(s) |
| **Mishanoke** | See **Mishannoke** | |
| **Mishauntatuk, Mishuntatuk** | See **Mashentuck** or **Me-shanticut** | Alternate spellings given in LaFantasie, vol. 1. are **Shanatuck, Shan-tatuck** |
| **Mishawomet** | See **Showomut** | |
| **Mishnic** | POND, West Greenwich, two or three miles south or south-west of Washington village. | They go, come by canoe; squirrel |
| **Mishnock** | Swamp, Lake, River, Cromp-ton | See **Mishnic** |
| **Mishoasakit** | | See **Niswasakit, Niswosakit** |

| | | |
|---|---|---|
| **Mishowomet** | Warwick neck, same as Shaomet. | See **Showomut** |
| **Mishquamicuk** | See **Misquamacut** | |
| **Mishquomacuck, Mishquomacuk** | See **Misquamacut** | |
| **Mishuntatuk** | See **Mashentuck** | |
| **Miskiana** | Camp | See **Miskianza** |
| **Miskianza** | BROOK [& Camp, Slocum], called also Shickasheen. Its waters come from Yarcoo, through Barber's pond. The Stonington Railroad crosses it a few rods south of the road. Nearly opposite to this was the great Indian swamp fight, on the north side of the Railroad. | Trout?; salmon?; grass?; (in Italian, a mixing?) |
| **Miskoasakit** | See **Niswosakit** | |
| **Misoaskit** | See **Niswosakit** | |
| **Misquamacoke** | See **Misquamacut** | |
| **Misquamacuck** | See **Misquamacut** | |
| **Misquamacut** | or coke Manquock, or Astomacut, means salmon [in Watch Hill]. It is the neck of land on the east side of Pawcatuck river. [See Potter, page 242.] The town of Westerly went by this name until it was incorporated in 1669. This tract extends to Wecapaug brook, or boundary line between Westerly and Charlestown. Steven's map erroneously represents Misquamacut to run far eastward of Wecapeug brook. [See affidavits of Indians, in Potter, 248.] | Salmon place |

| | | |
|---|---|---|
| **Misquamakuck** | See **Misquamacut** | |
| **Misquamicoke** | See **Misquamacut** | |
| **Misquamicut** | State Beach | See **Misquamacut** |
| **Misquitanset** | See **Misquitanxit** | |
| **Misquitanxit** | Washington County | At the place of the meadows |
| **Misquomacuk** | See **Misquamacut** | |
| **Misuckaskete** | R. Williams, page 96 | meadow |
| **Miswosket** | See **Niswosoket** | |
| **Mittaubscot** | See **Mettaubscot** | |
| **Mittaubscut** | Ancient Narragansett village, Kent County | See **Mettaubscot** |
| **Mohawk**[6] | | Cannibals |
| **Mohegan**[7] | Bluffs & Village[8], Providence County, Georgiaville | Wolf |
| **Mohegin** | See **Mohegan** | |
| **Molligwasset** | TRACT, sometimes called Wollimosset.  It is the same as Wannimosett,-Viall residence, in Barrington or Seekonk. | Valley place |
| **Monasses** | See **Manisses** | |
| **Monhegan** | Bluffs Beach, Washington County, Block Island | Place of islands |
| **Monotomyny** | See **Miantonomi** | |
| **Mont Haup** | See **Montop** | |
| **Montaup** | Country Club, Fall River | See **Montop** |
| **Montop** | HILL, changed by the English to Mount Hope [or Mount-hope], in Bristol. Near the residence of the late Hon. James D'Wolf. | Lookout place (seat of King Philip on grounds of Haffenref-fer Museum) |
| **Montup** | See **Montop** | |
| **Moohag** | See **Mohawk** | |
| **Moohegan** | See **Mohegan** | |

| Moonasachuet | RIVER. [Potter, 275.] It runs into the Pascachuto pond at the north end of Pettaquam-scott river, from a northerly and north-westerly direction, through Silver Spring factory. | Deep backward (re-versing ?) river |
|---|---|---|
| Moonassachuet | See **Moonasachuet** | |
| Moosehausic | See **Moshassuck** | |
| Mooseup | Valley, Historic District, Oneco | See **Moosup** |
| Mooshansick | See **Moshassuck** | |
| Mooshassuck | See **Moshassuck** | |
| Mooshausick | See **Moshassuck** | |
| Mooshawset | See **Moshassuck** | |
| Moosshausic | See **Moshassuck** | |
| Moosup | River, Providence County, Foster/Coventry & River, Oneco | Narragansett Sachem or Chief (See **Pessi-cus**) |
| Moquois | See **Mohawk** | |
| Morskituash | See **Mosskituash** | |
| Moscachuck | CREEK, north of Nayatt and running to the brick yard from the bay [in Barrington] | Place where rushes grow (see **Masqua-chug**) |
| Moscotage | RIVER, same as Narrow or Pettaquamscot. It runs between Pettaquamscott rock and the bay N. and S. at the east side of Tower hill, from Pascachuto pond to the beach, running N. and S. | Place where rushes grow |
| Mosep | Narragansett Sachem or Chief | See **Narragansett Tribe** |
| Moshantatut | See **Mashanticut** | |
| Moshanticut | BROOK, or Mashatatuck, running near Knightsvile and west of Gorton Arnold's and falls into the Pawtuxet. It was sometimes called Shantituck. | See **Mashanticut** |

| | | |
|---|---|---|
| **Moshassuck**[9] | RIVER, or Moosshausic, means moose hunting grounds, and passes by Gen. Barnes's and along south of Horton's Grove, and receives West river at or near Philip Allen's print works, and near Corliss & Nightingales' factory. It is also applied to a river S. W. of Pawtuxet, near where Samuel Gorton lived, and where he wrote a letter, signed by all his company to Massachusetts government. | Great brook in the marshy meadow; great fish; meadow |
| **Moshausick** | See **Mooshausic** | |
| **Moshosick** | See **Mooshausic** | |
| **Moshowunga-nuck, Moshowungga-nuck** | Washington County, Westerly & Hopkinton | At the place of the great bend (of Pawca-tuck River) |
| **Moshuntatuc** | See **Mashentuck** | |
| **Moshwaniscut** | See **Moshwaniscutt** | |
| **Moshwaniscutt** | POND, near and north of Smithville Seminary [in North Scituate], and within sight of it. The river leading from it through Scituate village has the same name. | Place of mist and fog; red hill at the great bend |
| **Moskituake** | Washington County (Also known as "Mosquito Hawk") | Grassy land |
| **Moskituash** | See **Mosskituash** | |
| **Mosquitohawk** | See **Moskituake** | |
| **Mosquitohawk** | Brook, Carolina | See **Musqueto-hauke** |
| **Mosskituash** | CREEK, in Barrington. it means grass or straw to lie on, or hay. It is now called Viall's creek, the mouth of it being in Barrington. | Meadow, grasses |

66

| | | |
|---|---|---|
| **Mosup** | Narragansett Sachem or Chief | See **Narragansett Tribe** |
| **Mouscochuck** | | See **Mascochuck** |
| **Moswaniscut, Moswansiscut** | See **Moshwaniscutt** | |
| **Mouwneit** | Hill, Washington County, Block Island | Lookout (or assembly?) place |
| **Mowshausick** | See **Mooshausic** | |
| **Mowshawset** | See **Moshassuck** | |
| **Mowshawsuck** | See **Moshassuck** | |
| **Muckqut** | See **Kittackamucket** | |
| **Mukquata** | Washington County | Place of rushes; meadow |
| **Mummaquog** | See **Mammaquaug** | |
| **Munnacommuck** | See **Minacommuck** | |
| **Muscachuge** | See **Masquachug** | |
| **Muschaug** | applied to two PONDS, N. E. by east, near Westerly, and near the ocean, sometimes called East and West Muschaug or Massachaug. The one farthest east is called Musquataug, and is also called Babcock's pond | Place of rushes |
| **Mushattchucka-peake** | Providence County | Pond at the great mountain; big hill near the edge of the bank of the pond |
| **Mushuaganic** | See **Mushuagusset** | |
| **Mushuagusset** | Pond, Washington County | Muskrat place |
| **Muskachaug** | See **Masquachug** | |
| **Muskachuge** | See **Masquachug** | |
| **Musquamacuk** | See **Misquamacut** | |

| | | |
|---|---|---|
| **Musquataug** | POINT, or Muxquataug, just within the S. E. of Westerly. | Places where rushes grow (see **Mukqua-ta)** |
| **Musquechuge** | Kent County | Place where rushes grow |
| **Musquetaug** | Washington County | Place of rushes |
| **Musquetohaug** | See **Musquetohauke** | |
| **Musquetohauke** | or haug, a BROOK, two or three miles north west of Smithville Seminary, and crosses Conn. and R. I. Turn-pike near Scituate Bank, and along the W. side of N. Scitu-ate village, to Aborn & Allen's factory. | Grassy place |
| **Musquetopaug** | See **Musquetohauke**? | Great pond (or place?) |
| **Musquetta** | See **Mukquata** | |
| **Musquetuxet** | TRACT, probably N. of' Paw-tuxet bridge. | Red brook?; brook in grassy place; grassy meadow brook land; place of herbs? |
| **Musqutah**[10] | See **Mukquata** | |
| **Mussachuck** | Creek, Bristol County, Bristol | At the place of flags or rushes |
| **Mussquetaug** | Washington County | Place of rushes |
| **Muxqua** | See **Mukquata** | |
| **Muxquata** | See **Mukquata** | |
| **Muxquataug** | See **Muyquatage** | |
| **Muxquetau** | See **Mukquata** | |
| **Muxquetaugh** | See **Mukquata** | |
| **Muxqutah** | a NECK OF LAND; same as Wecapatug, in Westerly. | Place of rushes |

| Muyquatage | or aug, LAND, between Ward's pond and Quona-quontaug pond, and Weca-paug brook, which here runs into Quonaquontaug pond at its west end, and was claimed as the eastern boundary of,-in or adjoining Charlestown. | Path to the pond place?; place of rushes |
|---|---|---|
| Muyquataug | See **Muyquatage** | |
| Myantanomy | See Miantonomi | |
| Myantonomey | See **Miantonomi** | |

(Footnotes)

1       Apparently not previously translated in Huden et al.; possibly related to **Machaquamagansett.**

2              Name of language (now "extinct") of Wampanoag Indians; formerly called Massachusetts or Massachusee.

3              "Pometacomet" is believed to be the full term.

4              Translation process: met(a) may mean "good or bad or great"; (a)cur may mean "long hill" or curs = "hills", and −est or (r=s)set means "little place of". One guess: "Place of large (or bad) hills" (**Massachuset or Mattachuset)**

5              See **Narragansett.**

6       New York Tribe described by Roger Williams (1643) as "Mohowaúgsuck  *or*  Mauquàuog  *from*  móho *to eate* (the Cannibals, or, Men-eaters, up into the west, two, three or foure hundred miles from us)". See LaFantasie, Vol. 1, for alternate spellings.

7              For other spellings see Trigger (1979), page 175. and LaFantasie, Vol. 1. Swanton's brief tribal summary:

     The Mohegan originally occupied most of the upper valley of the Thames and its branches. Later they claimed authority over some of the Nipmuc and the Connecticut River tribes, and in the old Pequot territory

8              Also "Tribe" (Connecticut).

9       Includes places in Providence and Pawtucket.

10      Rider ( page 284) relates this name to Wecapaug.

| Name | Historical & Geographical Information | Translation |
|---|---|---|
| **N** | | |
| Naaomuck | Neck, Washington County | Narrows fishing place |
| Nachick | Hill, Kent County, Warwick | My house |
| Naddock | See **Natick** | |
| Nahantic, Nah-antick | See **Niantic** | At the point? |
| Nahett | Peninsula or Point, Bristol County, Barrington/Warren | At the point |

| Nahigansett | River (Westerly) & Bay (Narragansett Bay) | See **Narragansett** |
|---|---|---|
| **Nahigonset, Nahigonsett** | Island, Washington County | At the small point |
| **Namacoke** | See **Namcook** | |
| **Namaock** | See **Namcook** | |
| **Namcock** | See **Namcook** | |
| **Namcook** | NECK, or Namacoke or Noomuck. It signifies *bank* in Indian. The English name is Boston neck. It extends from Anaquatucket south to Potter's factory, in North and South Kingstown. | At the fishing place |
| **Namcutt** | See **Nonquit** | |
| **Namecock** | See **Namcook** | |
| **Namecockeneke** | See **Namcook** | |
| **Nameoke** | See **Namcook** | |
| **Namkook** | See **Namcook** | |
| **Namococke** | See **Namcook** | |
| **Nampsic** | Pond, Providence County, North Smithfield | Fishing place |
| **Namquit**[1] | Point, Warwick (historic) | See **Nonequit** |
| **Namquoxet** | Shore, Providence County, Wickford | At the little beach; at the small fishing stand |
| **Namyak** | TRACT, or Namyake, on the west side of Pawcatuck. It was the country of the Pequots. Cassasiminum[2], or mon, was appointed Governor by the Commissioners, 1655. | Fishing place |
| **Namyake** | See **Namyak** | |
| **Nanaquonset** | Island (Fox Is.[3]), Narragansett Bay | Above the confluence of two streams?; narrow strait or long beach; long dry shore? |

| Nanequoxet | See **Nanaquonset** [Neck between Wickford and Annaquatucket River] | Same as **Homogansett & Kesickamuck** |
|---|---|---|
| Nanhiganset, Nanhigansett | See **Narragansett** | |
| Nanhiggonsick | See **Narragansett** | |
| Nanhygansett | See **Narragansett** | |
| Nanigonset | See **Narragansett** | |
| Nanipsic | See **Nampsic** | |
| Naniquoxet | See **Nanaquonset** | |
| Nannaquaket | Point, Neck & Hill, Tiverton | See **Nanquacket** |
| Nannaquokset, Nannaquoksett | See **Nonequasset** | |
| Nannequaket | See **Quacut** or **Nonequasset** | |
| Nannihiggonisk | See **Narragansett** | |
| Nanquacket[4] | POND or COVE, within a mile of the Stone bridge, Tiverton. Sold for Israel angell's soldiers, for revolutionary services. | Swamp dries up |
| Nanquit | See **Nonquit** | |
| Nantiganset | BAY, at the termination of Pawcatuck river, and bounded on the S. W. side by Tower Hill. It is the same as Narragansett, BAY. The name is derived from an island west of Wakefield, between Pettaquamscot and Misquamacook. "The original meaning of the word unknown," says [Roger] Williams. | At the small point; at the place where the river is no longer narrow (see **Narragansett**) |
| Nantusinunk[5] | ISLAND, called also Nomsusmuck. It is Goat Island in Newport Harbor [in Narragansett Bay], less than a quarter of a mile from the end of Long wharf. | Narrow ford or strait |
| Nantusunuk | See **Nantusiunk** | |

| Nantuzenunk | See **Nantusiunk** | |
|---|---|---|
| Naomcuck | See **Namcook** | |
| Naomuck | See **Namcook** | |
| Napatree | Beach & Point, Mystic & Watch Hill | Indian name? |
| Nariganset | See **Narragansett** | |
| **Narraganset**[6], **Narragansett** | Tribe, Indian Reservation & Church, [Hotel & Brewery, formerly], Beer, Pond, Beach, Lake, Bay, Electric Co., Ferry, School & many other references throughout State and region | At the small narrow point |
| Narragansett | Bay[7] | |
| Narragansett | Tribe[8] | |
| Nasauket | Kent County, Warwick | At the neck of land; land between rivers |
| Nashanticut | TRACT, Cranston, about the present place of the Friends' Meeting house. | See **Mashanticut** |
| Nassawket | SHORE, from Apponaug to Warwick neck, Green's point and Buttonwoods occupy a part of it. | See **Nasauket** |
| Natakonkanet | See **Neutaconcanut** | |
| Natchick | See **Nachick** | |
| Natick | FALLS and VILLAGE[9], or Natchick, HILL, S. W. of Providence, 8 miles [in East Greenwich] | My land, home, my house; the place I seek? |
| Nauquit | See **Nonquit** | |
| Nausaucat | See **Nausauket** | |
| Nausauket | Village, Kent County. East Greenwich | At the second outlet; between outlets |
| Nawwhun, Nawham | | In LaFantasie, Vol 1., page xci. |
| Nayanticut | See **Nianticut** | |

| | | |
|---|---|---|
| **Nayatt** | POINT [& other places], in Barrington, eight miles south of Providence [in Bristol] ; has a lighthouse. | At the point |
| **Nayhantic** | See **Niantic** | |
| **Nayot, Nayott** | See **Nayatt** | |
| **Neantick** | See **Niantic** | |
| **Neanticoet** | See **Nianticut** | |
| **Neanticot** | See **Nianticut** | |
| **Neastoquaheaga-nuck, Neastoquahea-gannuck** | See **Easterig** | Believed to be original name from which **Easterig**, **Echoheage** &c are derived in corrupted form |
| **Neataconcanitt** | See **Neutaconcanut** | |
| **Neataconconitt** | See **Neutaconcanut** | |
| **Neataconkonitt** | See **Neutaconcanut** | |
| **Neautoconconet** | See **Neutaconcanut** | |
| **Nedconconit** | See **Neutaconcanut** | |
| **Neekequaw** | See **Neekequawsee** | |
| **Neekequawsee, Nekeequoweese** | POND, probably Quonaquon-taug, in Charlestown; also called Narragansett pond. [see **Pespataug** as alternative name of pond, according to Trumbull, 1881] | My home place, house; double pond? |
| **Neequoweere** | See **Neekequawsee** | |
| **Neetmock** | River, Kent County | Fresh water place |
| **Nekeequoweewe** | See **Neekequawsee** | |
| **Nennecraft** | See **Ninecraft** | |
| **Neotaconckanett** | See **Neutaconcanut** | |
| **Neotaconckett** | See **Neutaconcanut** | |
| **Neotaconckonett** | See **Neutaconcanut** | |
| **Neotaconconitt** | See **Neutaconcanut** | |

| | | |
|---|---|---|
| **Neotaconkanett** | See **Neutaconcanut** | |
| **Neotaconkenitt** | See **Neutaconcanut** | |
| **Neotaconkinitt** | See **Neutaconcanut** | |
| **Neotaconkitt** | See **Neutaconcanut** | |
| **Neotaconquonitt** | See **Neutaconcanut** | |
| **Neotakonconitt** | See **Neutaconcanut** | |
| **Neotakonconitt** | See **Neutaconcanut** | |
| **Neotakonkanitt** | See **Neutaconcanut** | |
| **Neotakonkonitt** | See **Neutaconcanut** | |
| **Neoterconkenitt** | See **Neutaconcanut** | |
| **Neoterkernitt** | See **Neutaconcanut** | |
| **Neotoconenutt** | See **Neutaconcanut** | |
| **Neshunganes** | See **Neshunganset** | |
| **Neshunganset** | BROOK. [See Potter, page 65.] Near the junction of Asha-wake with Pawcatuck river [in Hopkinton]. | In the middle of the fishing place |
| **Nesquaheague** | See **Easterig** | |
| **Netaconkitt** | See **Neutaconcanut** | |
| **Netmocke** | See **Nipmuck** | |
| **Netop** | | My friend |
| **Neudaconkonet** | See **Neutaconcanut** | |
| **Neusneck** | See **Nooseneck** | |
| **Neutaconanut** | See **Neutaconcanut** | |
| **Neutaconcanut**[10] | MOUNTAIN[11] [& Hill, Park], two or three miles S. W. from Providence. A river or brook near its base has the same name, near which is An-taghantic neck. | At the short (scant) boundary mark |
| **Neutaconenutt** | See **Neutaconcanut** | |
| **Neutaconkanut** | See **Neutaconcanut** | |
| **Neutaconkanut** | See **Neutaconcanut** | |
| **Neutaqunkanet** | See Neutaconcanut | |

| Neutoconenutt | See **Neutaconcanut** | |
|---|---|---|
| Neutoconkenett | See **Neutaconcanut** | |
| Newdaconanet | See **Neutaconcanut** | |
| Newdaconkett | See **Neutaconcanut** | |
| Newdaconkonett | See **Neutaconcanut** | |
| Newtaconconut | See **Neutaconcanut** | |
| Newtakonkanut | See **Neutaconcanut** | |
| Newtaquenkanet | See **Neutaconcanut** | |
| Newtaqunkanit | See **Neutaconcanut** | |
| Newteconcanitt | See **Neutaconcanut** | |
| Niantic[12] | Washington County, Point Judith | Point of land at the tidal estuary |
| Niantick | See **Niantic** | |
| Nianticot | See **Niantic** | |
| Nianticut | or Neanticot, or Nyantic, COUNTRY of Ninigret, bounded by Wecapaug brook on the west [in Point Judith]. | At the tidal creek (or estuary) near the point |
| Ninecraft | Narragansett Sachem or Chief | |
| Niniclad | Narragansett Sachem or Chief | See **Narragansett Tribe** |
| Ninigrat | See **Ninigret** | |
| Ninigret[13] | Park, Inn , Pond, Statue in Charlestown, Beach in Carolina, Wildlife Refuge in Quonochontaug and Watch Hill | A Sachem of Niantic tribe |
| Ninigrett | See **Ninigret** | |
| Nipchoosuck | See **Nippsatchuck** | |
| Nipmuc | River, Chepatchet and Hill, Coventry | See Nipmuck |
| Nipmuck | HILL, a ledge a few miles N.W. of Washington village. | See alternative entry |

| Nipmuck[14] | COUNTRY, from Blackstone river westwardly, to the Connecticut, including north part of Smithfield and Burrillville, and probably Douglas and Thompson, but the chief headquarters was at Oxford. | Fresh water place; Fresh water fishing-place |
|---|---|---|
| Nippsatchuck | HILL, or Sachuck N. E. two miles from Greenville, in [North] Smithfield, probably Wolf's hill. | Water near the hill |
| Nipsachet | SWAMP, joins the S. E. corner of Burrillville. | See **Nippsatchuck**? |
| Nipsachook | See **Nippsatchuck** | |
| Nipsachuck | Hill and Swamp, Georgiaville | See **Nippsatchuck** |
| Nisquitianxet | See **Nisquitianxet** | |
| Nisquitianxet, Nisquitianxset | TRACT, east side of Misquamicut [in Westerly], and extending into Charlestown; bounded southerly by the sea, westerly by Wecapaug and Misquamacut, easterly by land bought by Smith and called Seepooke, and northerly by Machaquamaganset and Bapetaushat, a tract sold to William Vaughan, of Newport. | Defiled or unclean place? |
| Niswosaket | See **Niswosakit** | |
| Niswosakit[15] | TRACT, near Greenville, in Smithfield. [See page 163, Potter. Roger Williams's letter[16].] | Water broken up as it goes rapidly downward; two brooks place? |
| Niswosket | See **Niswosakit** | |
| Noadaconqunat | See **Neutaconcanut** | |
| Nockum | Hill, East Providence | Land can be seen far off; sandy? |
| Nomquid | Cove | See **Nonequit** |
| Nomsusmuck | Goat Island, Narragansett Bay | White beach place; infertile mud?; place of little heaps? (See **Nantusiunk**) |

| | | |
|---|---|---|
| **Nomsussmuc** | See **Nomsusmuck** | |
| **Nonequacket** | or quasset, SHORE, same as Homoganset. The shore between Sowanoxet, or Fox Island, and Wickford and Anaquatucket river. | Dry land place (shore) |
| **Nonequasset** | Washington County | Narrow swamp place?; above confluence of two rivers (see **Nanaquonset**) |
| **Nonequit** | or Namquit, POND, near Tiverton Four Corners & Newport. | Dry land (see **Nonquit**) |
| **Nonequoxet** | See **Nanaquonset** | |
| **Nonganeck** | See **Nonequit** | |
| **Nonnequaket** | See **Quacut** | |
| **Nonnequid** | See **Nonequit** | |
| **Nonniquatuc**[17] | See **Nonequit** | |
| **Nonquamquit** | See **Nonequit** | |
| **Nonquid** | See **Nonequit** & **Nonquit** | |
| **Nonquit** | or quamquit COVE or NECK [& Pond, Dam and School], south of Stone bridge, in Tiverton, and half-way to Seaconnet, and adjacent to the late Judge Durfee's residence, one mile south of four corners. | Fishing place |
| **Nonquit** | POINT, or Namquit, Gaspee point, or near it. [Judge Staples, page 229.] | See **Nonequit** |
| **Noomuck** | See **Namcook** | |
| **Nooseneck** | Hill and Post Office, Kent County, Hope Valley and River, Slocum | Beaver place/pond |
| **Noosup neck** | See **Nooseneck** | |
| **Nootas** | See **Nootash** | |

77

| | | |
|---|---|---|
| **Nootash** | Hill, Newport County, Tiverton | Carry loads on your back (i.e., baskets) |
| **Noozapoge** | See **Nooseneck** | |
| **Notacomanet** | See **Neutaconcanut** | |
| **Notaconckanet** | See **Neutaconcanut** | |
| **Notaconeanit** | See **Neutaconcanut** | |
| **Notaconkonott** | See **Neutaconcanut** | |
| **Notacunckanet** | See **Neutaconcanut** | |
| **Notakonanit** | See **Neutaconcanut** | |
| **Notakunkanet** | See **Neutaconcanut** | |
| **Notakunkanit** | See **Neutaconcanut** | |
| **Notakunkanut** | See **Neutaconcanut** | |
| **Notaquoncanot** | See **Neutaconcanut** | |
| **Notaquoncanutt** | See **Neutaconcanut** | |
| **Notaquonckanet** | See **Neutaconcanut** | |
| **Notaquonckanet** | See **Neutaconcanut** | |
| **Noteconkenett** | See **Neutaconcanut** | |
| **Notoconkanet** | See **Neutaconcanut** | |
| **Notoconkenett** | See **Neutaconcanut** | |
| **Notquonckanet** | See **Neutaconcanut** | |
| **Nowesit** | NECK, formed by Kickamuit, on the west side, and Montop or Mount Hope, on the east. | Little middle place |
| **Nowpaug** | TRACT, joined the latter. [See page 64.] Cashawasset was, at the same time, appointed Governor of the Pequots, at Pawcatuck and Wecapaug. | Dry pond ?;Beaver pond? |
| **Nudaconanet** | See **Neutaconcanut** | |
| **Nudaconanett** | See **Neutaconcanut** | |
| **Nudaconanit** | See **Neutaconcanut** | |
| **Nudaconganat** | See **Neutaconcanut** | |
| **Nudaconganet** | See **Neutaconcanut** | |

| Nudaconkenett | See **Neutaconcanut** | |
| --- | --- | --- |
| Nukkekummees | Newport County, Little Compton | Sought for place; desired home; small shelter? |
| Nummastaquyt | See **Nunnaquahgat** | |
| Nunnaquahgat | Neck, Newport County | Dry meadow |
| Nutaconquenitt | See **Neutaconcanut** | |
| Nutconkenut | See **Neutaconcanut** | |
| Nuteconkenett | See **Neutaconcanut** | |
| Nyantaquit | See **Nianticut** | |
| Nyantecutt | See **Nianticut** | |
| Nyantic | See **Nianticut** | |
| Nyatt | Hall, Bristol | See **Nayatt** |

(Footnotes)

1      Huden mentions another source indicating Namquit as a possible contraction for Quinnemquit ("high spring").

2      Alternate spellings in LaFantasie, vol. 1.

3      See Sonanoxet.

4      Probably "Nanaquaket" Pond, Neck and Road in Tiverton, RI.

5      Now called Goat Island.

6      Many variant spellings exist for this place name and tribal name; for sample of historical spellings, see Trigger (1978, pp. 160-178), LaFantasie, vol. 1, and Bartlett (RI Col. Records, Vol I). A capsule summary of Narragansett Tribe is from Swanton (1952):

> The Narragansett occupied the greater part of Rhode Island west of Narragansett Bay, between Providence and Pawcatuck Rivers. At one time they dominated the Coweset (see Nipmuc) north of them and the Eastern Niantic, and they drove the Wampanoag from the island which gives its name to the State of Rhode Island and the Pequot from some territory they held in the west.

7      Narragansett Bay extends N[orth]. 28 miles into the State of Rhode Island. Its climate is mild, as compared with the rest of New England; and it has many attractions in its numerous shore resorts, valuable fisheries, and points of historical interest. It receives the Providence, Pawtuxet, Warren, Taunton, and Apponaug Rivers; the last two through their estuaries, Mount Hope Bay and Greenwich, or Cowesett, Bay. The islands of Rhode Island [Aquidneck Island, commonly] and Canonicut [Jamestown] divide it at its mouth; forming three passages for vessels, known as the E[ast]., W[est]., and Middle Passages. The E[ast]. passage is also called Seaconnet [Sakonnet] River. ["King's Pocket-book of Providence, R.I." Moses King, Cambridge, Mass., 1882 Tibbitts, Shaw & Co., Providence, RI]

8      Here is an abbreviated listing (summarized from Brinley, 1900) of the names of some 17th century Narragansett Sachems [Chiefs] (prior to King Philip's war, 1675-1676) seen in the records of the early English; not all variant spellings are given:

❖ The first Narragansett sachem encountered by the English in the 1600s was Tashtassuck.

❖ Canonicus [1565-1647], the eldest of four sons of Tashtassuck, was the first Grand Sachem of the Narragansetts appearing prominently in the original records of the Colonists.

❖ Maxanno, the son of Canonicus, married Quaiapen, Ninegret's sister.    **79**

Ninegret was the sachem of the Niantics, or the Westerly Tribe, and since the division of that town, now the Charlestown Tribe.

❖ Mecksa, son of Canonicus, married Mattantuck ("The Old Queen" alias "Magnus") and together had sons Scuttop and Quequaquenuit (alias Gideon)

❖ Mascus was a brother of Canonicus.

❖ Canonicus had a sister (name?) who had a son Niniclad (and same-named son) and daughter Quinemique (Quineque)

❖ Miantenomi (or Miantomy or Miantonomi &c) was nephew of Canonicus and son of his brother Mascus. Other nephews of Canonicus were Cussucquunsh (alias Pessicus and Maussup or Mosep) and Cajanaquond. Quonepin was the son of Cajanaquond. Pessecus [Pessicus], the brother of Miantonomi, was admitted sachem with Canonicus. He was put to death by the Mohawks, in 1676. In the war between the Narragansetts and Mohegans, in 1643, Miantenomi was captured by Uncas, the sachem of the Mohegans, and executed.

❖ Canonchet, the son of Miantenomi, was the last sachem of the race up to 1676, the year native peoples were "conquered". He commanded the Indians at the Great Swamp Fight, in 1675. [He was executed by the English.]

　　o See Bartlett's RI Colonial Records (especially Vols. I through III) for other personages. Many alternative spellings in LaFantasie, Vol 1.

9　　　Also Pond in Crompton & East Greenwich, and Hill & Post Office in Crompton
10　　　Rider (page 207) lists many variant spellings (about 65).
11　　　Known more commonly as "Hill".
12　　　Tribal groups (Eastern & Western Niantic) in southwestern RI in Charlestown and Westerly. For other spellings see Trigger (1978), page 174, and LaFantasie, page xci. Swanton's summary:

The Eastern and the Western Niantic were parts of one original tribe split in two perhaps by the Pequot; the nearest relatives of both were probably the Narragansett.

13　　　Alternative spellings in LaFantasie, page xci.
14　　　A tribe in northwestern corner of RI and into Connecticut whose name has been spelled variously Nopnats, Nipnots, Neepnucks, Neepmoogs, Neepmucks, Nipnets, etc. Swanton's summary:

The Nipmuc occupied the central plateau of Massachusetts, particularly the southern part of Worcester County, but they extended into northern Rhode Island and Connecticut.

15　　　Ancient name for Woonsocket, RI.
16　　　See LaFantasie, Glenn W. (1988).
17　　　Parsons (1861) believes this name is from **Quacut**.

| Name | Historical & Geographical Information | Translation |
|---|---|---|
|  |  |  |
| **O** |  |  |
| **Occupaspawtuet** | Cove, Washington County (see **Occupasspatucket**) | Near the cove on the shallow tidal creek |
| **Occupaspawtuxet** | See **Occupasspatucket** |  |
| **Occupasspatuck-et** | COVE or uxet, near Gov. Francis's Warwick. It is printed in Walling's map, "Occu Pas Pawtuxet Cove." | Near the cove on the shallow tidal creek |

| | | |
|---|---|---|
| **Occupasstuxet** | Road, Kent County, East Greenwich | Small cove on tidal creek; cove on small tidal creek |
| **Occupassuatuxet** | See **Copassanatuxet** | |
| **Occupessatuxet** | Cove, East Greenwich | See **Occupessuatuxet** |
| **Occupessuatuxet** | Kent County, Warwick | Small cove on tidewater |
| **Occupesuatutuxit** | See **Occupasspatucket** | |
| **Ohasset** | See **Pocasset** | |
| **Ohomauke** | See **Ohomawauke** | |
| **Ohomawauke** | SWAMP, or Cappacommuck, place of concealment, near Owlshead [in Charlestown] | At the abode of owls; place of refuge or concealment |
| **Ok-wa-nesset** | Camp, Kent County, East Greenwich | At the small island? |
| **Oosamequen** | See **Osamequin** | |
| **Opponauge** | See **Apponaug** | |
| **Opponegansett** | See **Ponaganset** | |
| **Opponenaubock** | See **Apponaug** | |
| **Opponenauhock** | See **Apponaug** | |
| **Opuitowaxet** | Washington County, Wickford | Fording place at the end of the portage; ford at the wading place |
| **Orkatucket** | See **Anaquatucket** | |
| **Osamekin** | See **Osamequin** | |
| **Osamequin[1]** | Nature Trails & Bird Sanctuary, East Providence | Yellow Feather, Indian name of the Massasoit, the Grand Sachem of the Wampanoag Nation |
| **Osquepaug[2]** | River, Washington County, Kingston | At the end of the pond (see Usquepaug) |
| **Ossamequin** | See **Osamequin** | |
| **Ossapimsuck** | See **Assapumsik** | |
| **Ossapmsuck** | See **Assapumsic** | |

81

| Ossopimsuck | See **Assapumsik** | |
| **Ouchamanunka-net** | MEADOW. S. W. from Pawtuxet, and near it. | Cultivated plantation at the halfway place |
| **Ousa Mequin** | See **Osamequin** | |
| **Ousamequen** | See **Osamequin** | |
| **Ousamequin** | See **Osamequin** | |
| **Owsamequin** | See **Osamequin** | |
| **Owsamequine** | See **Osamequin** | |

(Footnotes)
1        Many historic spelling variants.
2        Does not mean "whiskey pond" at some suppose.

| Name | Historical & Geographical Information | Translation |
| --- | --- | --- |
| | | |
| **P** | | |
| **Pacanaset** | Providence County, Johnston | Little cleared place |
| **Pacanauket, Pacanaukett** | See **Pawconakik** | |
| **Pacanawkite** | See **Pawconakik** | |
| **Pacanoket** | Bristol, Warren, Barrington and parts of MA | See **Pawconakik** |
| **Pachanage** | See **Pachatange** | |
| **Pachasset, Pachaset** | See **Pocasset** | |
| **Pachatange**[1] | Washington County | Divided or boundary place |
| **Pachaug** | See **Pachauog** | |
| **Pachauog** | Washington County | The turning place;where they play games and dance?; they are playing? (See Pachaug) |
| **Pachawesit** | Same as **Pocasset**? | |

| | | |
|---|---|---|
| **Pachet** | BROOK, crosses the town line between Little Compton and Tiverton, soon joins the stream coming down from Nonquit point, and discharges into the bay, half-way between Stone bridge and Seaconnet point. | At the boundary; dividing place; turning place |
| **Packanocott** | See **Pawconakik** | |
| **Pa-co-ag** | See **Pascoag** | |
| **Pacousett** | See **Pocasset** (in RI?) | |
| **Pageacoag** | Providence County | Muddy place |
| **Pahcupog** | See **Cockumpaug** | |
| **Pahquopog** | Washington County | Clear pond; shallow pond |
| **Pakanoket** | Bristol County, Bristol ? | At the small plantation |
| **Pakanokick** | See **Pawconakik** | |
| **Pamechipsk** | Hills, Providence County, Smithfield | Cross-wise rocks; transverse rocks (across the path/trail) |
| **Pansacaco** | POND, or Ponscachuto, at north end of Pettaquamscot or Narrow river. It is half way between the Willet farm and Stuart's birth-place, in S. Kingstown. | Crooked outlet; crooked current |
| **Pantacunset** | Providence County, Cranston | At the round place |
| **Papanomscutt** | Peebles Neck | Place where we get winterfish (frostfish, tomcods); lookout place?; broken rocks? |
| **Papaquinapaug, Paupauqunnup-pog** | Pond and River, Providence County, Cranston | Shallow long pond; double long pond? |
| **Papaquinepaug** | See **Papaquinapaug** | |
| **Papasgush** | Washington County | A Counselor of King Philip |

83

| Papasqaush | PENINSULA, Bristol, R. I. It is so spelled in the original Indian deed, and not Pap-poose Squaw, as is generally supposed. | Broken rocks? ; double hill?; patridges? |
|---|---|---|
| Pappoose Squaw | Island | See **Poppasquash** |
| Paquaback | Providence County, Johnston | Clear or shallow pond |
| Paquabuck | See **Paquaback** | |
| Paquantack | or Poquanatack, STREAM, flowing from Poneganset pond, in Glocester, two miles east of Connecticut line, and south of a middle east and west line. | Clear or shallow stream |
| Paquantuck | Brook, Providence County, Thompson | See **Paquantack** |
| Paquattuk | Pawcatuck River, between Connecticut & RI | The clear, shallow tidal stream |
| Paquatuck | See **Pawcatuck** | |
| Paquinapaquoge | MEADOWS, near Cocumscus-sit, or northwest of Wickford. | Place of clear or shallow long pond |
| Paquinep-aguoque | See **Paquinapaquoge** | |
| Pascachute | See **Pansacaco** | |
| Pascachuto | See **Pansacaco** | |
| Paschucham-muck | See **Pasipuchammuck** | |
| Pas-co-ag | See **Pascoag** | |
| Pascoag² | or Pascoage, RIVER and FALLS, south side of Burrillville [in Chepatchet]. [See Registry of Deeds, Providence, page 160.] | The dividing place (rivers); land at the branch |
| Pascoage | See **Pascoag** | |
| Pascogue | See **Pascoag** | |
| Pascomattas | Washington County | Muddy place? |
| Pascommattas | See **Poscomattas** | |

| | | |
|---|---|---|
| **Pasconuquis** | Providence County | Muddy cove |
| **Pasipucham-muck** | or Paschuchammuck, COVE. It is an old mill cove in Warwick, says Judge Brayton. It runs from the shore between Nassauket and Warwick neck, in a N. W. direction. [See Stevens' map.] | Divided fishing place |
| **Paskhoage** | See **Pascoag** | |
| **Paskonucquish** | See **Passconuquis** | |
| **Paskuisset** | See **Pasquesit** | |
| **Paspalonage** | See **Paspatonage ?** | |
| **Paspatanage, Paspatonage** | BROOK, same as Weecapaug, near the line between Westerly and Charlestown. | Small inlet place; boundary at small inlet |
| **Paspataug** | See **Paspatonage** | |
| **Pasquesit** | ROAD, Paskuisset, running S. E. from Champlin's bridge, on the Pawcatuck river, at Mallerd's bridge, passing under it on the east side of the great Indian swamp, N. E. corner of Charlestown. A brook and pond of the same name, which enter Pawcatuck at Kenyon's mills. | Miry place |
| **Pasquiset** | Brook & Pond, Carolina | See **Pasquesit** |
| **Passagas sa waukeag** | See **Pessicus** | |
| **Passaiaco** | See **Paussachuco** | |
| **Passananoke** | Washington County | Muddy place |
| **Passanoquke** | See **Passananoke** | |
| **Passatuthon** | RIVER, about Devil's Foot, a little north by west from Wickford | Muddy shallow place; muddy ford |
| **Passcogue** | | See **Pascoge** |

| | | |
|---|---|---|
| **Passconuquis** | COVE, one mile and a third south of Pawtuxet. On the left of the entrance into it, is Gaspee point, where the Gaspee was taken. It is probably the same as Occupass, Pawtuxet river. | The miry place |
| **Passeonkquis** | Cove, East Greenwich | See **Passconuquis** |
| **Passpatanage, Passpatonage** | See **Paspatanage** | |
| **Passpataug** | See **Paspatanage** | |
| **Passquesit** | See **Pasquesit** | |
| **Paswonquitte** | Kent County | At the muddy bend |
| **Pataconconkset** | BOTTOMS. The Warwick north boundary line courses through Pataconconkset bottoms. | See **Pataconkset ?** |
| **Pataconkset** | Cranston | At the round place |
| **Patagumskocte** | Washington County | Place of the round rock |
| **Patawomuck** | See **Potowomut** | |
| **Patawomut** | River & Rocks, Washington County | Miry meadow place (See **Potowomut**) |
| **Patowomuck** | See **Potowomut** | |
| **Pattukett** | See **Pawtucket** | |
| **Patucket, Patuckett** | See **Pawtucket** | |
| **Patuxet, Patuxet** | River, Neck, Providence County (see **Pawtuxet**) | At the little falls |
| **Patuxit** | See **Patuxet** | |
| **Paucahak** | See **Pocasset** (in RI?) | |
| **Paucamack** | See **Paucamuck** | |
| **Paucamuck** | Pond, Providence County | Open or clear pond; shallow pond |
| **Paucatuck** | See **Pawcatuck** | |
| **Paucatuck** | See **Pawcatuck** | |

86

| | | |
|---|---|---|
| **Pauchasset** | See **Paucahak** | |
| **Pauchasit** | | See Pocasset |
| **Pauchauog** | See **Pachaug** | |
| **Paugachaug** | Newport County | At the clear open place?; pond near the hill? Bare hill? |
| **Paugamaug** | Pond, Washington County, Exeter | Shallow or clear fishing place |
| **Paugatuck** | See **Pawcatuck** | |
| **Paugeamapauge** | Pond, Providence County | Divided pond; shallow fishing place at pond |
| **Paukahak** | See **Pocasset** (in RI?) | |
| **Paukanawket** | See **Pawconakik** | |
| **Paukatuck** | See **Pawcatuck** | |
| **Paupasquachuke** | Kent County | Double Hill Place |
| **Paupausquatch** | See **Paupasquachuke** | |
| **Pauquabunke** | See **Paquaback** | |
| **Paussachuco** | POND, at the north end of Narrow river, and a little north of the boundary line between North and South Kingstown; same as Passaiaco. | Muddy place |
| **Pautucket** | See **Pawtucket** | |
| **Pautuckquitt** | See **Pawtucket** | |
| **Pautuckqut** | See **Pawtucket** | |
| **Pautuxit** | See **Patuxet** | |
| **Pauwanganset** | See **Pawawget** | |
| **Pawamack** | POND, same as Beach pond, north-west corner of Exeter | See **Pawawget** |

| | | |
|---|---|---|
| **Pawawget** | POND, or Powaget in Charlestown, sometimes called Ninigret. Half a mile east of Gen. Stanton's. An arm of this pond stretches north nearly to the highway, where is the Indian fort. It is very near the beach and begins S. W. from Champlin's farm. | Small clear meadow |
| **Pawcanokik, Pawcanakik** | See **Pawconakik** | |
| **Pawcatuck**[3] | BAY and RIVER [and Bridge, Church, Academy in Ashaway & Watch Hill], Westerly, the river rises partly in Connecticut, and makes a part of the boundary between it and Rhode Island. | The clear divided tidal stream; open divided stream |
| **Pawcatucket** | See **Pawcatuck** | |
| **Pawcawtuck** | See **Pawcatuck** | |
| **Pawchauquet** | Ancient Narragansett village, Washington County, "in western RI", according to Swanton (1952) | At the boundary or dividing place |
| **Pawcomet**[4] | Washington County, Arcadia (Beach Pond) | At the small beach |
| **Pawconakik**[5] | TRACT, or Pacanoket, embraced Bristol, Warren and Barrington, with part of Swanzey and Seekonk. It was also called Sowams, by the Narragansetts; but Pawcanokik, by the Wampanoags [an old Indian village]. | At the cleared land |
| **Pawkamauket** | See **Pawconakik** | |
| **Pawkeatucket** | See **Pawcatuck** | |
| **Pawkeesett** | See **Pocasset** ? | |
| **Pawkunnawkitt, Pawkunnawkutt** | See **Pawconakik** | |
| **Pawquabunke** | Providence County | Shallow pond |

88

| | | |
|---|---|---|
| **Pawsacow** | See **Pascachute** | |
| **Pawtucket[6], Pawtuckat, Pawtuckqut, Pawtuckut** | FALLS, four miles north of Providence, in North Providence. It means union of two rivers, and a fall into tide water, because there the fresh water falls into salt. [Potter, page 266. Pequot Testimonies.] | At the falls in the tidal stream |
| **Pawtuxcette** | See **Pawtuxet** | |
| **Pawtuxent** | FALLS, near Westerly, in the Pawcatuck river. | At the little falls |
| **Pawtuxet[7]** | FALLS, in the village of that name, four miles south of Providence [in Warwick]. | At the little falls |
| **Pawwanget** | See **Pawawget** | |
| **Pawwawget** | See **Pawawget** | |
| **Paynatuck** | See **Pawcatuck** | |
| **Pehhongansett** | See **Ponaganset** | |
| **Penhogansett, Penhungasset** | Pond | See **Ponaganset** |
| **Pequod** | See **Pequot** | |
| **Pequot** | RIVER, is Thames river, Connecticut. | See alternative entry |
| **Pequot[8], Pequott, Pequat, Pequt** | PATH, led along the bay through Wickford to Wakefield, and through Charlestown to New York. Post Road. It is the old count road from Providence, along shore to New London and New York. There are houses along this Pequot road wearing a very antique appearance. Alternative spellings in LaFantasie. | Destroyers (Connecticut Tribes) |
| **Pequt** | See **Pequot** | |
| **Pequt toog[9]** | The Pequots | See **Pequot** |

| | | |
|---|---|---|
| **Pesaum-kamesquesit** | POND, Providence County, now Blackmore Pond | Very small plain; meadow at its end |
| **Peskeomscut** | See **Pesquamscot** | |
| **Pespataug** | Pond, Washington County, Charlestown [another name for Nekeequoweese] | The land at the bursting-out place; at the small outlet |
| **Pesquamscot** | POND [the largest body of fresh water in RI] also, Worden's, making nearly the N. E. boundary of the Indian lands, which begin at Cross' Mill, and follow the brook up to a little west of the pond, and then strike a brook that runs into Pawcatuck river, at Zachery's bridge, and follows this to Shaddock's weir bridge, and thence south by Wec-capaug, to the great East and West road, and follows this to Christopher Champlin's farm. | At the cleft rock; split boulder place |
| **Pessacus** | See **Pessicus** | |
| **Pessicus** | Narragansett Chief or Sachem. Also called Maussup & Cus-sucquunsh | Little Bird |
| **Pesuponck** | Name found throughout the region | Hot house (Indian sweatlodge) |
| **Petacomscot, Petacomscott** | See **Pettaquamscot** | |
| **Petaqumskocte** | See **Pettaquamscot** | |
| **Petasquamscutt** | Historical Society, South Kingston | See **Pettaquamscot** |
| **Peteconset** | or quonset, BOTTOMS, on the border marshes of Pawtuxet river, near the village of Pontiac Mills, or Clarkeville. | At or near the small round place (either a hill, wigwam or sweatlodge) |
| **Petequamscot** | See **Pettaquamscot** | |
| **Petequomscutt** | See **Pettaquamscot** | |
| **Petequonset** | See **Peteconset** | |

| | | |
|---|---|---|
| **Pettacomscott** | See **Pettaquamscot** | |
| **Pettacomscutt** | See **Pettaquamscot** | |
| **Pettaconsett** | Kent County | At the small enclosure?; place of the round rocks? (cf. **Petequonset**) |
| **Pettakonsett** | | See **Pettaquamscot** |
| **Pettaquamscot** | TRACT, or PURCHASE; a strip of land, running east from the Pier, in South Kingstown, due west to Charlestown, and along the south side of Worden's pond. | See alternative entry |
| **Pettaquamscot** | ROCK, near the river of that name. It is on the west side of Narrow river, half a mile north east from Tower hill church, and half way, in a straight line to Narrow river, in South Kingstown. | See alternative entry |
| **Pettaquamscot[10], Puttaquomscut, Puttuckquomscut** | RIVER, or Metatoxet, NARROW RIVER, in South Kingtown], and runs parallel with the bay, from Pascachute pond to Whale rock, and is but a few rods East of McSparren and Tower hill. | At the round rock (cf. **Petequonset**) |
| **Pettaquamscutt** | Spring, Kingston | See **Pettaquamscot** |
| **Pettequomscott** | See **Pettaquamscot** | |
| **Pettiquamscut** | See **Pettaquamscot** | |
| **Pettiquamsott** | See **Pettaquamscot** | |
| **Pettycomscok** | See **Pettaquamscot** | |
| **Petusquamscutt** | See **Pettaquamscot** | |
| **Petuxet** | See **Patuxet** | |
| **Pisquasent** | LAND, in Charlestown. [Potter.] | Muddy (or slippery) rocks place |
| **Pissapoque[11]** | Washington County | See **Pesuponck** |

| | | |
|---|---|---|
| **Pittaquomscut** | See **Pettaquamscot** | |
| **Pocasset** | RIVER, over which is thrown the Stone bridge. It is also applied to the country adjoining, eastward, called Tiverton. [See another Pocasset, or Ohasset, page 39.] | See alternative entry |
| **Pocasset**[12] | RIVER, or Pochasset, rises in Johnston, passes Simmons' two factories and Sprague's print works, and enters the Pawtuxet at Whitman's rubber works, two miles from Pawtuxet village. It is also applied to Tiverton shore, as far south as the stone bridge [also in Portsmouth]. The Toskeyonke[13] Indians lived on the bank of this river. | Where the stream widens. This is a common name throughout New England meaning: Where the narrows or straits widen (depending on the type of waterway referenced) |
| **Poccassett** | See **Pocasset** | |
| **Pochasset** | See **Pocasset** | |
| **Pochoke** | See **Pauchauog** | |
| **Pockanocket** | See **Pawconakik** | |
| **Pockenocket** | See **Pawconakik** | |
| **Poggaticut** | Washington County | At the clear tidal creek (also a Chief's or Sachem's name) |
| **Poham** | Rocks Light House, East Providence | See **Pomham** |
| **Pohoganse** | POND, or Mushuagusset, or Mushuaganic is now Bailey pond, in South Kingstown. | See **Mushuagusset** |
| **Pohquantuck** | See **Paquantuck** | |
| **Pojac** | Point, East Greenwich | See **Pojack** |
| **Pojack**[14] | SHORE, south of the mouth of Hunt's river, a little below and S. E. of Greenwich | A Narragansett counselor |
| **Pokanoket** | Tribe & Historic location | See **Pawconakik** |

| | | |
|---|---|---|
| **Pomamganset** | Pond, Kent County, Warwick | At the small bend?; athwart the path?; place of tribute? (see **Mashapaug]** |
| **Pomecanset, Pomecansett** | See **Pomamganset** | |
| **Pometacom, Po-metacum** | See **Metacomet** | |
| **Pometacomet** | See **Metacomet** | He is highest of his generation (i.e., of his father's (Massasoit's) House) |
| **Pomham, Pumhom, Pumhommin, Pummakommins** | SHORE, in Seekonk, opposite Field's point and Pawtuxet [and Rocks in East Providence and Rocks Island, Bristol]. "Warwick Neck," says Judge Brayton, "belonged to Sachem Pomham. A controversy existed between Massachusetts and Rhode Island about the title to it, in which Benedict Arnold took part, and S. Gorton." | He travels by sea (Narragansett Sachem or Chief) |
| **Ponaganset** | RIVER, leading from the same, and uniting with the Moswansicut, to form the north branch of the Pawtuxet [Glocester—Foster—Scituate]. | See related entry |
| **Ponaganset**[15] | POND, near Pine hill, in Glocester. | Oyster processing place; waiting place at the cove? |
| **Poncamac** | See **Wolopeconnet** | |
| **Pondock** | RIVER, runs partly in Rhode Island and into Conn. near Moosup factory. | At the falls |
| **Ponham** | See **Pomham** | |
| **Ponquatist** | See **Puncoteast** | |
| **Ponscachuto** | See **Pansacaco** | |

93

| | | |
|---|---|---|
| **Pontiac** | Mills, Avenue & Highway, Warwick, Cranston & East Greenwich | The falls in the river (name of famous Ottawa Chief) |
| **Poonnock** | Rock, Kingston | Open/clear land? |
| **Pootatugock** | Providence County? | At the place of the cove in the river; shallow cove in the river? |
| **Pootowoomet** | See **Potowomut** | |
| **Popanompscut** | See **Poppanomscut** | |
| **Popanomscut** | See **Papanomscutt** | |
| **Popasquash** | Neck, Point in Bristol | See **Poppasquash** |
| **Poppanomscut** | LANDS, the south of Barrington, generally including Nayatt. [Gen. Fessenden.] Same as Phebe's neck. | Lookout hill place; winter-fish (frost fish) place?; place of the double boulder? (See **Papanomscutt**) |
| **Poppaqninna-paug** | POND, now Fenner's pond, one mile and a half N. W. from Pawtuxet bridge, in a straight line. | Shallow long pond; double long pond? **(See Papaquina-paug)** |
| **Poppasquash** | Neck, Point & Island, Bristol County, Bristol | Partridges; broken rocks? |
| **Poppy-squash** | See **Poppasquash** | |
| **Poquanatack** | See **Poquanatuck** | |
| **Poquanatuck** | Providence County | Shallow river; stream |
| **Poquatocke** | See **Pawcatuck** | |
| **Poquiant** | Brook, Carolina | See **Poquiunk** |
| **Poquinunk** | See **Poquiunk** | |
| **Poquiunk** | BROOK, or Poquinunk or Poquiant, in Charlestown, and runs from Chemunganse pond to Great, or Pawtuxet river | Clear or shallow stream; defender |

| | | |
|---|---|---|
| **Poquiunk** | BROOK, or Potquient runs from Chemagase, or Watchoag pond into Pawcatuck river, at the N. W. corner of Charlestown. Its course is N. W. from Watchaug pond to the river. | See alternative entry |
| **Poquyent** | See **Poquiunk** | |
| **Poscammattas** | POND, near the west end of Cedar swamp, in Westerly, probably Borden or Chapman pond. The line described in Potter, [page 65] began at the east end of Long pond, and ran N. W. crossing the shore road to a small pond and swamp, thence north to Borden's or Chapman's pond, and through this to an island called Minnacommuck, and through Aguntaug brook, and thence by said brook to the south bend of Pawcatuck. | Muddy place? |
| **Posneganset** | POND, or Punhanganset, or Pushaneganset one mile and quarter S. WV. of Pawtuxet [in East Greenwich]. | Oyster processing place; waiting place at the cove? |
| **Postatugock** | LOT. [See Registry of Deeds, Prov. page 48, vol. 1.] It is on the Pawtuxet river, and was sold by Wm. Field to Win. Carpenter. | At the place of the cove in the river; at the shallow cove in the river |
| **Potawomut** | See **Potowomut** | |
| **Potock** | See **Pojack** | |
| **Potowomett** | See **Potowomut** | |
| **Potowomuck** | Neck | See **Potowomut** |

| | | |
|---|---|---|
| **Potowomut** | or Pootowoomet, NECK OF LAND [& Golf Club, Pond, Dam, Post Office, River, Rocks, School], where the Ives live. South west from Warwick Neck light-house two miles [in East Greenwich]. | Low meadow land; where there is a going-to-bring-again (i.e. trading place[16]) |
| **Potowoomuck** | See **Potowomut** | |
| **Potquient** | See **Poquiunk** | |
| **Pottowomut** | See **Potowomut** | |
| **Potok** | | See **Potock** |
| **Potuck, Potucke** | Alternate spellings from LaFantasie, page xci: **Pa-watuck, Pawatuk** | Exercise to derive by reader using the Dictionary |
| **Powaget** | See **Pawawget** | |
| **Powakasik** | Newport | At the widening out place |
| **Powwow** | Indian events held throughout the region and the country involving dancing, drumming, singing and other customs | Medicine Man[17] |
| **Puckanokick** | See **Pawconakik** | |
| **Puckhunk** | or nuck, HILL, N. Stonington, near Hopkinton, R. I. It is also called Pendleton's hill. | Clear stream; smoke place; a bear? |
| **Pucknuck** | See **Puckhunk** | |
| **Pumgansett, Pumganset** | See **Pomecanset** | |
| **Pumham** | See **Pomham** | |
| **Puncateest** | See **Puncoteast** | |
| **Puncatest** | See **Puncoteast** | |
| **Punckatest** | See **Puncoteast** | |

| Puncoteast[18] | TRACT or NECK, the S. W. point of what is now called Tiverton. It is the neck between the east side of the bay and Nonquit pond, on the east. It was the field of several slight skirmishes between the Indians under Philip, and the soldiers under Church. | Low meadow; shallow when overflown |
|---|---|---|
| Punhanganset | See **Ponaganset** | |
| Punhunganset | See **Ponaganset** | |
| Punhungansth | See **Ponaganset** | |
| Punhunyun | See **Ponaganset** | |
| Punkatees | See **Puncoteast** | |
| Punkateest | See **Puncoteast** | |
| Puscommattas | See **Poscammattas** | |
| Pushaneganset | See **Posneganset** | |
| Puttaquamscuts , Puttaquamscut | See **Pettaquamscot** | |
| Puttuckqupmscut | See **Pettaquamscot** | |
| Putuomet | | See **Potowomut** |

(Footnotes)

1        Rider (page 284) relates this place to Wecapaug, and spells it Pachananage.

2        Two branches of the Blackstone River.  Also place name for Church, Post Office, Library, Race Track, Reservoir, Dam.

3        Alternate spellings (from LaFantasie, page xci) include Pawcatuk, Pwacatuck, Pwoacatuck, Pwoakatuck, Pwocatuck

4        Now called "Beach Pond".

5        Pokanoket in modern spelling; a Wampanoag tribe; an ancient village

6        Many places bear this name including City, Reservoir, Post Office, Boys Club, Red Sox baseball team, Church &c.

7        Many places bear this Indian name including City, Bridge, Cove, Park, Neck, River, Valley in Providence, Crompton & East Greenwich. Alternate spellings include Patuxet, Pautuxet, Pautuxett, Pawtuxit

8        Originally "Pepuot" in this and the next entry  (error in Parsons).  For other spellings see Trigger (1978), page 175.Swanton's brief statement about Pequots:

> The Pequot occupied the coast of New London County from Niantic River
> nearly to the Rhode Island State line. Until driven out by the Narragansett,
> they extended into Rhode Island as far as Wecapaug River.

9        Should read **Pequttoog**, ("The Pequots") ; from Roger Williams, *A Key into the Language of America,* 1643.

10        Also—Cove, Wildlife Refuge, Historical Society Building, Lake Shores, Park in **Pettaquamscutt.**

11        Possible origin for "Hothouse Pond".

12        Name for ancient Wampanoag village "near Tiverton, R.I." (Swanton, 1952). Today name for Golf Course, Avenue, Heights, Hill, Pond &c in Providence,        97

Bristol, North Scituate and Fall River.
13        Possibly **Toskaunk, Toskiounke** or **Toskeunke** ("Bridge, ford") in Kent County.
14        Perhaps related to **Pachauog** or **Pawtucket.**
15        Also place name for Middle/High School, River, Dam, Bridge, Fishing Area in
Chepatchet and Clayville.
16        Compare "Paudowaumset" (Pequot-Mohegan language) in New London County, CT.
17        The Narragansett word Taúpowaw ("A wise speaker") may be related.
18        Sometimes called Pocasset Neck (Church, 1716).

| Name | Historical & Geographical Information | Translation |
|---|---|---|
|  |  |  |
| **Q** |  |  |
| **Quacataug** | Washington County, Charlestown | Swampy place; where the land trembles |
| **Quacompaug** | Lodge | See **Cocumpaug?** |
| **Quacut** | NECK, abbreviation of Nonniquatuc, near Howland's ferry, in Tiverton. | Narrow swampy place |
| **Quahaug** | Point, Quonochontaug & Rock, Kingston | See **Quoaug** |
| **Quaket** | Creek & River, Newport County | See **Quacut ?** |

| | | |
|---|---|---|
| **Quamatucumpic** | LAND, near Yawgoo, (or loo,) pond, and Barber's pond, within from one to two miles from North Kingstown depot. It makes the N. E. corner of Hall's purchase, so called, of two miles square; whilst Chippachuac makes the S. E. corner of said two miles purchase, to the brook south of South Kingstown depot. Quowachauk or Whatchaug, makes the S. W. the corner of Hall's purchase, or " Usquepaug river on the west, Pettiquamscot purchase, on the east." [Hall's purchase. By this be it understood, that John Warner bought of a sachem, two miles square, and then deeded it to Henry Hall; and hence called Hall's purchase. East side of it being the west side of Pettaquamscot, or Narrow river, and called Quanatumpic] | Rocks in the long stream |
| **Quamquit** | Cove, Newport County, Tiverton | Wide place (see **Nonquit**) |
| **Quanacontaug** | Pond, Washington County, Quonochontaug | Extended deserted place; at the long beach?; two long ponds in succession |
| **Quanaquataug** | See **Quonacantaug** | |
| **Quanatumpic** | Washington County, Exeter | Long ford; wading place |
| **Quanduck** | Brook, Providence County, Oneco | Long stream |
| **Quanopen** | Alt. spellings in LaFantasie, page xci: **Quawnepum, Qwanipund** | Exercise for reader: to derive using Dictionary |
| **Quanquajawatchuck** | See **Cawcawnjawtchuck** | |

| | | |
|---|---|---|
| **Quanuntowock** | See **Quassaconkanuck** | |
| **Quassakonka-nuck** | POND, N. W. from the snuff mill at the head of Narrow river, South Kingstown. | Stone fence boundary mark; place at the stone wall |
| **Quatenus** | See **Quotenis** | |
| **Quatocanit** | Providence County, North Smithfield | Large plantation; large enclosure |
| **Quatuck** | RIVER, or Quequatasia or Quequatage, two miles up Pawcatuck river, near where Crandall's mill stood in 1681, [Potter,] on the north side, and near the centre of Charlestown. | The long (tidal ?) stream |
| **Quawawehunk** | about the swamp fighting ground, two or three miles west of South Kingstown depot. | Where the land shakes and trembles |
| **Quawquinnip-pau** | POND, south of Pawtuxet, called also Long pond | Stream with a wide turn |
| **Quebaquauge** | See **Aquebapaug** | |
| **Quequachanoke** | Washington County | Place of a strong rapid current |
| **Quequaganewet** | See **Quequaquenuit** | |
| **Quequaken** | Tiverton | See **Quequechan** ? |
| **Quequakenuit** | See **Quequaquenuit** | |
| **Quequanuit** | See **Quequaquenuit** | |
| **Quequaquenuit** | Narragansett Sachem or Chief (alias "Gideon") | See **Narragansett Tribe** |
| **Quequatage** | See **Quatuck** | |
| **Quequatasia** | See **Quatuck** | |
| **Quequataug** | UPLAND, running into the Great Indian Cedar Swamp, in Charlestown. [Potter.] | See **Quacataug** |
| **Quequathanock** | See **Quatuck** | |
| **Quequecham** | See **Quequechan** | |

| | | |
|---|---|---|
| **Quequechan** | SHORE, from Fall River to Taunton. | Very swift current |
| **Quequegusewet** | See **Quequaquenuit** | |
| **Quetenis** | See **Quotenis** | |
| **Quidnesit** | or Aquidesit, or Opuitowaxet, from Pootowoomet to Cocumscusset or Wickford, along the shore [in East Greenwich]. | At the small island |
| **Quidnesset** | Golf & Country Club, East Greenwich and Church, Cemetery and School in Wickford | See **Quednesit** |
| **Quidnessett** | See **Quidnesset** | |
| **Quidnic** | RIVER, one of the western branches of the Pawtuxet river, through Washington village. Its reservoir is near Harkney mills in Coventry, and Quidnic pond. It is near Week's hill. | Place at the end of the hill (see **Aqueednuck**) |
| **Quidnick** | Brook, City & Resevoir, Kent County, Coventry | At the end of a hill |
| **Quidy** | See **Aquidneck** | |
| **Quinamoge** | See **Quinamogue** | |
| **Quinamogue** | MEADOW, in Westerly purchase. [See Potter, 204.] N. W. corner of Westerly, near Weir bridge. | Long fish place; eels (lampries?) |
| **Quinamogue** | MEADOW, in Westerly purchase. It is near the N. W. corner of Charlestown. | See alternative entry |
| **Quinemique** | Narragansett Sachem or Chief | See **Narragansett Tribe** |
| **Quineque** | See **Quinemique** | |
| **Quinimiquet** | See **Quinamogue** | |
| **Quinnihticut** | Connecticut River | On the long tidal river |

101

| | | |
|---|---|---|
| **Quinsnaket** | LEDGE OF ROCKS, S. W. and near the residence of the late Stephen Smith, Esq., and extending west to the Louis-quisset turnpike, near Esquire Olney's [in Lincoln]. The name means rock-house, and is applied to places under shelving rocks. Another place of like form and name is near Woonsocket. | At my stone house |
| **Quinsnicket** | Hill, Pawtucket | See **Quinsnaket** |
| **Quinsniket** | See **Quinsnaket** | |
| **Quinsnikit** | See **Quinsnaket** | |
| **Quinunicut** | See **Canonicut** | |
| **Qunnunnagut** | | See **Cononicut** |
| **Qumatumpick** | Washington County | At the long ford; long wading place; sinking swamp |
| **Qummunagat** | Beaver Tail Point, Jamestown | See **Canonicut** |
| **Qunnihticutt, Qunniticutt, Qunnticut, Quoneticut** | Given in LaFantasie, Vol. 1, page xc | See **Connecticut** |
| **Quoaug** | ROCK, on the shore N. E. of Point Judith. | Round clam |
| **Quoheset, Quohesett** | See **Quonset** | |
| **Quomatumpick** | See **Qumatumpick** | |
| **Quonacantaug, Quonacontaug** | Pond, Washington County, Westerly/Charlestown | At the extended pond; at the long beach |
| **Quonanicut** | See **Canonicut** | |
| **Quonapaug** | See **Canopaug** | |
| **Quonaquatog** | See **Quonacantaug** | |
| **Quonaquontaug** | See **Quonacantaug** | |

| Quonepin | Narragansett Sachem or Chief | See **Narragansett Tribe** |
|---|---|---|
| Quonnaquonset | MEADOWS, in Little Compton. | See **Quonset** ? |
| Quonnoquon | RIVER, enters the north side of Tiverton. | Very long place |
| **Quonny, Quonnie** | Pond | See **Quonochontaug** |
| Quonochontaug | Neck, Post Office, Ponds & Beach, Washington County, Quonochontaug | At the long pond |
| Quonocontaug | Pond, Washington County, Quonochontaug | At the extended pond; at the long beach |
| Quononagutt | See **Canonicut** | |
| Quononaqutt | See **Canonicut** | |
| Quononaquut | See **Canonicut** | |
| Quononicut[1] | See **Canonicut** | |
| Quononiquit | See **Canonicut** | |
| Quononiquot | See **Canonicut** | |
| **Quononoquot, Quononoquott** | See **Canonicut** | |
| Quononoqutt | See **Canonicut** | |
| Quonopataug | See **Quonacantaug** | |
| Quonopaug | Brook, Kent County, North Scituate | Long pond (see **Canopaug)** |
| Quonotamaquot | See **Canonicut** | |
| Quonset | POINT [& Aviation Museum and Airport] makes the right border of the entrance into Wickford bay, being the most projecting point [in Wickford]. | Long place; a round shallow cove |

| Quotenis[2] | ISLAND, in Narragansett bay, was made an Indian fur trading place by the Dutch West India Company, settled in New York, 1617 or 18 and is now called Dutch island. [See page 268 Broadhead's[3] history.] | |
|---|---|---|
| Quowachauck | See **Quowatchaug** | |
| Quowatchaug | Washington County, Westerly | High Hill (See **Watchaug)** |
| Quowchauk | See **Quowatchaug** | |
| Quttonckanitnu-ing | Providence County | Wide planted place; wide garden |

(Footnotes)
1        Original name for Jamestown, in one spelling variant.
2        Not an Indian name according to Huden, but of Latin origin which became Dutch Island.
3        Should read "Brodhead".

| Name | Historical & Geographical Information | Translation |
|---|---|---|
| | | |
| **R** | | |
| Retacumuckut[1] | Washington County | On the west mainland opposite (See **Neutaconkonut)** |
| Romicanset[2] | Providence | See **Pomecanset**? |

(Footnotes)
1        The letter "R" is not found in the Algonquian Indian languages/dialects of Rhode Island.
2        Pomecanset? (Rider's Map, ff. page 58); see above footnote re "R".

| Name | Historical & Geographical Information | Translation |
|---|---|---|
| | | |
| **S** | | |
| Saccanosset | HILL, a coal mine, in Cranston, near Gorton Arnold's, three and half miles west by south from Pawtuxet. | Black earth place; along the little sea-shore trial |

| | | |
|---|---|---|
| **Sacanocho** | Narragansett Sachem or Chief | See **Narragansett Tribe** |
| **Sachem**[1] | Pond, etc., Newport County, Block Island & elsewhere | "The strong one" (tribal leader—akin to "Chief"); also a small, brave bird |
| **Sachimma Co-maco**[2] | Kent County | Sachem's House |
| **Sachuck** | Hill, Providence County | At the mountain (See **Nippsatchuck**) |
| **Sachueeset** | POINT and BAY, making the S. E. point of Rhode Island, mentioned in Church's History of the Indian Wars. It is nearly opposite and N. W. from Sea-connet point. | See **Sachuest** |
| **Sachues** | See **Sachuest** | |
| **Sachuest** | Bay, Beach, Point, River, Golf Club Newport County, Middle-town and Golf Club, Prudence Island and National Wildlife Refuge, Sakonnet Point | At or near the great hill; little hill at the outlet |
| **Sachuset** | See **Sachuest** | |
| **Sackett, Sacket** | School, Providence County, Providence | See **Sauga** ? |
| **Saconaset** | See **Sockanosset** | |
| **Saconet, Sa-conett** | See **Saconnet** | |
| **Saconnet** | POINT, or Seaconnet. South west termination of Little Compton. In 1700, there were 100 Indian men here, and a smaller settlement north east, near Dartmouth. The boundary of the Saconnet Indians, on the north side, was a line from Packet brook to the head of Coaxet. The word, Secon-net, means black goose, like Seekonk. [See introductory remarks.] | Rocky outlet; at the outlet; black goose abode |

| | | |
|---|---|---|
| **Sagamore**[3] | See **Sachem** | |
| **Sahnnock** | Historic District, Washington County, Carolina | See **Shannock** |
| **Sakannet** | Vineyards and Historic District, Tiverton | See **Saconnet** |
| **Sakonet** | See **Saconnet** | |
| **Sakonnet**[4] | See **Saconnet** | |
| **Sapowet** | SHORE [& Cove, Creek, Wildlife Refuge], or Espowet, between Dr. West's house and the bay in southwest part of Tiverton. | By the river; wet miry place (See **Espowet**) |
| **Sassafras** | Island, Tivereton and Point and Cove, Providence | See **Saxafrax** |
| **Sassawitch** | BEACH, next beyond the present one of bathing in Newport. | Eel trap |
| **Satuit** | See **Setuat** | |
| **Sauga** | Point, Washington County, Wickford | At the outlet |
| **Saugatuck** | See **Saugatucket** | |
| **Saugatucket** | Camp, Pond, River at Narragansett Pier | See **Sawcatucket** |
| **Saugkonnate** | Tribe, Little Compton | See **Saconnet** |
| **Sauks** | Island, Washington County, Quonochontaug | Outlet; black mud; yellow earth people (Sauk Tribe) |
| **Sautaug** | POND, north end of Long Island. | Outlet place? |
| **Sawcatucket** | RIVER, South Kingstown, runs from Moore's field, nearly due south, through Peacedale to Wakefield. | At the outlet of the tidal river |
| **Sawgoge** | Sawgoge, or -goog, POINT, in North Kingstown, extension of Sawgogue Meadows. | Loose shell beads (wampum) unstrung |

| Sawgogue | MEADOWS, near Cocumscus-sit, mentioned in Coquino-quand's lease to R. Smith. [See Potter, page 33.] It is between Wickford and Devil's Foot. | See **Sawgoge** |
|---|---|---|
| Sawgoog | See **Sawgoge or Sawgogue** | |
| Sawsumsit | See **Causumset** | |
| Saxafrax[5] | Point & Cove, Providence | Eels? Place of the upright rocks? |
| Scamscammuck | SPRING, near Rumstick point, in Barrington [& Warren]. [Gen. Fessenden.] | Rocky enclosure |
| Scamscamnek | See **Scamscammuck** | |
| Scamscamnet | See **Scamscammuck** | |
| Scatacoke | See **Scatacook** | |
| Scatacook | LANDS, or Scatacosh, part of Kent County [in Coventry]. | Fork in river |
| Scatacosh | See **Scatacook** | |
| Schichmachute | See **Setamachut** | |
| Scituate | Town, Reservoir, Post Office, School, Hall/House, Provi-dence County, Scituate | At the cold springs or cold brook; between tides |
| Scoakequanock-sett | See **Sockanosset** | |
| Scoakequanoc-sett | See **Scoakequanocksett** | |
| Scoconaxit | See **Sockanosset** | |
| Scutabe | See **Scuttop** | |
| Scuttape | See **Scuttop** | |
| Scuttop | Narragansett Sachem or Chief | See **Narragansett Tribe** |
| Seaconk | See **Seekonk** | |
| Seaconke[6] | See **Seekonk** | |
| Seaconnet, Sea-connett | See **Saconnet** | |

| | | |
|---|---|---|
| **Seacunck, Sea-cuncke** | See **Seekonk** | |
| **Seakunk** | See **Seekonk** | |
| **Sec-e-sa-kut** | See **Secasakut** | |
| **Secesakut, Sec-esakutt** | Hill, Providence County, North Scituate | Black rocks place |
| **Seconiganset** | See **Quonset** | |
| **Seconiquonset** | See **Quonset** | |
| **Seconit** | See **Saconnet** | |
| **Seconnet** | See **Saconnet** | |
| **Seconocho** | See **Sacanocho** | |
| **Secunk, Secunke** | See **Seekonk** | |
| **Secunnit** | See **Saconet** | |
| **Seeconnet** | See **Saconnet** | |
| **Seekhouk** | See **Seekonk** | |
| **Seekonk, Secunck, Secunk, Secunke** | RIVER and TOWN [& Park, Plain], opposite Providence, in Massachusetts. Name derived from Seki, black, and konk, goose. It has recently been decided to annex this town to Rhode Island. It is believed from tradition, that wild geese, in migrating, stop here to feed. | Black goose abode; outlet; mouth of the stream |
| **Seepoke** | or Sepooke, TRACT of land R. Smith bought of the Indian, Hermon Garret, [Potter's History,] adjoining the west side of Weecapaug line, where Charlestown and Westerly join, probably including the eastern part of the town of Charlestown, and the western part of South Kingstown. | Salt pond in water |
| **Seepoocke** | See **Seepoke** | |
| **Seepooke** | See **Seepoke** | |

| | | |
|---|---|---|
| **Seewamuck** | POINT, nearly three miles northwest of Slade's Ferry, a point of land where Taunton river enters Montop bay. [De Barre's map.] | At the place where we catch bream (porgies[7]); at the place of early summer fish; big plain or meadow place; place of *sewan*[8] |
| **Seippog** | See **Seepoke** | |
| **Sekescute** | See **Secesakut** | |
| **Sekonit** | See **Saconnet** | |
| **Sekunk** | See **Seekonk** | |
| **Senechataconet** | TRACT, between Abbott's run and the Blackstone or Sneachteconnet river, and extending north to the Massachusett's boundary line. It is a part, if not all, of Cumberland gore. [See old map in Arnold's History, 2d vol.] | Stony angle (corner) of plantation; stepping-stones ford |
| **Sepooke** | See **Seepoke** | |
| **Setamachut** | Hill, Providence County, Johnston | At the great stony hill; place of strong currents? |
| **Setamechut** | See **Setamachut** | |
| **Settemeechut** | See **Setamachut** | |
| **Setuat** | Providence County, Cranston | Cold brook; salt, cold stream? |
| **Shaganiscalhauk** | Washington County | Land at the side of the hills; land of the green hills?; land between hills |
| **Shamcook** | BANK or SHORE, same as Namcook or Naomuck, Boston neck, in North Kingstown. | Great salmon (or fishing) place |
| **Shanatuck, Shantatuck** | | See **Mashentuck, Meshantic** |
| **Shannock** | RIVER, in North Stonington, runs into Pawcatuck river, N. W. corner of Westerly. It means squirrel river. | Where two streams meet; big squirrel; morning star |

| | | |
|---|---|---|
| **Shannock, Sha-nock** | HILL [& Mill & Post Office], or Mishannoke, HILL, S. E. corner of Richmond [in Carolina]. The name means squirrel. | See **Shamcook** |
| **Shannuck** | See **Shannock** | |
| **Shantituck** | BROOK, Cranston, called also Meshautituck. A Quaker Meeting house was not far from here. [See Staples, page 430.] | Large trees near the river |
| **Shaomet** | See **Shawomut** | |
| **Shawhomett** | See **Shawomut** | |
| **Shawmut** | Historical place, Providence | See **Shawomut** |
| **Shawnnuck** | See **Shannock** | |
| | | |
| **Shaw-omet** | See **Shawomut** | |
| **Shawomock** | See **Shawomut** | |
| **Shawomut** | NECK. Warwick Neck. The Indian word means a spring. Boston was so called, from a spring. Also, a tongue of land, running from Slade's ferry, south west, near Tiverton. | At the neck of land; canoe landing place |
| **Sheganiscalhoke** | LANDS. It applies to the east side of the boundary between Westerly and Charlestown. | See **Shaganis-cathoke** |
| **Sheganiscathoke** | See **Shaganiscathoke** | |
| **Sheganiska-choke** | See **Shaganiscathoke** | |
| **Shenskonet** | Brook & Hill, Providence County, Glocester | Strong field; wholly enclosed place?; level land? (see **Shinskatuck**) |
| **Shewatuck** | See **Showatucquese** | |
| **Shewatucket** | Stream, Providence County, North Kingston | At the place between tidal streams |
| **Shewatucquese** | See **Showatucquese** | |
| **Shewotuck** | Brook [also called Phillip Brook], | See **Shewatucket** |

| | | |
|---|---|---|
| **Shewtuck** | RIVER or CREEK, see Show-auckese [in North Kingston]. | See **Shewatucket** |
| **Shewtuk** | See **Shewatucket** | |
| **Shichemachute** | See **Setamachut** | |
| **Shickasheen** | same as Miskianza, BROOK. It runs from Yagoo and Barber's pond, in South Kingstown. | Great spring |
| **Shinscot** | Brook, Georgiaville | See **Shinskatuck** ? |
| **Shinskatuck** | Brook & Hill, Providence County, Glocester | Spring-fed river (see **Shenskatuck)** |
| **Shippaquonset** | LAND, near Passanoke, or quke, in South Kingstown. [See Potter | Place apart from big point, or from long point |
| **Shippee** | | Large lake |
| **Shogonaug** | Providence County, Glocester | Land on the side of the hill |
| **Showatucquese** | STREAM, or Shewatuck, very small, near Wickford or Cocumscusset bay. [See Potter's History, page 33. Land Records, page 57.] | Place between small streams; small place between streams |
| **Showaukese** | See **Showatucquese** | |
| **Showomet** | Post Office, Bristol | See **Shawomut** |
| **Shumack** | Stream, Washington County | A beaver?; the sumac bush (Arabic word)? |
| **Shuman Kanuc, Shuman Kanuk** | See **Shumunkanuck** | |
| **Shumunkanuc** | Hill, Carolina | See **Shumunka-nuck** |
| **Shumunkanuck** | HILL, N. W. corner of Charlestown, near the Stonington Railroad [in Carolina], and south side of it, midway between Watchaug pond and Richmond Switch, which bears due north one and a half miles. | High enclosed place; place of refuge high up |
| **Sickkibunkiaut** | Hill, North Scituate | See **Setamachut** |
| **Sikunke** | See **Seekonk** | |
| **Sissamachute** | See **Setamachut** | |

| Situate | See **Scituate** | |
| --- | --- | --- |
| **Skamscommuck** | See **Scamscammuck** | |
| **Sneachteconnet** | See **Senechataconet** | |
| **Sneech** | POND, in Cumberland, a mile N. E. of Cumberland hill. | Rocks at the outlet |
| **Sneechteconnet**[9] | RIVER, is the Blackstone river, running through Woonsocket and Mannville. | Rocks in or along the river |
| **Soansacut** | See **Moshwaniscut** | |
| **Soansakant** | See **Moshwaniscut** | |
| **Sockanosset, Sockanossett** | Cross Road , Hill, School for Boys Providence County, Cranston | Dark colored little place |
| **Soewompsit** | See **Sowampsett** | |
| **Sogkonate** | POINT, same as Seeconnet [in Little Compton]. | See **Saconnet** |
| **Sogkonet** | See **Saconnet** | |
| **Sogkunate** | Point, River, Village, Newport County. Little Compton | Haunt of the black goose; land at the outlet; a path along the seashore? |
| **Sonanoxet** | Washington County, Narragansett Bay | Place too strong (hard) to dig; crushed by heavy stone (as in a trap). Now called Fox Island[10] |
| **Sowaams** | See **Sowams** | |
| **Sowampsett** | Pond & River, Bristol County, Warren | Red rocks place |
| **Sowams**[11] | LAND, or Sowamset, part of Barrington and all of Warren and Bristol. | South country |
| **Sowamset** | RIVER, now Warren river; also the name of the present site of Warren village, and of a bank there. | See **Sowamsett** & **Sowams** |

| | | |
|---|---|---|
| **Sowamsett** | Bristol County, Bristol | At the south country; strong plain?; beach trees? |
| **Sowanoxet** | ISLAND. Fox Island, near Wickford. Shickasheen, same as Miskianza, BROOK. It runs from Yagoo and Barber's pond, in South Kingstown. | Place of small shells[12] (see **Sonanoxet**) |
| **Sowhomes** | See **Sowams** | |
| **Sowonexet** | Sowanoxet | |
| **Spoart** | LAND, between Nomquit pond and Nonequacket neck, Tiverton. | Large cove (see **Es-powet**) |
| **Squakheag, Squakeage** | See **Sawgoge** | |
| **Squakheag**[13] | See **Squakheague** | |
| **Squakheague** | Washington County | Waiting, watching place |
| **Squamcut** | Providence County | See **Misquamicut** |
| **Squamicott** | WESTERLY, same as Misquamicutt. | See **Misquamicut** |
| **Squamicut** | See **Misquamicut** | |
| **Squammicott** | Washington County, Chepachet | Salmon fishing place |
| **Squannakonk** | River, Warwick | Salmon fishing place; bream[14] taking place |
| **Squantum** | Association, Providence and Point & Park, East Providence | Angry god?; door, gateway |
| **Squaw**[15] | SQUAW HOLLOW [was] the name given to a district bet[ween]. Orms and Martin St[reet]s [in Providence]. and adjacent to Bull-dog Hill.  It was formerly inhabited almost wholly by negroes and a low class of white people[16]. | Woman |
| **Squepaug** | Washington County | Red pond; end of pond |
| **Squomacuk** | See **Misquamacut** | |

| Suamicut | Burriville | See **Misquamacut** |
|---|---|---|
| **Succotash** | Point, Washington County, Kingston & Road, Wakefield, South Kingston | Shelled corn kernels separated and beaten to a pulp |
| **Suckatunkanuc** | Hill, North Scituate | See **Suckatunkanuck** |
| **Suckatunkanuck** | HILL, a mile or two west of Newtaconquenut hill, in Johnston, and ranging nearly parallel with it. | Dark colored earth (rocks) at the summit |
| **Suckquansh** | See **Cussucquunsh** | |
| **Suckuansh** | See **Cussucquunsh** | |
| **Sugkonate** | See **Saconnet** | |
| **Suker** | POND, runs into Chepachet river, one mile northeast of the village, from a north direction. | It pours forth |
| **Susquansh** | See **Cussucquunsh** | |
| **Sutamachute** | See **Setamachut** | |
| **Swamcot** | NECK, on the east side of Pawcatuck river; same as Misquamacut. | See **Misquamicut** |
| **Swamicott** | VALLEY, two miles S. E. of Chepachet. East of it is Matomy hill, running north and south. | South plantation |
| **Swammicott** | See **Swamicott** | |

(Footnotes)
1        Sometimes spelled "Sachim".
2        Original word, recorded by Roger Williams (1643), is *Sachimmaacômmock* = Sachem's wigwam
3        A Sagamore was thought to be a "subchief", but may mean "He is the Sachem".
4        Also name for Bridge, Point, River, Harbor, City, and one recorded name of Indian Tribe that lived in Little Compton, RI, as described by Church (1716).
5        Sassafras [Sasafrash, Bed & Breakfast, Block Island].
6        Also Tribe of Wampanoag Nation.
7        See **Squannakonk** (footnote).
8        Wampum which the Dutch called *sewan*.
9        Local name for Blackstone River.
10       Several Native American names (Sonanoxet , Sowananoxet, Azoiquoneset, Nonequasset, Nanaquonset) are associated with Fox Island in Narragansett Bay; there appears to be three distinct names describing parts or all of the place Fox Is.
11       Also Bay, School and Playground in East Providence.

12        Probably *sewan* (or wampum)
13        Also an Indian Tribe.
14        A porgy or related fish; any of various freshwater sunfishes, *especially* : Bluegill . Porgy:
**1** : a blue-spotted crimson food fish of the eastern and western Atlantic; *also* : any of various fishes
of the same family. **2** [alteration of *pogy*] : any of various bony fishes (as a menhaden) of families
other than that of the porgy.
15        The only instance of this word discovered in RI place names. "Squaw" is considered
offensive [as discussed in the author's essay—
"The Word 'Squaw' in Historical and Modern Sources" http://www.docstoc.com/profile/waabu].
Some States have changed names involving "squaw".
16        From, "King's Pocket-book of Providence, R.I." Moses King, Cambridge, Mass., 1882
Tibbitts, Shaw & Co., Providence, RI.

| Name | Historical & Geographical Information | Translation |
|---|---|---|
| | | |
| **T** | | |
| **Tabamapaug, Tabamapauge** | Pond, Johnston | Sufficient fish in pond?; clear or shallow pond |
| **Takekamuit** | Bristol County | Place of the spring; fountain |
| **Tauskounk** | or Toskiounke, MEADOW, below Pontiac [in Warwick]. There was an Indian tribe here. [See Vol. 5, page 9, of Providence Records. | A ford or a bridge |
| **Tautog** | Cove, Carolina | Place of fish called Sheepshead ? |
| **Tauton** | River, Watershed &c, RI and MA | On the principal (or great) river |
| **Teapannock** | POND, near the sea shore, probably Babcock's pond in Westerly. It has another Indian name | At the great clearing at the great cove |
| **Teapanocke** | See **Teapannock** | |
| **Tepannock** | See **Teapannock** | |
| **Tepee** | Pond, Providence County, Chepachet | Indian dwelling (not New England) |

115

| | | |
|---|---|---|
| **Tiogue** | Lake, Providence County, Chepachet & Dam, Crompton | Low place; low land it is low? |
| **Tippecan** | See **Tippecanaurit** | |
| **Tippecanaunit** | See **Tippecanaurit** | |
| **Tippecanaurit** | POND, or Tippecanset, or Tippecan, S. W. corner of West Greenwich. | Small place at the great clearing |
| **Tippecanset** | See **Tippecanaurit** | |
| **Tiscatuck** | a small, round swamp, near the centre of Westerly. | At the ford or wading place |
| **Tiscatuk** | See **Tiscatuck** | |
| **Tishcottic** | See **Tishcottie** | |
| **Tishcottie** | FARM, in Westerly, once owned by Samuel Ward. The name is still retained. | At the wading place or ford |
| **Tishmattuck** | See **Tismatic** | |
| **Tismatic** | Washington County, Westerly | Wading place; crude bridge over the water; river over which we cross on a driftwood bridge |
| **Tismattue** | LINE, same as Weacapaug or Weepacannock, between Westerly and Charlestown. | See **Tismatic** |
| **Tismatuc** | See **Tismatic** | |
| **Tismatuck** | See **Tismatic** | |
| **Titicutt, Titticut** | ROAD, leading out from Newport. [See Bartlett, Vol. 1, page 57.] | Place of the principal (or great) tidal river |
| **Toaskeunck** | Kent County | A bridge (made of wood)? |
| **Tobyan** | SWAMP, between Cockompaug pond and the county road, within one mile due north from the old Dutch or Indian fort, in Charlestown. | Camp? |

| | | |
|---|---|---|
| **Tockwotten** | TRACT, S. E. portion of Providence city. | Steep ascent to be climbed; shaped like a pounding mortar; frozen hill |
| **Tockwotton** | Hill, Park, House, [& formerly Hotel], Providence | See **Tockwotten** |
| **Tomaquag** | Indian Memorial Museum, Hope Valley, Exeter | See **Tommaquaug** |
| **Tommany** | HILL, an abbreviation of Wannametonomy[1] or Wonnemetonomy, north of Newport. | Good lookout |
| **Tommaquaug** | or Tommocweague, BROOK, runs from Hopkinton South to Pawcatuck river, near the N.E. corner of Westerly. | They who cut (beavers) |
| **Tommocweague** | See **Tommaquaug** | |
| **Tommoeweague** | See **Tommaquaug** | |
| **Tompe[2], Tompee** | Swamp(s), Little Compton | Camp? Desereted place? |
| **Tonissit** | NECK lower or south end of Warren-mostly in Warren. | Pine place |
| **Toothos[3]** | Path, Little Compton | Small crossing? (Indian name?) |
| **Topamisspauge[4]** | Washington County, Johnston | Little camp at a pond; little twisting river pond? |
| **Toskaunk** | Warren | A bridge or ford |
| **Toskeunke** | See **Tauskounk** | |
| **Toskibunke** | Providence County | A wooden bridge |
| **Toskiounke** | See **Tauskounk** | |
| **Totawamscut, Totawamscutt** | Kent County, Warwick | At the crossing, by means of (stepping) stones |
| **Touisset, Touiset** | Fire Station, Highlands, Wildlife Refuge, Bristol County (Fall River[5]) | Fording place; worn out fields (see **Toweset**) |

| Touskounkanet | Providence County | An enclosure near the (stone) fording place |
|---|---|---|
| Toweset[6] | or Towesit, NECK [& Point], on the Swanzy line, N. E. from Bristol three miles, and two miles N. by E. from Montop, and E. side of Warren. | Near the old fields?; at the place of the pines? |
| Towesit | See **Toweset** | |
| Towoset | See **Toweset** | |
| Toyaskquit | River, Providence County, North Smithfield/Smithfield line | Place of the bridge |
| Toyusqut | See **Toyaskquit** | |
| Tuckonoma | Narragansett Sachem or Chief ? | |
| Tueskennekinck | Location uncertain | A fording place |
| Tuisset | See **Tonissit/ Toweset** | |
| Tummunkque | See **Tommaquaug** | |
| Tuncowsden | POINT, India point, in Providence. [See map of 1741, inserted in history of boundary line in Massachusetts. | On a fast flowing little stream ? |
| Tunipus | POND, very small, in Little Compton. It means little herring, is near the S. E. corner of the town. | Turtle, tortise; small herring? |
| Tunissit | See **Tonissit** | |
| Tunk[7] | Hill, North Scituate | River or wood, tree ? |
| Tuscatucket | RIVER [& Brook], three miles E. N. E. of Apponaug [in East Greenwich]. | At the ford (or wading) place in the tidal stream |

(Footnotes)
1  Narragansett Sachem or Chief.
2  Mentioned in Church (page 38), and called Wilbour's Woods in Little Compton.
3  From Church (1716); called Taylor's Lane, near Patchet Brook on north side of Swamp Road.
4  Now called Randall's Pond.
5  According to GNIS database.
6  Rider (page 140) claims this name is same as **Coweset**.
7  Not certain if Indian name.

| Name | Historical & Geographical Information | Translation |
|------|----------------------------------------|-------------|
|  |  |  |
| **U** |  |  |
| **Uncas**[1] |  | The fox ("circler") (Famous Mohegan Sachem) |
| **Unquawomuck** | Kent County | Beyond the fishing place farther away |
| **Usquebaug** | RIVER, or Osquepaug, or Wawaskepaug, west boundary of S. Kingstown [in Kingstown] , running from Exeter due South till it meets a stream coming from Warden's pond, and thence running to Shannock mills. | At the end of the pond |
| **Usquepaug** | River, Reservoir, Post Office & Historic District, Slocum | See **Usquebaug** |
| **Usquepaugh** | See **Usquebaug** |  |
| **Ussamequen** | See **Osamequin** |  |

(Footnotes)
1        Alternate spellings given in LaFantasie, page xcii. (including Okace, etc.)

| Name | Historical & Geographical Information | Translation |
|------|----------------------------------------|-------------|
|  |  |  |
| **W** |  |  |
| **Wabaquasset** | Providence County, Glocester | Place of flags or rushes for making mats |
| **Wachemottuck** | See **Watchamoquot** |  |
| **Wainsokett** | See **Woonsocket** |  |
| **Wainsokit** | See **Woonsocket** |  |
| **Wakamo** | Park, Park Resort in Wakefield,  East Matunuck, South Kingston | Crooked, bent? End of fishing place? |

| | | |
|---|---|---|
| **Wallum** | Lake, Village, Pond, Dam, Post Office, Providence County, Oxford & Thompson | See **A'wumps** & **Alum** |
| **Wamkeag** | HILL, or Wayunkeak. [Roger Williams.] Two miles north east of Greenville, and extending to Farnum's, or Slaterville turnpike, | White land or place |
| **Wampanoag**[1] | Shopping Mall, East Providence & other places | People of the East or Dawn |
| **Wampanoo**[2] | See **Wapanoos** | |
| **Wampnesick** | applies to Pawtucket. [See page 292. Potter. Deed to Fones.] | Place of chesnut trees? Place at or in the east? |
| **Wanamataneme** | Wannemetonomy/Tommany | |
| **Wanamoiset** | Country Club, East Providence | See **Wannamoiset** |
| **Wanasquatucket, Wanasquatuckett**[3] | See **Woonasquatucket** | |
| **Wanasquatuckqut** | See **Wanasquatucket** | |
| **Wanepoonseag** | Providence County, Hughsdale | Place where (hunting) nets are set?; where the brook floods (see **Wawepoonseag**) |
| **Wannametonomy** | See **Tommany** | |
| **Wannamoisett** | Country Club, East Providence | See **Wannomoisset** |
| **Wannamoisset** | See **Wannomoisset** | |
| **Wannasquatockitt** | See **Wannuchecoecut** | |
| **Wannassquatucket** | See **Wanasquatucket** | |
| **Wannemetonomy** | See **Tommany** | |

| Wannomoisset | TRACT. Viall region, head of Bullock's Cove, near which, on the Warren and Providence road, was the residence of Thomas Willett, who was buried on the east bank of the cove. | At the good fishing place |
|---|---|---|
| Wannuche-coecut | a part of Boston neck, in North Kingstown. | Enclosed camping place; plantation at end of hill |
| Wannuchecom-ecut | Brook, Wickford | See **Wannuche-coecut** |
| Wannumene-tomey | See **Wannemetonomy/ Tommany** | |
| Wanonitonimo | Hill | See **Wannemeton-omy** |
| Wansaukit | See **Woonsocket** | |
| Wansecutt | See **Woonsocket** | |
| Wanshuck | MEADOWS, in North Providence, probably where Wainscott factory is. [See deed, vol. 11, page 36, City Records.] | At the steep place (See **Winscot**) |
| Wanskuck | Park, Boys School, Historic District, Library & Pond, Providence County, Providence | At the end place |
| Wanskuk | See **Wanshuck** | |
| Wansockett | See **Woonsocket** | |
| Wansocott | See **Woonsocket** | |
| Wansocut | See **Woonsocket** | |
| Wansoket | See **Woonsocket** | |
| Wansokett | See **Woonsocket** | |
| Wansokut | See **Woonsocket** | |
| Wansokutt | See **Woonsocket** | |
| Wanuchecom-ecut | See **Wannuchecoecut** | |
| Wanuchecom-ecut | See **Wannuchecoecut** | |

| Wanumetonomy | Golf Club, Prudence Island | See **Wannemeton-omy** |
|---|---|---|
| **Wanwaskepaug** | same as Usquepaug. It is the north west corner of Hall's two mile purchase, at Miumford's mills. | See **Usquebaug** |
| **Wapanoo** | See **Wapanoos** | |
| **Wapanoos** | POINT, is Point Judith. By the Dutch, the name was applied to all Narragansett. [See Broadhead's[4] map in Dutch History of New York.] The Indian name before the Dutch arrived was We-nan-na-toke. [See the word.] | Place in the east? East wind blowing |
| **Wapenocks** | See **Wampanoag** | |
| **Wappewassick[5]** | ISLAND. Prudence. [See Bartlett's Records, vol. 1, page 31.] | At the narrow straits |
| **Wapping** | Road, Newport County, Newport | East land; dawn place |
| **Wapwayset** | See **Weybosset** | |
| **Washouset, Woshonset** | Point, Providence | Place by the hill; boundary brook |
| **Washquisset** | Pond, Providence County | Boundary brook |
| **Washukquatom** | HILL. [See vol. 1, of recorded deeds.] It is in Burrillville. | Summit of hill |
| **Wasquadomesit** | or Westquadomesit, RIVER and LAND, between Limerock and Mansville. [Page 14, vols. 1 and 4, Providence Records.] It extends north to Judge Mann's. On Steven's map, called Crookfall. [See deed, vol 4, page 177.] | Place at the end of the hill; place of walnut trees |
| **Wassamegon** | See **Osamequin** | |
| **Watachun** | SPRING, on the south side of Greenwich, near the mouth of Muscachowage river. | On a hill, hillside |

122

| | | |
|---|---|---|
| **Watchamoquot** | Pond, Washington County, Carolina | Place of the great spring |
| **Watchaug** | POND, near the centre of Charlestown [in Carolina]. It discharges into the Pawcatuck river, by Poquiunk brook, near Brown's bridge. Same as Chemunganock. | Hill country |
| **Watcheer** | ROCK, where Roger Williams is supposed to have landed. This, however, is an expression in old English, equivalent to "How do you do?"— and was used by Indians to welcome Roger Williams when he landed. | Not Indian name |
| **Watchemoket** | Cove & Point, Providence | See **Watchamoquot** |
| **Watchemottuck** | or moyket, NECK, from India bridge to Bowers' cove, and near Kettle point. [See note in Bliss' History,] from which it appears to include all between Ten Mile river and Bullock's cove and Pawtucket river. | See **Watchamoquot** |
| **Watchemoyket** | See **Watchamoquot** | |
| **Watchimoquet** | See **Watchamoquot** | |
| **Watchkecum** | See **Kickamuit** | |
| **Watchymoquett** | See **Watchamoquot** | |
| **Watesamoon-suck** | TRACT and HILL, west of Hopkinton. | Other side of the outlet; junction of brooks |
| **Watuppa** | NORTH, POND, in the southeast corner of Tiverton. It lies chiefly in Massachusetts, the south part being in Rhode Island. | Roots for sewing |

| | | |
|---|---|---|
| **Watuppa** | SOUTH, POND, in the northeast corner of Tiverton, near North Watuppa. The road from Fall River to New Bedford crosses between the two Watuppas. | See alternative entry |
| **Waubosett** | Hill. | See **Weybosset** |
| **Waubosset** | See **Weybosset** | |
| **Wauchimoquot** | See **Watchamoquot** | |
| **Wauwoskepog** | See **Usquebaug** | |
| **Wawaloam** | School, Slocum | See **Wawalona** |
| **Wawalona[6], Wawalonah** | Providence County, Glocester | She roams about? (see **Aspatnansuck**) |
| **Wawashekit** | LAND, north west of Pawtucket Falls. | See **Watchamoquot** |
| **Wawaskesepaug** | See **Usquebaug** | |
| **Wawattaquatuck** | TRACT, or corner of the tract owned or claimed by Herman Garrett, in Charlestown, —northwest corner of it. | Twisting, turning, meandering tidal stream |
| **Waweonk** | See **Wethungamet** | |
| **Wawepoonseag** | Providence County, Lonsdale (see **Wawweponseag**) | Place where the stream overflows; where birds are snared? |
| **Wawoskepog** | See **Chippuxet** | |
| **Wawweonke** | See **Weeweonk** | |
| **Wawweponseag** | SHORE. Blackstone's residence, near Lonsdale. It means place for snareing water fowl. | Place where the stream overflows |
| **Wawwepoon-seag** | See **Wawepoonseag** | |
| **Wawwoskepog** | See **Usquebaug** | |
| **Waxcadowa** | See **Weecapaug** | |
| **Wayanitoke** | Point Judith | Twisting current?; waves around a bend |
| **Waybausset** | Neck, Providence | See **Weybosset** |

| | | |
|---|---|---|
| **Waybousett** | Hill, Providence | See **Weybosset** |
| **Wayboussett** | Hill, Providence | See **Weybosset** |
| **Waypoyset** | NARROWS, at the entrance of Kickamuit river, which runs north and south through the eastern part of Warren | See **Weybosset** |
| **Wayunckeke** | See **Wiorickheague** | |
| **Wayunkeage** | See **Wiorickheague** | |
| **Wayunkeak** | See **Wamkeag** | |
| **Weacapaug** | See **Weecapaug** | |
| **Wecacheconet** | See **Witchetseconnet** | |
| **Wecapaug** | See **Weecapaug** | |
| **Wecatheconnet** | See **Witchetseconnet** | |
| **Wechenama** | MEADOW, or Nonganeck, between Old Warwick and Pawtuxet river. West and south west from the bridge | See **Nonganeck** |
| **Wechenoma** | See **Wequeehackomuck** | |
| **Weecapaug**[7] | NECK and BROOK, or Musqutah, or Paspataug, or Paspalonage, or Tismatuc, or Waxcadowa. It runs southerly, and enters the west end of Quanaquataug pond. It was regarded as the boundary between the Pequot and Nyantics. | At the head (or end) of the pond |
| **Weekachommet** | TRACT. Same as Weequechacommuck | Place at the end of the enclosed field; house in the enclosed field |
| **Weekapaug** | Post, Point (Watch Hill) & Beach, Yatch Club (Quonochontaug) and Breachway, Beach, Watch Hill | See **Wecapaug** |
| **Weenachasett** | Street, Naval Station, Newport (See **Woonachasset**) | At the divided, winding place (or hills)? |
| **Weepacannock** | See **Tismattue** | |

125

| | | |
|---|---|---|
| **Weepoiset** | in Swanzey. [Church's Indian Wars, page 87.] | At the small ford; the narrow strait |
| **Weequechacom-muck** | See **Weekachommet** | |
| **Weetamo, Weet-amoe, Weeto-more, Wetamo** | Woods, Tiverton | Lodge Keeper (Female Sachem or Chief ("Queen") of Pocasset Tribe) |
| **Weeweonk** | CREEK, or Wawweonke, that makes in near Nassawket from Greenwich bay, not far from the Buttonwoods. | Turning, bending place |
| **Wekepaug** | Location unknown, historical | At the end (or head) of the pond (see **Weecapaug**) |
| **Wenannatoke** | or Weyanitoke, POINT JUDITH, or JUDA-NECK [in South Kingston], deeded by Tumtockoro, Indian chief, 1659, to Winthrop and others. [See Land Evidence, vol. 1, page 29.] | A sweep around a high point?; winding river |
| **We-nan-na-toke** | See **Wenannatoke** | |
| **Wennanatoke** | Point Judith | Winding River (see **Wenannatoke**) |
| **Wepoiset** | Entrance of Kickemuit River | See **Weepoiset** |
| **Wepoiset** | See **Weybosset & Weepoiset** | |
| **Wepitamock, Webtummacks, Wepitammock, Wepieammock** | | Given in LaFantasie, page xcii |
| **Wequashcook, Wequashcuck** | | Given in LaFantasie, page xcii |
| **Wequapaugset** | Kent County | At the end of the small pond |
| **Wequapunock** | See **Wawattaquatuck** | |
| **Wequatucket** | Cove, Washington County | At the end of the river |

| | | |
|---|---|---|
| **Wequatuxet** | Cove, Washington County | At the end of the small stream; at the head of a small cove |
| **Wequeehacko-muck** | LAND, south of Natick, and near Emanuel Rice's farm. | See **Wecatheconnet** |
| **Wequepogue** | Washington County | End (head) of the pond |
| **Wequetequock** | Westerly | Place at the end of the tidal stream; as fas as the tidal stream goes |
| **Wesaquanage** | See **Wesquanage** | |
| **Wesaquanaug** | See **Wesquanage** | |
| **Wesauamog, Wissowyamake** | | Given in LaFantasie, page xcii. |
| **Wesconnaug** | See **Connaug** | |
| **Wesconnaug** | See **Westquanoid** | |
| **Wesquage** | Pond, Narragansett Pier | See **Wesquogue** |
| **Wesquanage** | or aug, SETTLEMENT. [Bartlett, page 440, vol. 1. See Arnold, vol. 1, page 5.] | The end place; a cove? |
| **Wesquogue** | TRACT and POND, near Watson's Pier, a little north of it, and northeast from Tower Hill, and between Pettaquam-scot and the bay [in South Kingston, Narragansett Pier]. | The end place; a cove? Maker of clay pots? |
| **Westconnaug** | RESERVOIR [& Dam, and Brook], south of Clayville, in Foster. | See **Connaug** |
| **Westeonnaug** | See **Connaug** | |
| **Westototucket** | RIVER, either Beaver or Usquepaug. [See Potter, page 66.] It is in S. Kingston | At the river's end; as fas as the end of the stream |
| **Westquadomesit** | See **Wasquadomesit** | |
| **Westquage** | Beach, So. Kingston | See **Wesquogue** |

| Westquanoid | PURCHASE, or Westeonnaug, being a strip of land, the south line of which runs through the State E. and W. from Connimi-cut point, opposite Nayatt on the bay, through the centre of Punhanganset or Great pond, through Natick to the Connecticut line. [See page 72, Vol. 4, Providence Records.] | Walnut trees? |
|---|---|---|
| Westquodniake | See **Westquanoid** | |
| Wetamo | See **Weetamo** | |
| Wethungamet | CREEK, or Waweonk, CREEK, east or north of Baker's station, Coweset shore | House on the other side |
| Wethunganet | Washington County | See **Wethungamet** |
| Wewaskepaug | See **Usquebaug** | |
| Weyanitoke | See **Wenannatoke** | |
| Weybosset | STREET [& Bridge], in Providence. It means half way. | Narrow place or crossing |
| Wickaboxet | POND [& State Forest, Coventry], north of the southwest corner of West Greenwich. | At the end of small pond |
| Wickerboxet | POND, west side of West Greenwich, probably same as Boxet. | See **Wickaboxet** |
| Wicketiquack | COVE, in Stonington, midway between Stonington and Westerly | See **Wequatucket** |
| Wigwam | Many locations | Indian lodge, dwelling |
| Wimatompic | LAND. Part of Hall's purchase [in Richmond]. [See vol. 1 of recorded deeds] | Place at the top of the rock?; place at the end of the rocks? |
| Winatompick | See **Wimatompic** | |
| Wincheck | POND. The eastern one on the beach, in Charlestown [Voluntown], called on Stephen's map, Green hill pond. | At the pleasant place |

| | | |
|---|---|---|
| **Wincheck** | POND, at Rockville village, near the northwest corner of Hopkinton [Voluntown —according to GNIS database]. | See alternative entry |
| **Winkheigues** | See **Wiorickheague** | |
| **Winnapaug** | Pond and Golf Course, Washington County, Watch Hill | A good pond |
| **Winnapauket** | Kent County | Land/place at the good pond |
| **Winscot** | RIVER, or Wanshuck, or Manchuck, where Wainscott factory is, in North Providence. | See **Wanshuck** |
| **Winsokeit** | See **Woonsocket** | |
| **Winsokett** | See **Woonsocket** | |
| **Wionkeage** | See **Wiorickheague** | |
| **Wionkhiege** | Schoolhouse, Georgiaville | See **Wiorickheague** |
| **Wiorickheague** | or Winkheigues, or Wayunckeke, SETTLEMENT. [Potter, page 163.] North from Greenville, and including a hill [in Georgiaville]. [Bartlett, vol. 4, page 871.] | At the bend; land at the bend |
| **Wiorikeague** | See **Wiorickheague** | |
| **Wishquatenniog** | See **Westquanoid** | |
| **Wishquodiniack** | See **Westquanoid** | |
| **Wissowyamake, Wesauamog** | | Given in LaFantasie, page xcii. |
| **Witchetseconnet** | LANDS, or Wecatheconnet, between Apponaug and Arnold's factory, and between Natick and Apponaug. | Place at the end of the enclosed field; house in the enclosed field |
| **Wixerboxet** | See **Wickaboxet** | |
| **Wollomoisset** | See **Molligwasset** | |
| **Wolopeconcet** | POND, or Pawcomet. Beach pond, on Lockwood's map | Shallow enclosed cove; fine cleared land |
| **Wolopeconnet** | POND, Poncamac, or BEACH POND, probably Babcock's pond, Westerly. | See alternative entry |

| | | |
|---|---|---|
| **Wompimish** | R. Williams | Chestnut tree |
| **Wonnamaton-namee** | See **Wanumetonomy** | |
| **Wonneme-tonomey** | See **Wonnumetonomy/ Tommany** | |
| **Wonnometony** | See **Tommany** | |
| **Wonnumeton-omy** | HILL, see Metonomy, north of Newport. | See **Tommany** |
| **Wonosoket** | See **Woonsocket** | |
| **Wonsocket** | See **Woonsocket** | |
| **Wonsocut** | See **Woonsocket** | |
| **Wonsoket** | See **Woonsocket** | |
| **Woonachasset**[8] | or Coasters Harbor, off Newport [in Narragansett Bay]. The site of the Asylum. It is a peninsular. | Crooked little hill?; at the place of separation (boundary) |
| **Woonasquatuck-et** | RIVER [& Park], divides North Providence from Johnston. | At the head of the tidal river |
| **Woonsocket**[9] | HILL and FALLS. The hill is a mile or two south west from the compact part of the village or falls. It was formerly spelled Wonsocket. [Providence Records, vol. 4, page 28.] | Place of steep descent; two brook place? |
| **Woonsoket** | See **Woonsocket** | |
| **Woonsoquett** | See **Woonsocket** | |
| **Woosamequin** | See **Osamequin** | |
| **Woquagonset** | POND, or LITTLE POND, in Old Warwick, south side of the road that runs from Pawtuxet to Apponaug. On Stevens's map it is called Sand point, or pond. | At the end of the plain; as far as the end of the plain |
| **Woquogonset** | See **Woquagonset** | |
| **Wosamequin** | POND, which sends a branch into Ashaway river in Hopkinton, and is on the Connecticut line. | See **Osamequin** |

| Wotchaugh | See **Watchaug** | |
|---|---|---|
| **Wotesamoon-suck** | same as Wecapaug, being the boundary between Pequots and Niantics [in Hopkinton]. | Junction of brooks |
| **Wowoskepog** | See **Usquebaug** | |
| **Woxeodawa** | LAND, or Maskaeowage, or Cocumscusset, bounded by the brook on the west side [in Westerly]. | End (or head) of the pond |
| **Wusamequin** | See **Osamequin** | |
| **Wuyunckeke** | See **Wiorickheague** | |
| **Wuyunckeke** | See **Wiorickheague** | |
| **Wyapumseat, Wyapumseatt** | a RIVER, in the north part of Quidnesit [in North Kingston]. Same as Mascachowage. | Place of rushes; place at the end of the rocks; hill (or rocky hill) at the end of the cove |
| **Wyaxcumscut, Wyaxcumscutt** | PONDS, about two and half miles northwest from South Kingstown station, and on the line between Exeter and Richmond. | See **Wyapumseat** |
| **Wyoming** | Pond, Dam, Post Office, Park & Village Historic District, in Hope Valley | The large prairie (Delaware language) |
| **Wyunkeke, Wayunckeke** | | See **Wionkhiege** |

(Footnotes)
1	Tribal groups throughout Rhode Island and Massachusetts. See alternate spellings in LaFantasie, page xcii. Swanton's brief summary:
  The Wampanoag occupied Rhode Island east of Narragansett Bay; Bristol County, Mass., the southern part of Plymouth County, below Marshfield and Brockton; and the extreme western part of Barnstable. The Indians of Martha's Vineyard should also be added to them, and it will be convenient to treat under the same head those of Nantucket and the Saconnet, or Sakonnet, of Sakonnet Point, R. I., whose connection was more remote. They controlled Rhode Island in Narragansett Bay until the Narragansett tribe conquered it from them.
2	Word may basis for present day "Wampanoag"; see Trigger (1978), page 171.
3	Part of Providence River; cf. **Moshassuck** and **Masswasscutt**.
4	Should read "Brodhead".
5	Now "Prudence Island".
6	Wife of Narragansett Sachem, Miantonomi.
7	**Weexcodawa** was Pequot-Mohegan name (Trumbull, 1881); see **Woxeodawa**.
8	Now called Coaster's Harbor Island.
9	Many variants in spelling in Rider and many place references including 131

City, City Hall, Library, House, Post Office, Reservoir.

| Name | Historical & Geographical Information | Translation |
|------|---------------------------------------|-------------|
| | | |
| Y | | |
| Yagompoh | See **Yayompoh** | |
| Yagunsk | See **Yawgunsk** | |
| Yawcook | Ponds, about two and half miles northwest from South Kingston station, and on the line between Exeter and Richmond. | See **Yawgoo** |
| Yawgoag | See **Yawgoog** | |
| Yawgoo | WOODS, west from Gardner's Mill, and north of Yawgoo pond | Red pond; fire place; as far as this place |
| Yawgoog | POND [& Valley Ski Area, Exeter and School, Slocum], on the corner line and northwest corner of Hopkinton, and Woods, Kingston | One side of the pond; here are many lice? |
| Yawgook | See **Yawgoog** | |
| Yawgunsk | BROOK [& Dam, Camp, and Pond], on the east side of Ninagret's fort. It is probably the Cross' Mill brook, in Charlestown. | As far as that rock |
| Yawloo | See**Yawgoo** | |
| Yayompoh | Brook, Washington County | That opening (mouth of stream) is crooked |
| Yomtonoc | Washington County | Flood tide there; here go to the right-hand side |
| Yomtunnock | See **Yomtonoc** | |

# Algonquian Dictionary

"(see ___)" is a reference to dictionary, Understanding Algonquian Indian Words (1996/2001), which provides full Algonquian derivation for the original language meaning. See http://www.docstoc.com/profile/waabu.

NOTE: ∞ = oo as in food.

| Algonquian Fragment/Root | Translation |
|---|---|
| | |
| **A** | |
| *-ab-*, *-abon-* (see *áppu*) | resting place (e.g., *Mattabesec* = "at the end of carrying place of portage (resting place")) (one possible meaning) |
| *abaga-* (from *abaohquos* = "a tent, covert") | concealing, hiding, haven, refuge |
| *abaqu-* (from *ashapo* = "flags, rushes, flax" ) | flags, rushes, flax, &c (e.g., *Abaquag* = "place where rushes grow") |
| *abriga-* (from *abaohquos* = "a tent, covert) | concealing, hiding, haven, refuge |
| *absalon-* (see *âshâp* or *hashâp*) | hemp or fishing-net, spider web (e.g., *Absalonomiscut* = "place of fish trap") |
| *-absc-* (see *-ompsk*) | rock, of rocks, standing or upright rock |
| *abscu-* (see *ogguhse* ) | little in quantity, small |
| *ac-* (see *aûke*) | land, ground, place, country (not enclosed or limited). |
| *acadia-*, *arcadia-* | land, ground, place, place of abundance (e.g., *Acadia* = "the earth, land, or place") |

| | |
|---|---|
| *acap-* (see *aucùp*) | cove (e.g., *Acapasket* = "at the small cove") |
| *acawmen* (see *ongkome*) (Narr.) | on the other side of, beyond |
| *accom-, aco-* (see *ogkome*) | across, other side of, over against (e.g., *Accomonticus* = "beyond the little river"; *Acoont* = "place on the other side") |
| *ach-* (1), *acha-* (see *ask* (1), *ascoscoï*) | green or raw (e.g., *Achagomi-conset* = "where there are green meadows") |
| *-ach-* (2), *-achu-* , *-chu-* (see *wadchu*) | mountain, hill (e.g., *Massachu-setts* = "at or near the great hills") |
| *acha-* (see *ask* (1), *ascoscoï*) | green or raw (e.g., *Achagomi-conset* = "where there are green meadows") |
| *-achus-* (see *wadchu, -ash*) | mountains, hills (e.g., *Massachu-setts* = "near the great hills") |
| *-ack-* (1) (see *agu*) | concealing, hiding, haven, refuge, bog, swamp |
| *-ack-* (2) , *-acke* (see *ag* (1)) | land, place of (e.g., *Ascocompa-macke* = "small place closed in by boulders"). Sometimes includes a preceding "glide" *w* or *u* or *y* or l, etc. |
| *acoa-* (see *koua*) | pine, pine tree (e.g., *Acoaxet* = "at the place of pines, " one possible meaning) |
| *-acoic-, coic-, ajcoyijc-* (from either *ohkuk, ohkuhk, ahkuhq* = "an earthen pot or vessel") ? | |

134

| | |
|---|---|
| *acqu-, acqui-* (see *ukque*) | at the end of, beyond (e.g., *Acquedneseth* = "place beyond the hill") |
| *acqui-* (see *agwe*) | under, underneath, below (e.g., *Acquiunk* = "under a tree") |
| *acquid-, acquedn-, acqueedn-* (see *ahquidne*) | island, floating mass (e.g., *Aquid-neck* = "at the island") |
| *acu-, acush-* (see *aucùp*) | cove (e.g., *Achushnet* = "at the cove") |
| *-ad-* (see *adchaü*) | hunting, of hunting (e.g. *Chepados* = "principal hunting place") (one possible meaning) |
| *adchaü* (see *ahchu*) | he hunts (e.g., *nuttahchun* = "I hunt") |
| *-adchu-* (see *wadchu*) | mountain, hill |
| *-adn-, -aden-, -adene-, -atn-* (see *adene, tn, dn*) | mountain (e.g., *Adden* = "a mountain") |
| *adt* (*át, ahhut*) (see *ut*) | at, a place, to, in (e.g., *nôadt* = "far off") |
| *aē taï* (*éhtái*) (see *ta*) | on both sides of (see *aē taiseep*); (e.g., *aē taiseep* = "on both sides of the river") |
| *-ag* (see *og* (2)) | pluralization stem for "animate" forms, nouns (e.g., *Wampanoag* = "People of the first light"). Sometimes includes a preceding "glide" *w* or *u* or *y* or *l* as in *–uag* or *–wag*. |

135

| | |
|---|---|
| *-ag-* (1), *-agee-* (see *aûke*) | land, ground, place, country (not enclosed or limited). (e.g., *Agawam* = "lowlands along the water"). Sometimes includes a preceding "glide" *w* or *u* or *y* or l, etc. |
| *-ag-* (2) (see *agu*) | bog, swamp, hiding-place, wet ground |
| *-ag-* (3) (see *mogke*) | great, huge |
| *agame-, agamen-* (see *ogkome*) | other side of, over against (e.g., *Agamenticus* = "other side of the little river") |
| *agami-* (see *ogkome*) | other side of, over against |
| *-agan-* (see *-hegan*) | instrument of, agent, tool for |
| *-agi-, -aigio* (see *agu*) | concealing, hiding, haven, refuge, , bog, swamp (e.g., *Agicomook* = "sheltered haven") |
| *agome-* (see *ogkome*) | other side of, over against |
| *-agu-* (see *agu*) | concealing, hiding, haven, refuge, bog, swamp |
| *agun-* (1) (see *agwe*) | under, underneath, below (e.g., *Aguntaug* = "under a tree" or "big tree place") |
| *agun-* (2) (see *mogke*) | great, huge (e.g., *Aguntaug* = "under a tree" or "big tree place") |
| *águshau* (see *agwe, -shau,* ∞*m*) | he goes below it (for shelter or concealment) |
| *agwattin* (see *agwe, attin*) | under a hill |
| *-agw, -ogw* (1) (see *agwe*) | under, underneath, below (e.g., *Agwonk* = "under a tree") |

| | |
|---|---|
| *-agw-* (2) (see *-uhku*) | floating or appearance of |
| *agwonk* (see *agwe, -unk* (2)) | under a tree |
| *ahánu, ohanu* (*hanánu*) | laugh (onomatopoetic) (e.g.,*ahquompi adt ohanimuk* = "a time to laugh"; e.g., *aháhuock* = "they laugh) |
| *-aham-* (see *acawmen*) | beyond, other side of |
| *-ahap-* (see *âshâp*) | hemp, rushes (e.g., *Ahapaconsett* = "place of flags or rushes") |
| *ahchu* (see *audchaonk*) | he strives after |
| *-ahd-* (see *adene*) | mountain |
| *-ahdin-* (see *adene*) | mountain |
| *ahkeit* (*ohkeit*) (see *ohke, -it*) | of or on the earth |
| *ahki* (*aki* ) (see *ohke, aûke*) | land, place of |
| *-ahkk-* (see *aûke*) | land, ground, place, country (not enclosed or limited).Sometimes includes a preceding "glide" *w* or *u* or *y* or *l*, etc. |
| *-ahkta-* (see *aûke*) | land, ground, place, country (not enclosed or limited). Sometimes includes a preceding "glide" *w* or *u* or *y* or *l*, etc. |
| *ahshim* (see *ashim*) | water spring |
| *ahtuck* (*ahtuk*) (see *-ag* (2), *tuck* (2)) | orchard |
| *ahtuhquog* (see *ahtuk, -og* (2)) | many deer (see next entry) |
| *ahtuk, ahtukq* (see *tuck* (2)) | a deer ("at the tree"?) or roe or hart or roe-buck |

137

| | |
|---|---|
| -ahum- (see *acawmen*) | beyond, other side of (e.g., *Ahum-patunshaug* = "beyond the round pond") |
| *ahwk* (see -*unq*, *weque*) | |
| -*aig*- (see *agu*) | concealing, hiding, haven, refuge, bog, swamp (e.g., *Aigiocommack* = "sheltered harbor") |
| -*ak* (1) (see –*ag*(1)) | place of (e.g., *Pissak* = "swampy place"). Sometimes includes a preceding "glide" *w* or *u* or *y* or *l*. |
| -*ak* (2) (see -*og*(2)) | pluralization stem for "animate" forms, nouns |
| -*ake*- , -*ahki*- , -*aki*- (see *aûke*) | land, ground, place, country (not enclosed or limited).Sometimes includes a preceding "glide" *w* or *u* or *y* or *l*, etc. |
| -*aki*-, -*ake*- (see *aûke*) | land, ground, place, country (not enclosed or limited). (cf. *Abenaki*). Sometimes includes a preceding "glide" *w* or *u* or *y* or *l*, etc. |
| -*alk* (see *aûke*) | land, ground, place, country (not enclosed or limited) |
| -*aloam*- (see *∞m* ) | s/he flies (*Wawaloam* = "s/he flies about" ?) |
| *alum* , *allum* (see *anúm*[1]) | dog (e.g., *Alum* (Lake) = "Dog Lake") |
| *allum*- (see *wunni*) | good, beautiful, pleasant |

| | |
|---|---|
| *-am-*(1) , *-ame-*, *-amos-*, *-om-* (see *-âm, nâmaus*) | fish (taken by hook) (e.g., *Amoskeag* = "place of fish traps") |
| *-am-*(2)  (see *-ompsk*) | rock, of rocks, standing or upright rock |
| *-ama* (see *moeonk*) | meeting (e.g., *Amataconet* = "meeting place") (one possible meaning) |
| *-amag* (see *-âmaug*) | fishing-place, fish-curing place (e.g.,  *Amagansett* = "at the fishing-place") |
| *amareck* (see *âmaug*) [r-dialect] | fish |
| *-âmau-* (see *-âm*) | fish |
| *-amaug* (see *-âmaug*) | fishing-place, fish-curing place |
| *-amelake*  (see *-amaug*) ("*l*" dialect) | fishing-place, fish-curing place |
| *-ameock*  (see *-âmaug* ) | fishing-place, fish-curing place |
| *-ameugg*  (see *-âmaug* ) | fishing-place, fish-curing place |
| *amisque* (*amisq, mecq*) (see *mecq, mech*) | beaver ("water beast") (about 30 distinctions) |
| *-amock*  (see *-âmaug* ) | fishing-place, fish-curing place |
| *-amond*  (see *-âmaug* ) | fishing-place, fish-curing place (e.g., *Congamond*  = "long fishing place") |
| *-amoq*  (see *-âmaug*) | fishing-place, fish-curing place (e.g., *Amoqut* = "place of fish") |
| *-amps-* (see *-ompsk*) | rock, of rocks, standing or upright rock (e.g., *Cowamps* = "sharpening stone, used a whetstone" |

139

| | |
|---|---|
| *-ampsc-* (see *-ompsk*) | rock, of rocks, standing or upright rock<br>(e.g., *Swampscott* = "at the red rock place") |
| *-amsc-* (see *-ompsk*) | rock, of rocks, standing or upright rock<br>(e.g., *Pettaquamscot* = "at the round rock") |
| *-amsk-, -amske-* (see *-ompsk*) | rock, of rocks, standing or upright rock<br>(e.g., *Pabaquamske* = "split rock") |
| *-amuck , -amuc* (see *-âmaug* ) | fishing-place, fish-curing place<br>(e.g., *Congamuck* = "long fishing place") |
| *-amug* (see *-âm, -ag* (1 )) | fishing-place, fish-curing place<br>(e.g., *Chickamug* = "principal fishing place") |
| *-amyock* (see *-âmaug, -ick* ) | fishing-place, fish-curing place |
| *-an-, -en-, -n-* (see *-an-*) | spread out, going beyond (e.g., *Kitthan* = "ocean, great expanse") |
| *an , ane* (see *unne*) | thus, to |
| *ana-, anna- , annaqua-* (see *weque , ukque*) | at the end of (e.g., *Anaquacutt* = "at the end of the river") |
| *anâwsuck* (see *anna, -suck*)<br>(cf. *suckaúhock, -hogk*) (Narr.) | shells (from shellfish) |
| *-anck-, -unck-* (see *'tugk*) | tree, wood |
| *-anish* (see *-anish*) | stink |
| *aneq-, anequass-* (from *anequs* = "squirrel") | squirrel (e.g., *Anequasset* = "at the abode of the squirrel") |

| | |
|---|---|
| *-anit-* (see *manit*) | spirit, supernatural being (e.g., *Ketahanit* = "The Lord God" ("place of Great Spirit")) |
| *anko-, ankoke-* (see *ongkoue*) | beyond, end place (e.g., *Ankoke-maug* = "fishing-place at the end") |
| *-anna-* (see *anna* (Narr.)) | shell |
| *annachim* (see *anna, min*) | a nut |
| *Annawan* (see *ánnŭau* ) | he conquers (name of famous war captain, *Annawan,* King Philip's war) |
| *-annaqua-, -annisqu-* (see *wanasq*) | upon the top, the top, end-place |
| anue | - more, rather (used when choosing something) <br> - above (cf. *anit*) <br> - it exceeds, surpasses, expresses more of something (e.g., *anue mohsag* = "that which is great"," a great thing," "the greatest") |
| *-annusk-* (see *-sk-*) | broken up, plowed, cultivated (such as land) (e.g., *Annuskumi-kak* = "broken up land") |
| *anque-* (see *ukque*) | at the end of (e.g., *Anquepogskit* = "at the end of the small pond") |
| *-ans-* (see *nái, -es* (1)) | point-little-at (cf. *Narragansett* = "people of the small point') |
| -ansett | little point (of land); cf *–ans-,* above |
| *-ant, -antam* (see *-antam*) | indicating states, activities of mind, believing, praying (in compound words) (e.g., *noántum* = "I am well minded") (e.g., *Bantam* = "he prays") |

141

| | |
|---|---|
| *-ante-* (see *adene*) | mountain |
| *-antep, -antup* (cf. *-ontop, montup*) (root is *t-p*) | head (combining form) |
| *anúm* ("*n*" dialect) | a dog (from *annumaü* = "he holds with his mouth") |
| *-aog* (see *aûke, -aug, -og* (2)) | - pluralization stem for "animate" forms, nouns<br>- where it goes |
| *ap-* (1), *ab-* (see *api, apwonat*) | bake or roast (e.g., *Apponaug* = "where we roast oysters") |
| *-ap-* (2) (see *apè - hana*) | fish-trap, traps (e.g., *Aptucket* = "at the fish trap in the little river") |
| *apè* (Narr.) | trap (for hunting); *apè -hana* = "traps" |
| *api* (see *appuonk*) | sit, be there, to dwell (e.g., appin = "a bed") |
| *appo-* (see *app∞au*) | shell fish (cf. *ap* (1), above);e.g., *Apponaug* = where we roast oysters") |
| *appon-* (see *áppu*) | sitting, waiting (e.g., *Apponequet* = "sitting or waiting place") |
| *aqu-* (see *ahquidne*) | floating mass or island (e.g., *Aquednesset* = "place of the small island") |
| *aqua-* (see *weque , ukque*) | at the end of (e.g., *Aquapauksit* = "at the end of the small pond") |
| *aquabe-* (see same) | on this side, before, in front of |
| *aque-* (see *ukque* ) | at the end of (e.g., *Aquebagapaug* = "beyond the pond") |

| | |
|---|---|
| *aquène* (Narr.) (from *ahque*) | "peace" or "cessation of hos-tilities" (e.g., *aquène ut*= "treaty camp") |
| *aqueduen-* (see *ahquidne*) | the island[2] (e.g., *Aquedenesick* = "at the small island") |
| *aquee, aqueed-* (see *ukque*) | at the end of (e.g., *Aqueednuck* = "place beyond the hill") |
| *aquethn-* (see *ahquidne*) | the island (e.g., *Aquethneck* = Aquidneck) |
| *aquidn-* (see *ahquidne*) | the island (cf. *Aquidneck* = "the floating mass-at"; i.e., "an island") |
| *aquidn-* , *ahquedne-* (from *edn* ?) | island (root implies a sitting, or suspension, as a floating mass) (e.g., *Aquidnet* = Aquidneck) |
| *aquin-* (see *aquène, ahque*) | "peace," cessation of hostilities, treaty (e.g., *Aquinnah* (Gay Head) = "peace or treaty camp") |
| *aquene* (see *aquène*) | peace, cessation of hostilities, treaty (e.g., *Aquene-ut* = "peace (treaty) camp") |
| *-aquoddy* (from *aquoddy*) (see *mónáe*) | abundance, as in *Passamaquoddy* ="abundance of Pollock", North-ern New England tribe |
| *arcadia-, acadia-* | land, ground, place, place of abun-dance (e.g., *Acadia* = "the earth, land, or place") |
| *aroos-* (see *wohsi*) | shining or slippery (e.g., *Aroos-took* = "shining river") |
| *-as-* (1) (see *-is*) | little (e.g., *Ascocompamacke* = "small place closed in by boul-ders") |

| | |
|---|---|
| *as-* (2) , *-ass* (see *–ash*) | many, much of (pluralization stem for "inanimate" forms, nouns). Sometimes includes a preceding "glide" *w* or *u* or *y* or *l*, etc. |
| *-as-* (3) (see *-is*) | brook, rivulet |
| *-âs* (4) | referring to an  animal (cf. *ôâas*) |
| *-asa-* (see *hassen*) | rock, stone, of rocks or stones, ledge, cave, den (e.g., *Asa* = "stone or stoney") |
| *asa-* , *assa- ash-*  (from *ashapo* = "flags, rushes, flax, &c") | flags, rushes, flax, &c  (e.g., *Asabeth*  = "wild flax place") |
| *asab-* (see *âshâp*  or *hashâp*) | hemp or fishing-net, spider web (e.g., *Asabeth*  = "wild flax place") |
| *asam-* (see *nashaue*) | midway, fork (e.g., *Asamu* = "between or midway" |
| *-asc-*  (1) (see *msque, muski*) | red (e.g., *Ascomacut* = "red fish (i.e., salmon place" ) (one possible meaning) |
| *-asc-*  (2), *-ask-, -sk-* (see *ask* (1), *ascoscoi*) | green or  raw |
| *-asem-* (see *ashim*) | spring of water |
| *ash-* (see *ash-*) | pluralization stem for "inanimate" forms, nouns (e.g., *Mosskituash* = "meadow, grasses") Sometimes includes a preceding "glide" *w* or *u* or *y* or *l*, etc. |
| *ashant-* (see *assóúshaü*) | backwards in motion, turning, lobster (e.g, *Ashanteaug* = "lobster place") |

| | |
|---|---|
| *ashap-* (see *âshâp* or *hashâp*) | hemp or fishing-net, spider web (e.g., *Ashappaquonset* = "place where nets are spread") |
| *-ashaw-*  (see *nashaue*) | midway, fork (e.g., *Ashaway* = "a place in the middle") |
| *ashawa-*  (see *nashawe*) | midway, fork (e.g., *Ashawa* = "land in the middle or between") |
| *ashaway-*  (see *nashawe*) | midway, fork (e.g., *Lashaway* = "place between") |
| *ashcan-* , *ashcannan-*, *ashcan(a)-* (from *askuhum*= "he watches, waits") | observation, watching, waiting |
| *ashim-*(1) (see *ashim*) | spring of water (e.g., *Ashimuet* = "at the spring") |
| *ashim-* (2) (see *-ashim*) | of animals |
| *-ashin-* (see *hassen*) | rock, stone, of rocks or stones, ledge, cave, den |
| *-ashp(a)-* (see *esph*) | up above, high, elevated (e.g., *Ashpatuck* = "high place") |
| *-ashquo-* (see *askútasquash*) | squash(es), pumpkin(s) |
| *-ashun-*  (see *hassen*) | rock, stone, of rocks or stones, ledge, cave, den (e.g., *Ashunaiunk* = "rocky point") |
| *-ask-* (1) (from *quon∞asq* = "long gourd") | bottle, flask, jug (for water) |
| *-ask-* (2), *-ash-* (see *ask* (1), *ascoscoi*) | green or raw (e.g., *Askoonkton* = "green tree"?) |

| | |
|---|---|
| *askug* (*askꝏk, askooke, skug*) (see *sk*) | a snake or worm (e.g., *móaskug* = "a black snake") |
| *askunkq* (see *ask* (1), *-unk* (2)) | a green tree |
| *askútasquash* (see *ask* (2), *ash*) | squash, pumpkin (common Indian staples) |
| *-asn-, -asna(n)-* (see *hassen*) | rock, stone, of rocks or stones, ledge, cave, den (e.g., *Asnantuck* = "rocky stream") |
| *asóúshan* (see *assóúshaü*) | lobster ("he goes backwards") |
| *-asp-* (1) (see *uspunnumun*) | up above, high, elevated (e.g., *Aspanansuck* = "high place") (one possible meaning) |
| *asp-* (2) (see *âshâp* or *hashâp*) | fishing net or hemp (e.g., *Aspinet* = "at the net place") |
| *asquo-* (1), *asquee-* (see *ukque*) | at the end of (e.g., *Asqueebagga-muck* = "at the end of the double pond") |
| *asquo-* (2) (see *askútasquash*) | squash, pumpkin |
| *-ass-,-assa-, -assin-, -ashin-, -ossi-, hassa-* (see *hassen*) | rock, stone, of rocks or stones, ledge, cave, den (e.g., *Assawompset* = "white stone place") |
| *assawa-* (see *nashaue*) | midway, fork (e.g., *Assawas-san* = "place between fork of the brook") |
| *-assen-, -ahsun-* (see *hassen*) | rock, stone, of rocks or stones, ledge, cave, den |
| *-asset* (see *–es*(1), *-et*) | at something small (e.g., *Mono-hasett* = "at the small island") |

| | |
|---|---|
| *-assin-* (see *hassen*) | rock, stone, of rocks or stones, ledge, cave, den (e.g., *Assinippi* = " rocky water") |
| *-assinash-* (see *hassen, -ash* ) | plural of *assin*: rocks, stones |
| *assinek (hassunnek)* (see *hassen,-ik*) | a cave, den (basis for place, Horseneck) |
| *-asson-* (see *hassen*) | rock, stone, of rocks or stones, ledge, cave, den (e.g., *Assonet* = "the rock place") |
| -asuonk | suffix meaning "a mark, sign, token" |
| *-at* (see *át* (or) *–et, -ut*) | at, in, by near, (popularly, "place of") |
| *-atan-* (see *adene*) | mountain |
| *-atch-, -atchu-* (see *wadchu*) | mountin, hill |
| *athaam-* (see *agwe*) | under, underneath, below |
| *-atin- , -adn- , -aden-, -adene-, -atn-* (see *adene, tn, dn*) | mountain |
| *-atoot-* (see *adt*) | on something |
| *-attan-* (see *utan, otan*) | village, town, city (e.g., *Manhattan* = "island place") |
| *attaq-* (see *ahtuk*) | deer (e.g., *Attaquahunchonett* = "at the hill of plenty deer") |
| *-attin-* (see *adene*) | mountain |
| *-attiny-* (see *adene*) | mountain |
| *auc-* (see *aucùp*) | cove (e.g., *Aucoot* = "at the cove") |
| *aucup- , acu-, aku-* (see *aucùp*) | cove |
| *aucùppâwese* (see *aucùp, paw, -ese*) | a smaller cove, creek |

| | |
|---|---|
| *-aue* (see *aûke*) | land, ground, place, country (not enclosed or limited) |
| *-aug-* , *-auge* (see *aûke*) | land, ground, place, country (not enclosed or limited) (e.g., *Apponaug* = "shell fishing-place"). Sometimes includes a preceding "glide" *w* or *u* or *y* or l, etc. |
| *-auk-* , *-ak-*, *-ahki-* , *-ohki-* (see *aûke*) | land, ground, place, country (not enclosed or limited) (e.g., *Montauk* = "fort placehigh land"; *Nasauket* = "At the neck of land; land between rivers"). Sometimes includes a preceding "glide" *w* or *u* or *y* or *l*, etc. |
| *-auke-* (see *aûke*) | land, ground, place, country (not enclosed or limited). Sometimes includes a preceding "glide" *w* or *u* or *y* or *l*, etc. |
| *-aum-, -am-, -om-, naum-* (see *−am*) | fish (taken by hook) |
| *aumaûi* (see *-âmau*) | he is fishing ("he fishes with a hook") (e.g., *paponaumsúog* = "winter fish") |
| *-auq-, -auqu-, -ockqu-* (Narr.) | of a tree, long, tall, deep (e.g., *qunnauqussu* = "He is tall (like a long tree)". |
| *auqua-* , *auque-* (see *ukque*) | top, end of (e.g., *Auquebatuck* = "top of tree") |
| *aûsup-* | raccoon ("face washer") (related to root for "fan"; "fanner") |
| *-auwa-, -awo-* | people, relations, kin |

148

| | |
|---|---|
| *a'wumps, a'waumps* (from *whauksis* = "fox," or *wonqŭssis* ="fox") | the fox (Quinebaug tribe Indian Chief or Sachem) |
| *-awgoo, -awgoog, -awgook, -awloo* (see *aûke*) | land, ground, place, country (not enclosed or limited). Sometimes includes a preceding "glide" *w* or *u* or *y* or *l*, etc. |
| *awk-* (see *acaw*) | adhere, be on |
| *-awussi-, -ous, -hous-* (see *wussi*) | other side of |
| *Awoshonks* (see *sonksq, sohk, squa*) | woman who rules (name of female sachem (Chief)of the Sakonnet Tribe, Little Compton, RI) |
| ayeu | he is here, there (e.g., *noh ayeu kah áp*pu = "he dwells and abides") |
| *azoi-* (see *koa* or *wesaui*) | gum, tree sap or yellow(e.g., *Azoiquoneset* = "small island where we get spruce pitch" or "yellow point [spruce] place) |

(Footnotes)

1        Anum is a good illustration of the four regional dialects: "n", "r", "l", "y". Those tribes saying *anùm* called N-dialect by linguists. Those tribes saying *ayìm* called Y-dialect speakers. Those tribes saying *arúm* called R-dialect speakers, and those tribes saying *alúm* called L-dialect speakers.

2        Two words for "island" were translated and are seen in place names: *ahquidne* & *munnoh* (see Goddard, 2002); *munnoh* (the more common term in the *Indian Bible*) may imply any dry place or refuge like an island (perhaps derived from *m'nunnu* = "dry place"); *ahquidne* may imply a floating or suspended mass, as related to other Algonquian words for "canoe".

| Algonquian Fragment/Root | Translation |
|---|---|
| | |
| **B** | |
| *bab-*  (see *pohsh*) | between-two, half, part of, divided, split (e.g., *Babaquamshk* = "split rock") |

149

| | |
|---|---|
| *badda(c)-*  (see p'etùk'qui) | round  (e.g., *Baddacook* = "at the round place") |
| *-bag-* , *-baga-* , *-bago-*  (*-paug* (1)) | watery open area, lake, pond, bay still-water <br> (e.g., *Umbagog* = "clear pond") |
| *-bagga-* (from *abaohquos* = "a tent, covert") | concealing, hiding, haven,  refuge |
| *bapet(au)-* (see *puhpúkki*) | hollow (e.g.. *Bapetaushat* = "hollow place" <br> (one possible meaning) |
| *baqua-*  (see *pohque*) | clear, open, bare, shallow <br> (e.g., *Baquag* = "clear water") |
| *bash-* (see *pashk*, *-pisk* (1)) | bloom, blossom, burst forth  (e.g., *Bashbish* = "it bursts forth") |
| *bassoq-* (see *pashk* (*paashk*)) ? | split, burst (e.g., *Bassoqutoquaug* = "where trees were split") (one possible meaning) |
| *-baug* (see *paug* (1), (2)) | - flat, flat land, level, still  (as water pond) <br> - lake, pond, bay, still water  (e.g., *Musquebaug* = "red pond") |
| *-be-* , *-bi-*  (see *p*) | of water (e.g.,  *Beseck* = "at the water place") |
| *-bec-*  (see *peauke*) | lake, pond, bay, still water <br> (e.g.,  *Sennebec* = "rocky pond") |
| *-beek-*  (see *peauke*) | lake, pond, bay, still water |
| *bet, betuck-* , *betuckqua-* (see p'etùk'qui) | round, round about ("turning at the end") (cf. *Petuckqunneg*) (The root is *p-t*) (e.g., *Betuckqua*pock = "Round Pond") |
| *-bequi-* (see *peauke*) | lake, pond, bay, still water |
| *-bi-*(1)  (see *p*) | water |

| | |
|---|---|
| *-bi-*(2)  (see pè tùk'qui)  (cf. *p-t*) | round, round about  (e.g., *Aque-binocket* = "round Island"; Bicknell, 1920) |
| *-bog-, -bagga-*  (see *-paug*  (1)) | watery open area, lake, pond, bay still-water  (e.g.,  *Quanabog*  = "long pond") |
| *boggoch-, boggach-*  (see *pauchag*) | turn, place of turning  (e.g., *Boggochaug*  = "at the turning place") |
| *-bogue-*  (see *-paug*  (1)) | watery open area, lake, pond, bay still-water |
| *-box- ,-boxo-*  (see *-boxy*  below) | watery open area, lake, pond, bay still-water  (e.g., *Boxet* = "small pond" |
| *-boxet*  (see *-paugeset*) | little pond  (e.g.,  *Boxet*  = "little pond") |
| *-boxy*  (see *-paugeset*) | little pond  (e.g., *Oxyboxy*  = "very little water") |
| *-bsk-*  (see *-ompsk*) | rock, of rocks, standing or upright rock |
| *b-t*  (see p'etùk'qui)  (cf. *p-t*) | round, round about  (root word) (e.g., *Betcumcasick* = "round bend with a gravely bottom") |
| *-buck-* (see *-paug*  (1)) | watery open area, lake, pond, bay still-water |
| *bun-* ? | boundary  (e.g.,  *Bungee*  = "a boundary") ? |

| Algonquian Fragment/Root | Translation |
|---|---|
| | |
| **C** | |
| *cad-, cod-, cud-* (see *kehte*) | large, great, principal |
| *caj-* (see *kowaw*) | fir-tree (e.g., *Cajoot* = "Fir-tree place"?) |
| *calumet* | pipe for tobacco, "peace pipe" |
| *-camoco* (see *-kōmuk*) | enclosed place, building |
| *can-, cano-* (see *quinni*) | long (e.g., *Canopaug* = "long pond place") |
| *canon-* (see *quinni*) | long (e.g., *Canonicus* = "of the long place") |
| *canonch-* (from *quanunkquaéan* = "he dwells high, in a high place," Trumbull, 1903, p. 137)? | he is high (in office, importance) (e.g., *Canonchet*, famous Narr. Sachem or Chief) |
| *caneun-* (see *qunnuhqui*) (cf. *can*) | tall, high, elevated (e.g., *Caneun-squisset* = "high place") |
| *-cap-, -kup-* (see *kup* (2)) | closed-up, stopped-up, refuge place, thick (e.g., *Capowack* = "the refuge place") |
| *capat* (*kuppadt*) | ice |
| *-capp-* (see *kup* (2)) | closed-up, stopped-up, refuge place, thick (e.g., *Cappacommock* = "refuge or hiding place") |
| *-cassa-, -casso-, -cassom-* (see *hassen*) | rock, stone, of rocks or stones, ledge, cave, den (e.g., *Cassomacook* = "rocky place") |

| | |
|---|---|
| *cassac-* (see *kussukkoe*) | high (e.g., *Cassacubque* = *Cos Cob* = "high rock, great ledge of rock") |
| *cat-* , *cata-*, *catu-* (see *kehte*) | principal, greatest, large (e.g., *Catumb* = "at the place of the great rock") |
| *cau-*, *caun-*, *cawn-* (see *kē̄ nai* ) | sharp, splintered, jagged, thorn-like (e.g., *Caucaujawatchuk* = "sharp mountain") (one possible meaning) |
| *caucau-*, *cawcaw-* (see above, *cau-*) | very sharp, very splintered, very jagged, very thorn-like |
| *caucumsqussuck* (see *-umpsk, qussuck*) | a marked rock |
| *cauompsk* (see *cauompsk*) | sharpening stone, whetstone, sharp (e.g., *Consumpsit* = "at the sharp or sharpening stone") |
| *caute(e)-* (see *kehte*) | large, great, principal |
| *caw-* (1) , *cau-* (see *ko*) | sharpening stone, whetstone, sharp (e.g., *Cawsumsett* = "sharp rock place") |
| *caw* (2)- (see *kowaw*) | pines, firs (e.g., *Cawaude* = "pine place") |
| *cawcau-*, *caucau-* (see above, *cau-*) | very sharp, very splintered, very jagged, very thorn-like |
| *cawkin-*, *cawgen-* (see *quinni* ?) | long or long-long |
| *cawncawn[1]-* (see *quinni*) | very long (e.g., *Cawncawnja-watchuk* = "very long hill") |
| *ceac-*, *cea-c* (see *sucki*) | dark, black (e.g., Cea-Concke = *Seekonk*) |

| | |
|---|---|
| *-ch-*  (see *-ch, -tchuan*) | running water (root) (e.g., *Chicopee* = "rushing water") |
| *chadchab-, chabchab-*(see *chippe-*) | divide and divide ("frequentative form") (e.g.,*chadchabenum* = "he divides by hand") |
| *chaba-* , *chab-* , *chaub-*  (see *chepi, ch-p*) | separated, boundary, apart, divided (e.g., *Chaubunakungamaug* = "at the boundary fishing-place" or "a divided-island-lake²" or more popularly translated as "you fish on *your* side of the lake, I'll fish on *my* side") |
| *chabe-* , *chapa-*, *chop-*  (see *chepi, ch-p*) | separated, boundary  (e.g., *Chabatawece* = "little separated place") |
| *chac-* (see *chepi, ch-p*) | separated, boundary  (e.g., *Chachacust* = "where stream divides and opens") (one possible meaning) |
| *chach-* , *chacha-*  (see *k'che*) | large, great (e.g., *Chachapacasset* ="at the great widening") |
| *chack-* (see *chepi, ch-p*) | separated, boundary  (e.g., *Chackapaucasset* = (" where stream divides and opens") (one possible meaning) |
| *chagum*  (see *chógan*) | black bird-black birds (imitative) (from *chogq* = "spot "?) (e.g., *Chagu*m) |
| *-cham-*(1), *chan-* (see *ch-, -tchuan*) | running water, currents (e.g., *Keequechan* = "place of swift water") |
| *-cham-* (2), *-chem-*  (see *shim*) | animal |

| | |
|---|---|
| *cha(n)-* (see *k'che*) | big, large, great   (e.g., *Chanan-gongum* = "great reed place; great paint place") |
| *chap-* (see *k'che*) | big, large, great   (e.g., *Chapom-pamiskock* = "big fishing place near boundary rock?") |
| *chappa-*  (see *chepi, ch-p*) | separated, boundary  (e.g.,  *Chap-paquiddick* = "separated island  land") |
| *-chas-, -chass-* (see *chepi, ch-p*) | separated, boundary  (e.g., *Ween-achasett* = "at the divided, winding place (or hills)?" |
| *chau-, chaub-* (see *chab* above) | separated, boundary  (e.g.,  *Chau-bongum*  = "the boundary mark") |
| *chaug-* (see *chepi, ch-p, aûke*) | separated, boundary |
| *che-* (1), *chee-*  (see *k'che*) | big, large, great   (e.g.,  *Chep-achaque*  = "at the principal turn-ing place") |
| *che-*  (2) (see *kehte*) | principal, greatest, large (e.g., *Chepachague* = "principal turning place) |
| *check-* (see *chepi, ch-p*) | separated, boundary  (e.g *Check-echnusset* = "At the boundary (one possible meaning) |
| *-checke-*  (see *chekee*) | violent, dashing, falling, rushing, swift (such as water) |
| *-chee-*  (see *chekee*) | violent, dashing, falling, rush-ing, swift (such as water)  (e.g., *Quechee*  = "quick, whirling falls") |
| *-cheeb-* (see *chepi, ch-p*) | separated, of spirits (e.g., *Cheebee-antups* = "a separated head") |

155

| | |
|---|---|
| *cheek-* (see *chickot*) | fire (e.g., *Cheekeck* = "fire place") |
| *cheep-* (see *chepi, ch-p*) | separated, boundary (e.g., *Cheep-auke* = "A place apart; an isolated island") |
| *cheke-* , *checheke-* (see *cheke (checheke)*) | slowly |
| *chekee* (*cheche*) | violently |
| *chep-* (see *chepi, ch-p*) | separated, boundary (e.g. *Chep-inoxet* = "little place of departed spirits") |
| *-chep-* , *-chip-* (see *chab*) | separated, boundary (e.g., *Chep-achet* = "boundary place") |
| *chepachet* (see *chepi, -et*) | a place separated, or apart (a modern place name) |
| *-chet* (see *-et*) | at, in, by, near (cf. *–chep* below) (e.g., *Chepachet* = "place of separation where stream divides; boundary place") |
| *-chib-*, *-chiba-* (see *chepi, ch-p*) | separated, boundary (e.g., *Chiba-coweda* = "little place separated by a passage" (from Prudence Island) |
| *chic-* , *chio-*, *chicup-* (see *chekee*) | violent, dashing, falling, rushing, swift (such as water) (e.g., *Chi-coppe* = "rushing water) |
| *chick-* (1), *shick-*, *chock-* (see *chickoht*) | fire, of burning (e.g., *Chickons* = "burned place for farming") |
| *chick-* (2) (see *k'che*) | big, large, great (e.g., *Chickamug* = "principal fishing place") |

| | |
|---|---|
| *chickoht* (*chikohteau*)(see *chekee,* *-ohteau*) (cf. *yote, n∞tau*) | fire[3] |
| *chick-* (3) (see *ch*) | swift (as water) (e.g., *Chichabi* = "swift water") |
| *chip-* , *chipp-* (see *ch-p*) | divide at, separated (e.g., *Chiponaug* = sepatated place") |
| *chippo-, chippu-* (see *ch-p*) | divide at, separated (e.g., *Chip-pachooag* = "place of separation; where the stream divides") |
| *chis-* (1), *chisa-, chisaw-* (see *kehchis* ) | old (e.g. *Chisawamicke* = "at the old field") |
| *chis-* (2) (see *k'che*) | big, large, great (e.g., *Chisawan-nock* = "Principal fishing place) (one possible meaning) |
| *chógan*(Narr.) | black bird (imitative ) (from *chogq* = "spot "?); plural is *chóganeuck* |
| *chock-* (1) (see *ch*) | swift (as running water) |
| *chock-* (2) (see *chipohke* ) | unoccupied or separated land |
| *chock-* (3) (see *chickoht*) | fire |
| *chockal-* (see *wonqŭssis*) ? | fox (e.g., *Chockalaug* = "fox place") |
| *-choo-* (see *wadchu*) | mountain, hill |
| *chop-* , *chope-* , *chomp-* (see *chepi*) | separated, boundary (e.g., *Chomp-ist* = "boundary or dividing place") |
| *ch-p* (*ts-p*) (see *chippe*) | Root-word for ghost, spirit, de-parted spirit, evil spirit, "devil", separated; (common root: sepa-rated, physically or from life) |

157

| | |
|---|---|
| *-chu-* (1) (see *wadchu*) | mountain, hill (e.g., *Chusick* = "mountain place"; e.g., *Massachusetts* = "near the great hills") |
| *-chu-* (2) (see *-ut*) ? | at, in, by near, (popularly, "place of") ? |
| *chupp-, chuppi-* (see ch-p) | divide at, separated |
| *co-* (1) (see *quinni*) | long (e.g., *Cohasset* = "long stone place" or *Coginchaug* = "long swamp") |
| *-co-* (2) (see *koua*) | pines, firs (e.g., *Oxecoset* = "place of small fir trees") |
| *coc-* (see *k*; see *caw-, cau-* above) | sharpening stone, whetstone (e.g., *Cocumscusset* = "At the place where there are small sharpening stones," one possible meaning) |
| *coch-* (1) (see *kowaw*) | pines, firs (e.g., *Cocheset* = "a place of small pine trees") |
| *coch-* (2) (from *kenupshau* = "he is swift") | fast, swift (e.g, *Cochituate* = "place of swift water") |
| *coch-* (3) (see *wutche, ooche*) ? | issuing from, flowing from ? |
| *cod-, cad-* (see *kehte*) | large, great, principal |
| *codd-* (see *pohquettahun*) | broken up, cultivated (e.g., *Coddank* = cleared land") |
| *coh-* , *cohan-* (see *quinni*) | long (e.g., *Cohanit* = "at the long place"?) |
| *coha-, cohe-* (see *kowaw*) | pines, firs ("thorny, pointed") (e.g., *Coheassuck* = "pine tree place") (one possible meaning) |

158

| | |
|---|---|
| *coho-* (see *kowaw*) | pines, firs ("thorny, pointed") (e.g., *Coheassuck* = "small pine place") |
| *-coic-* (from *ohkuk, ohkuhk, ahkuhk, aúcuck* = "a kettle") | |
| *-comacock* (see *-komuck*) | a building or enclosed place (usually *not* a *wétu* = *wigwam*) (e.g., *Nacommuck* = "enclosed point of land") (one possible meaning) |
| *-comuc* (see *-komuk*) | a building or enclosed place (usually *not* a *wétu* = *wigwam*) (e.g., *Comet* = "at the house") |
| *-commuck* (see *-komuk*) | a building or enclosed place (usually *not* a *wétu* = *wigwam*) |
| *con-* (1) , *cohan, cona* (see *quinni*) | long (e.g., *Conanicut* = "the especially long place") |
| *-con-* (2) , *-kon-* (see *muskon*) | bone, horn, raw hide |
| *conaquotoag-* (see *qunnuhqui*) | tall, high, elevated (e.g., *Conaquotoag* = "at the long beach"?) |
| *-conkan-, -conkon-, -conckan-, -concan-, -conan-, -conk-, -concon-. -conck-,-conckon-, -conkin-, -conken-, -conk-, -conquon-, -conen-,* &c ( from *kuhkuhheg* = "a (land)-mark, boundary, limit") | land boundary (e.g., *Neutaconkanut* = "at the short (scant) boundary mark"); many other variant spellings in RI Place Names section. |
| *-conn- , -conne-* (see *quinni*) | long (e.g., *Sepaconnet* = "at the long stream") |
| *-coon-* (see *quinni*) | long (e.g., *Coonempus* = "long gravelly place" (one possible meaning) |

159

| | |
|---|---|
| cop-, coppa-, coppo- (see *kup(2)*) | covered up, closed up, refuge place, thick (e.g., *Copicut* = "at the closed-up place") |
| cons- (see *kous* , *ko* or *kē nai*) (cf. *cauompsk*, above) | sharp (e.g., *Consumpsit* = "at the sharp rock or sharpening rock ") |
| -cook (see *aûke*) | land, ground, place, country (not enclosed or limited). (e.g., *Suncook* = "rocky point of land") |
| cos- (see *kussuhkoe*) | High (e.g., *Cos Cob* = "high rock") |
| cot- (1) (see *pohquettahun*) | broken up, cultivated (e.g., *Cotuit* = "at the planting fields") |
| cot-(2), cote- (see *kehte*) | principal, greatest, large (e.g., *Coteticutt* = "on the great river") |
| cottin- , cotting- (see *pohquettahun*) | broken up, cultivated (e.g., *Cottinackeesh* ="place of little farms") |
| cow-, coww- (see *kowaw*) | pines, firs ("thorny, pointed") (e.g., *Cowaude* = "pine place") |
| cowas-, cowes- (see *kowaw*) | small pines, firs ("thorny, pointed") (e.g., *Cowesit* = "pine place") |
| cows-, cau-, cow- (see *kous*) | sharp (e.g., *Cowsumsett* = "place of sharp rocks") |
| cowwaus (see *kous*, -es) | small pine |
| -ctic- (see *tuk*) | a tidal river, broad river (e.g. Connecticut = "on the long tidal river") |

| | |
|---|---|
| *-cuck* , *-cook* (see *-uck, -ut*) | at, in, by near, (popularly, "place of"). Appears to be a double locative→here is the approximate location where something is (e.g., *Squamicuck* = "salmon fishing place") |
| *cum-* , *cumma-* (see *kob* , *kobpag*) | enclosed place, harbor (e.g., *Cummaquid* = "harbor") |
| *cup-* (see *aucùp*) | cove (e.g., *Cupheag* = "at the cove") |
| *cuppa-* (see *kup* (2)) | enclosed place, harbor, refuge, haven, , thick |
| *cus-* , *cush-* (see *aucùp*) | cove (e.g., *Cushena* = "wet land") |
| *cut-, cutto-* (see *kehte*) | principal, greatest, large (e.g., *Cuttoquat* = "at the great tidal river") |
| *cuttyhun-* (1) (see *pohquettahun*) | broken up, cultivated (e.g., *Cuttyhunk* = "broken land"?) |
| *cuttyhun-* (2) (see *kehte-hunk* under *k't*) | principal stream |

(Footnotes)
1       Repetition of syllable cawncawn ("long-long") is called reduplication or frequentative form, a very common grammatical feature in Algonquian languages.
2       See Goddard, NY Times, 1990, who provided this new and best translation vice Trumbull's rendition (1881/1974) based on a similar Algonquian language and knowledge of geographic reference.
3       Nòte= Fire [in general]; Yòte = [domestic] fire; Chíckot = [destructive] fire; Squtta= fire in general & a fire spark ?

| Algonquian Fragment/Root | Translation |
|---|---|
| | |
| D | |
| *-dge-* | running water |
| *-dn-* , *-edn- -tn-* (see *adene*) | mountain (e.g., *Aqueednuck* = "place beyond the hill") |

| Algonquian Fragment/Root | Translation |
|---|---|
| | |
| **E** | |
| *each- eack-* (see *weque* , *ukque*) | at the end of (e.g., *Eackhonkᵢ*, = "This is the end of the fishing place; as far as the migratory fish go" (other possible meanings) |
| *-eag* (see *ag* (1)) | place of (e.g., *Namkeag* = "eeling place). Sometimes includes a preceding "glide" *w* or *u* or *y* or *l*, etc. |
| *-eage* (see *ag* (1)) | place of (e.g., *Wachaqueage* = "country near the mountains"). Sometimes includes a preceding "glide" *w* or *u* or *y* or *l*, etc.. |
| *east-* (see *weque* , *ukque*) | at the end of (e.g., *Easterig* = "This is as far as the spear-fishing goes" (several other possible meanings for this high-noise place name) |
| *eataw* (Narr.) | old, abandoned (see *eataw aûke*, below) |
| *eataw aûke* (see *eataw, aûke*) (Narr.) | old, abandoned land |
| *-ece-* (see *-ese*) | little (e.g., *Chabatawece* = "little separated place") |
| *-eck* , *-ek* (see *-ik -ick*) | at, in, on, by, near, (popularly, "place of") (e.g., *Aquidneck* = "on (some kind of) island; at the island"). Sometimes includes a preceding "glide" *w* or *u* or *y* or *l*, etc. |

| | |
|---|---|
| *-edn-* (1) (see *adene, tn, dn*) | hill (e.g., Acqueednuck = "place beyond the hills") |
| *-edn-* (2) , *-idn-*  (see *ahquidne*) | something jutting or floating over a flat surface (an island) (e.g., *Aquednesset* = "place of small island") |
| *-ees-* (1) , *-ett* (see *neese*) | brook or rivulet (cf. *nis*) |
| *-ees-* (2) (see *-es* (1)) | little  (e.g., *Tooksees* = "little stream") |
| *-egan* (see *–hegan*) | instrument of, agent, tool for |
| *-ege-* (see *aûke*) | land, ground, place, country (not enclosed or limited). |
| *éhtái* (*aetawe*) (see *ogkome*) | on or at both sides |
| *-ehtekw-* (see *ihte, tukkoo*) | wavy waters  (root in *Connecticut*) |
| *-ek*  (see *-ut*) | at, in, on, by, near, (popularly, "place of")<br>Sometimes  includes a preceding "glide"<br>*w* or *u*  or *y* or *l*, etc. |
| *-ekan-* (see *-hegan*) | instrument of, agent, tool for |
| *-elen-* (proto-Algonquian[2] root) | ordinary (as an ordinary tribal man) |
| *-ehte* (*-ahtu, -ehtu, -uhtu, -ehten*) (see *-ut*) | the term *-ut* is a common suffix meaning: at, in, on, where something is, place of, near (e.g., *kehtompskut* = "at the great rock"). Also used as a preposition (e.g., *ut ohkeit* = "on the earth") |
| *-emaug-* (see *-ompsk-*) | rock, of rocks, standing or upright rock |

| | |
|---|---|
| *-emes* (see *-es* (1)) | diminutive, "lesser or least"" (e.g., *ogguhsemese* = "smallest of something") |
| *-emsc-* (see *-âmaug*) | fishing-place, fish-curing place |
| *-en, -an* (see *-an* ) | spread out, going beyond (e.g., *Mashentuck* = "Many trees; well forested place") |
| *-enin (-anen, in)* | suffix meaning "doer of some-thing" (e.g., *adchaénin* = "some hunter, any hunter, a hunter") general form for "man", "male" |
| *en kussohkoiyeu wadchuut* (see *en, kussuhkoe, yeu, wadchu,* ut) | into a high mountain |
| *en wadchue ohkeit* (see *en, wadchu, ohke, -it*) | to the hill country |
| *es-* (see *missi-*) | big, large, great (e.g., *Espowet* = "At the large cove") |
| *-es-* (see *-es* (1)) | little (e.g., *Hassanamesit* = "place of small stones") |
| *esco-,* (see *each-, eack-* above) | |
| *-ese-* (see *-ese, -es* (1)) | little (e.g., *Pimsepoese* = "extended little river") (one possible mean-ing)) |
| *-eset* (see *-es* (1) & *-et*) a compound diminutive and primary locative | place of small (something) (e.g., *Azoiquoneset* = "Spruce-pitch small-island place") |
| *-esh* (1) (see *-ash*) | more than one of something (e.g., *Cottinackeesh* = "place of little farms") |

| | |
|---|---|
| *-esh-* (2) | sudden or violent motion (in composition) (e.g., *queshau* = "he leaps, jumps") <br> motion verbs ("to go"); e.g. *acâw-muck notéshe*m = "I came over the water) |
| *-eshp-* ,*-asp-*,*-ashp*, *ishpmin-* (see *uspunnumun*) | up above, high, tall, elevated (e.g., *Aspanansuck* = "High place; brook near the high hill?") |
| *-esit*  (see *-es* (1), *-et*) | place of small (something) (e.g., *Hassanamesit* = "place of small stones") |
| *-esset* , *-essett*, *-eset* (see *-es* (1), *-et*) | place of small  (something)  (cf. *-edn-*, above) |
| *-esuck*  (see *-og* (2)) | pluralization stem for "animate" forms, nouns |
| *-et*[3] , *-ett* (see *-et, -ut*) (cf. *−etu-*) | at, in, on, by, near, proximity of (less than exact location specified); specifies a definite location for a single feature; *-et* is popularly given as "place of" <br> (e.g., *Paugusset* = "place of  small pond" ?) |
| *-etic* ( see *−et, -ick*) | at, in, on, by, near (a double locative) |
| *-eton-*  (see *adn*) | mountain (e.g., *Wannemetoname* = "red paint hill") |
| *-ett* , *-et, -etts*  (see *-et* , *-ut*) | at, in, on, by, near (e.g.,  *Cochessett*  = "a place of small pine trees") (see *Massachusetts* under *ach-* (2) |
| *-etu-* (1), *ettu-*, *-ittu* (see *−et, -ut*) | for plural nouns,  and "at, in, by, near"  for a definite number of features (popularly given as  "place of") |

| | |
|---|---|
| *-etu* (2) , *-ittu* (cf. *kin*) | of growth (compound words) (e.g., *netu* = "he grows") |
| *-euck* (1) (see *-êuck*) | people, folk of an area  (e.g., *Muhhekekannêuck* = "wolf people (Mohegan Nation)") |
| *-euck* (2) | pluralization stem for "animate" forms, nouns |
| *-eum* (see ∞*m*) (many variant spellings*)* | indicates possession for some nouns (e.g. *numoskehteum* = "my herb"; *num-Manitt∞m* = "my God") |
| *-eutten-*  (see *adene*) | mountain |
| *ewáchimin*(see *min, wachu ?, ash*) (Narr.) (see *weatchimmineash*) | corn (maize), ("the plant  in the field") plural = *ewáchiminneash* |

(Footnotes)

1          Multiple meanings with this word: "This is as far as the spear-fishing goes; fork in the river where we spear-fish; three forks in the river; source of three rivers; red land; a meadow". Other place-name spellings include Eascoheague, Escoheage, &c

2          The original or ancestral language from which the Algonquian languages/dialects derive.  See Goddard, "Eastern Algonquian Languages" and http://en.wikipedia.org/wiki/Proto-Algonquian_language.

3          Trumbull (1870, pp. 23-4) makes many useful distinctions regarding singular/plural, definite/indefinite location suffixes for (-et, -it, -ut), -set, (-ettu, -ittu, -uttu), -kontu, -ehtu.

| Algonquian Fragment/Root | Translation |
|---|---|
| | |
| **F** | |
| *-fen-*  (cf. *pen*) (there is no *f* in southeastern Algonquian languages) | descending, falling, sloping (e.g., *Fennapoo* = "sloping seat") (one possible meaning) |
| *fox-, pox-* (see *puck-, -paug* (2) | flat, flat land, level, still (e.g., Foxon = "flat stone" or "level rock") |

| Algonquian Fragment/Root | Translation |
|---|---|
|  |  |
| G |  |
| *-gam-, -gami-, -gomi* | lake, pond (northern Algonquian languages root) |
| *-gan-*, *-gon-*, *-gan*, *-goni* | lake, pond (e.g., *Michigan* = *michi* + *gan* = "large lake") |
| *-gan*, *-gun* (see *–egan*, above) |  |
| *-(g)ansett* (see *naiag* & *-es*) ? | small point of land (cf. Narragan<u>sett</u>)? |
| *gash-*, *gesh-* (see *kesu*) | warm, hot (e.g., *Gashee* = "at the warm pond") |
| *-ge (-ege)* | means "the thing that" (e.g., *Puttuckqunnége* = "the thing that is long and round" [long bread]) |
| *gen-* (see *wunni*) ? | good, beautiful, pleasant (e.g., *Genesee* = "Beautiful valley"; "there it has fine banks") (other possible meanings) |
| *-gin*, *-cogin* (see *quinni* ?) | long |
| *-gomuck* (see *hamuck*, *-komuk*) | a building or enclosed place (usually not a *wétu* = wigwam) |
| *got-* (see *kehte*) | large, great entity (e.g., *Gotomska* = "big rocks") |
| *-gun-*, *-gunk-* (see *-unk* (2)) | tree (e.g., *Aguntaug* = "under a tree" or "big tree place") |

| Algonquian Fragment/Root | Translation |
|---|---|
| | |
| **H** | |
| -*hamuck* (see -*komuk*) | a building or enclosed place (usually *nota wétu* = *wigwam*) |
| -*hanne* (1), -*han* (from −*tchuan* = "a swift or rapid stream, a current, flowing water") | used for river names (not typically seen locallyin place of common river names□-*tuk*- or −*sepu*-); see Trumbull, 1870, pp. 12-13. |
| *hanne*- (2) | of or relating to an island (e.g., *Munnohhane* =" of an island") |
| *hank*-, *hoank*- (from −*tchuan* = "a swift or rapid stream, a current, flowing water") | rapid stream |
| *hassa*- (1) (see *oggushki*) | bog, swamp, wet ground, refuge (e.g., *Hassacky* = "swamp, meadow") |
| *hassa*- (2) , *hassu*-, *hassun*-, *horsen*- (see *assen*, *hassen*) | rock, stone, of rocks or stones, ledge, cave, den (e.g., Horseneck = *Hassunek* = "at the stony place" or "at the ledge") |
| *hassen* (*hassun, hussun, ohsun*) | a stone (root may imply something that cuts or penetrates) |
| -*hauk*-, -*hauken*- (see *aûke*) | land, ground, place, country (not enclosed or limited). (e.g., *Musquetohauke* = "grassy place") |
| -*hd*-, -*hde(n)*- (see *adene*) | mountain (e.g., *Keetahden* = "principal mountain") |
| -*hegan*- , -*hegin*-, -*hican*-, -*igan*-, -*agan*-, -*ekan*-, -*ogan*- (see -*hegan*) | instrument of, agent, tool for (e.g., *Higganum* = "tomahawk stone-quarry") |

| | |
|---|---|
| *heikto-* (see *kitthan*) | sea, open sea |
| *-hep-* (see *agu*) | concealing, hiding, haven, refuge, bog, swamp |
| *higgan-*( see *tomheganompsk*) | concerning a tomahawk (cf. *–hegan-* above) |
| *-hoank* (cf. *ch*, above) | dashing, rapid stream |
| *hobomoco-* (see *hobbamoco*, Trumbull, 1881, p. 27) | "devil," "evil spirit," (European understanding) The Healing Spirit, The Spirit of Death, the dark, underworld, or northeast wind (all recorded meanings or interpretations) |
| *hoccanum* (see *uhquan*) | hook, so shaped |
| *-hock-* (1) , *-hocq-* (see *uhquan*) | hook, so shaped (e.g., *Hockamock* = "hook-shaped place") |
| *-hock* (2), *-hog,* *-hogh* (see *hogki*) | - any external covering for body of an animal or man shell, thick shell (e.g., *Aponahock* = "where he roasts oysters") |
| *-hocken-* (see *aûke*) | land, ground, place, country (not enclosed or limited). |
| *-hog* (see *–hogki*) | - any external covering for body of an animal or man<br>- shell, thick shell |
| *-hogh* (see *-hogki*) | - any external covering for body of an animal or man<br>- shell, thick shell |
| *hogki* (see *–hogk,-i*) | it covers, serves as a covering (e.g., *wuhhogki* = "a shell") |
| *-hom* (*-ham*) (see ∞*m*) | common endings for some motion verbs using ∞*m*, stating a going from one place to another ) (cf. *sohham = soh +* ∞*m*) |

| | |
|---|---|
| *homo-* | - "at the fishing place" (e.g., *Homoganset* = "At the fishing place") (one meaning) <br> - "at low tide there are fresh springs" <br> - "hunting grounds" |
| *hònck* (Narr.) | A Canadian goose (imitates honking sound of bird) |
| *hónckock* (Narr.) | Canadian geese (plural) |
| *-hoos-* (1) (see *hassen*) | rock, stone, of rocks or stones, ledge, cave, den (e.g., *Hoosac* = "rock- place") |
| *hoos-* (2) | kettle (e.g., *Hoosicwhisic* = "at the place of the small kettle") |
| *hopuónck* (see *uhp∞onk*) (Narr.) | a tobacco pipe |
| *horse-* , *horsen-* (see *hassen*) | rock, stone, of rocks or stones, ledge, cave, den (e.g., *Hassunegk* = Horseneck = "a rock shelter") |
| *hous-, hos-* (see *wussi*) | Beyond, on other side of (e.g., *Housatonic* = "place beyond the mountains") |
| *h'tugk* (*h'tugh, tug, tugk, tugq*)) (see *m'tugk*) | tree (imitative sound) (e.g., *mis-hun*tugk = "much wood") |
| *hum-* (1), *humm-* (see *–am-*) | fish (taken by hook) (e.g., *Hummock* = "fishing place" (one meaning)) |

| | |
|---|---|
| *hum*-(2), *humm*- (see *–komuck*-) | a building or enclosed place (usually *not* a *wétu* = *wigwam*) (e.g., *Hummocks* = "enclosed place" (one meaning)) |
| (*h*)*umsk*- (-*ompsk*) | rock, of rocks, standing or upright rock |
| -*hus*- (see *hassen*) | rock, stone, of rocks or stones, ledge, cave, den (e.g., *Huson* = "a stone") |
| *hussun*(see *hassen*) (cf. *qussuk*) | a stone; plural = *hussunash* |
| *hutt*- (see *kt*-) | principal, greatest, large (e.g., *Huttmoiden*[1] = "of the principal fishing place") |
| *hyannis*- (from *ayeuhteáu* "he makes war, warrior) | Name of a Sachem (Chief) *Anayanough* |

(Footnotes)
1        From Morton, 1669, page 67

| Algonquian Fragment/Root | Translation |
|---|---|
| | |
| **I** | |
| -*iak*- (see  -*ch* ?, -*tchuan*) | running water, perhaps a stream |
| -*ibsk*- (see -*ompsk*) | rock, of rocks, standing or upright rock |
| -*ic* (see -*ick*) | in, at, on, near, place of (e.g., *Meshantic* = "woody place") (one meaning). Sometimes includes a preceding "glide" *w* or *u* or *y* or *l*, etc. |
| -*ich*- , -*ch*- (see –*ch*, -*tchuan*) | flowing, flows, current (cf. *coch* (2)) |

| | |
|---|---|
| *-ick* (1) (see *-ick*) | in, at, on, near, place of (e.g., *Natick* = "my land"). Sometimes includes a preceding "glide" *w* or *u* or *y* or *l*, etc. |
| *-ick* (2) (see *-ick , aûke*) | land, ground, place, country (not enclosed or limited). (e.g., *Chappaquiddick* = "separated island place"). Sometimes includes a preceding "glide" *w* or *u* or *y* or *l*, etc. |
| *-idge-* (see *–ch, -tchuan*) | running water, currents, perhaps a stream |
| *-idn-* (see *adene, ahquidne*) | something jutting or floating over a flat surface (an island) (e.g., *Aquidny* = "island") |
| *-ig* (see *-ick*) | in, at, on, near, place of. Sometimes includes a preceding "glide" *w* or *u* or *y* or *l*, etc. |
| *-igan-* (see *-hegan*) | instrument of, agent, tool for |
| *-iggon-* (see *kitthan*) | ocean, open sea |
| *-ihte* (*-ihteu*) (see *-ut*) | locative |
| *-ik* (see *-ick*) | in, at, on, near, place of (e.g, *Assapumsik* = "place where wild hemp is gathered to make cords or net"). Sometimes includes a preceding "glide" *w* or *u* or *y* or *l*, etc. |
| *-in,-on,-an* (see *–in*) | in, at, on (or) a suffix meaning "a doer of something" |

| | |
|---|---|
| -*ing* (see -*ick*) | in, at, on, near, place of (e.g., *Ossining* = "place of little stones"). Sometimes includes a preceding "glide" *w* or *u* or *y* or *l*, etc. |
| -*ink* (see -*unk* (1), -*uck*) | in, at, on, near, place of. Sometimes includes a preceding "glide" *w* or *u* or *y* or *l*, etc. |
| -*ipsk*- (see -*ompsk*) | rock, of rocks, standing or upright rock |
| -*is* (1) | - brook or rivulet (cf. *nis*)<br>- small (cf. *us*) |
| -*is*, -*s*- (2) (see –*ash*) | pluralization stem, inanimate forms |
| -*ish* (see –*ish*) | - denoting a bad, useless quality of something (e.g., *anish* = "it stinks")<br>- denoting continuous action (in composition) (e.g., *ásekesukokish* = "every day, daily"; e.g., *wunníish*= "farewell") |
| *ishpmin*- , -*esph*-, -*asp*-, -*asph*- (see *uspunnumun*) | up above, high, elevated (e.g., *Ishpeming* ="up aloft") |
| -*iset, -isset, -issett, -issitt* (see -*eset*, -*esett*)<br>(cf. –*eset*, above) | place of small something (e.g., *Weepoiset* = "at the small ford") (one possible meaning) |
| -*it, -itt* (see -*it* , -*ut*) | at, in, on, by, near, (popularly, "place of") (e.g., *Kawamasohkakannit* = "at the place with pines and the brook") |
| -*itch*- (see –*ch, -tchuan*) | dashing, rapid, stream |

173

| | |
|---|---|
| *-itt* (see *-it* , *-ut*) | at, in, by near, (popularly, "place of") (e.g., *Capanagansitt* = "place of the enclosed (or plugged-up) well," one possible meaning |
| *-ittu* (see above entry, *-etu-*) | |
| *-iutten-* (see *adene*) | mountain |

| Algonquian Fragment/Root | Translation |
|---|---|
| | |
| **K** | |
| *-kaddy, -kadia* | ground, land, place, place of abundance |
| *kam(e)-* (see *kehte*, *-âm*) | large or great fish |
| *-kap-, kappo-, kuppo-* (see *kup* (2)) | closed-up, stopped up, refuge place, thick (e.g., *Kappowongamick* = "place shut in by river bend") |
| *kat-, kata-* (see *kehte*) | large or great |
| *katam-* (see *kehte*, *-âm,* ) | large or great fish |
| *kaukont* (Narr.) | a crow ("caw! caw!"); plural = *kaukontuock* |
| *kaw-* (see *kowaw*) | pines, firs (e.g., *Kawamasohkakannit* = "at the place with pines and the brook") |
| *kawam-* (see *kehte*, *-âm*) | large, great large or great fish |
| *-ke-, -ki-* (see *-ke* (2)) | land, earth, "place of " (e.g., *Namkeag* = "fishing place") |

| | |
|---|---|
| -keag- , -kheag- (see -ke (2), ag) | land, place of (e.g., *Squakheag* = "watching (look out) place" ?) |
| *kedinket* (from *kitônuck* = "a ship (Narr.)) | a ship, resembling a ship (Narr.) (e.g., *Kedinket* = "A ship"; "on the ship"; "it resembles a little ship") |
| *keek-* (see *kehte*) | large, great entity (e.g., *Keeka-manset* = "at the great valley") |
| *keeck* (from *ohkuck* = "kettle") | a kettle, (e.g., *Keeck* = "kettle pond") |
| *keenai* (*keeneh, keneh, keene, keen*) | sharp, keen (used in composition) |
| *kees-, kuss-, kesi-* (see *kussuhkoe*) | high, high land |
| *keeshk* (see *sk, 'sh*) | cut through, sever (imitative?) |
| *keet-* (see *kehte*) | large, great entity (e.g., *Keetah-den* = "principal mountain") |
| *keght-* (see *kehte*) | large, great entity |
| *kehchis* (*kutchissu*) (see *kehche*) | he is old, he is an old man |
| *keht-, kehtah-* (see *kehte*) | large, great entity (e.g., *Kehtah Hanit* = "principal salt bays") |
| *kehtompsk* (see *kehte, -ompsk*) | the great rock |
| *kek-* (see *kehte*) | large, great entity |
| *keih-* (see *kehte*) | large, great entity |
| *keheihtukqut-* (see *kehte, tuk, ut*) | on the great river |
| *keihtanit* (see *keht-, anit*) | where the Great Spirit (*Keihtan*) lives |
| *kehteâmaug* (see *k't, -âmaug*) | great fishing-place |
| *kehtoh* (*keihtoh*) (see *'k, -ohteau*) | name of the sea, ocean ("it is going on", "it is indefinitely extended") |

175

| | |
|---|---|
| *kehtpaquonunk* (see *k't, pauqua, -unk*) | at the great clearing |
| *ken-* (1) , *kenne-* (see *quinni*) | long (e.g., *Kennebec* = "long water land") |
| *ken-* (2) (see *quinni, ôâas* ) | pike, pickerel (e.g., *Kenoza* = "a pike or a pickerel") |
| *kenag* (see *kēnai* ) | that which is sharp, when it is sharp |
| *-kenw-* (cf. *quinni*) | long |
| *kenunck-* (see *qunnunkque* ) | tall, high, elevated |
| *kenoi-* , *ko-* (see *kēnai* ) | sharp, splintered, jagged, thorn-like |
| *kenugke* (see *kenawun*) | among, mixed (related to *kōhukkehtahwhaü* = "he pierces, penetrates") |
| *kenún* (*kinúm*) (see *annuu*) | to bear or carry (used with animate form verbs) |
| *-kep-* (see *kup* (3)) | covered up, closed up, refuge place, thick |
| *keq-*, *keqt-* (see *kehte*) | principal, greatest, large (e.g., *Kequassagansett* = "at the place of the principal wells") |
| *kes* (see *qussuk*) | stones (e.g., *Kesickamuck* = "Stony fishing place"; "stone we stand on when fishing") |
| *kesi-* (see *kussuhkoe*) | high, high land |
| *keshy-* , *keshi-* , *gesh-* , *gash-* (see *kesu*) | warm, hot (cf. *gash*) |
| *keshyi* (*keshyii*) | speedy |

| | |
|---|---|
| *késu (see késuk)* | it warms or is warm (e.g., *kussit-tau* = "the sun is hot") |
| *ket-, kete-* (see *kehte*) | principal, greatest, large (e.g., *Keticut* = "on the great river") |
| *keta-, kehta-* (see *keihtanit*) | spirit, supernatural being |
| *-ki-* (see *ke* (2), *aûke*) | land, ground, place, country (not enclosed or limited). (e.g. *Winooski* = "onion country"). |
| *kichci-* (see *k'chi*) | principal, greatest, large |
| *kick-* , *kicka-* (see *nkeke*) | otter (e.g., *Kickamuit* = "place where otters pass") |
| *kikigat-* , *kickigat-* (see *kēsuk* ?, or *kesŭkod* = "day") | day or clearness |
| *-kil* (see *kenugke* ?' "*l*" dialect) | mixed |
| *-kin* (cf. *-etu*) | of growth (in composition, inanimate forms) (e.g., *neekin* = "it grows") |
| *kishki* | broad, great, from side-to-side |
| *kit-* , *kite-*, *kita-*, *kitt-* (see *kehte*) | principal, greatest, large (e.g., *Kitemaug* = "the principal fishing-place") |
| *kitthan-* , *wechekum-* (see *kehte*, *-an*) | the sea |
| *kitsuog* (see *k't*, *-suog*) (Narr.) | cormorants |
| *kitts* (see *kitsuog*) | cormorants (e.g., *Kitts* = cormorants) |
| *ko-* (see *ko* ) | sharp, splintered, jagged, thorn-like |
| *koa* (see *azoi*) | gum, tree sap |
| *-kob-* (see *kep*) | closed up, stopped-up, refuge place |

| | |
|---|---|
| *kobpak-* , *kobpag-*  (see *kobpag*) | haven, harbor  (e.g., *Kobpakom-mocket* = "refuge place") |
| *kodchu-* , *kodchuhki-*  (see *ke* (2)) | fragment, small piece |
| *kodt-* (see  *kodt* ) | up above, high, elevated  (e.g., *Kodttukoet* = "at the summit of a hill") |
| *kodtuhkoag* (see *kodt, ohke, -ag* (1)) | a high place, summit, top of a hill |
| *koess-*  (see *kowaw*) | sharp, splintered, jagged, thorn-like (e.g., *Koessek* = "at  the pine tree place") |
| *-komek, -komuk*  (see *-komuck*) | a building or enclosed place (usually *not* a *wétu* = *wigwam* ) (cf. *kup*, below); (e.g., *Shekomeko* = "principal house (headquarters)") |
| *-komuk* , *-komuck*  (see *-komuck*) | a building or enclosed placdemn(usually *not* a *wétu* = *wigwam* ) (cf. *kup*, below) |
| *kon-*(1), *kono-*  (see *quinni*) | long  (e.g., *Konomoc* = "place of long  fish (eels, lampreys)") |
| *-kon-* (2), *con* | bone, horn, raw hide |
| *-konkan-*, *-koncon-*, *-konkon-* &c (from *kuhkuhheg* = "a (land)-mark, boundary, limit") | boundary (e.g., *Natakonkanet* = "At the short (scant) boundary mark"); other variant spelling forms exist.[1] |
| *konnoh* (see *ukkonnoh, nukkonnoh*) | place where something is, at |

| | |
|---|---|
| *-kontu* (see *-kontu*) | much, quite a bit, where many are, place of abundance (e.g., *Namessikontu* = "where there are many fish") |
| *-k∞g* (see *-og* (2)) | pluralization stem for animate forms (e.g., *muhhogk∞g* = "bodies") |
| *-kook* (see *ook*) | place of (e.g., *Namcook* = "eeling place") |
| *koppo-* (see *-kup*(2)) | covered up, closed up, refuge place, thick |
| *koune-* (see *quinni*) | long |
| *kous; uhq* (see *cauquat*) | arrow, thorn, sharp thing |
| *kowpi-* (see *kup* (2)) | closed up, shut in, refuge place, thick |
| *kt-* (see *kehte*) | principal, greatest, large |
| *kehte -hunk* (see *kehte, tuk*) | principal stream (e.g., *Kittyhunk* = "place of principal straem") |
| *kôshki* (see *kough* ?, *kushki*) | rough |
| *koua* (see *kowa, kenoi, cowes*) | pine, fir tree |
| *kough* (see *koue, kous*) | sharp (see *kôuhquodt*) |
| *kôühquodt* (*kôunkqoudt*) (see *kóüs, uhq, -ohteau*) | arrow ("that which has a point at the end") |
| *kóüs* (see *koua, cowes*) (cf. *uhq*) | a thorn, briar, a sharp thing (e.g., *kôühquodt* = "arrow") |
| *kowaw* (*kowa, kowas*) (see *koua*) | pine, fir (especially white pine) |
| *kowawese* (see *kowaw, -ese*) | young, small pines, firs |

179

| | |
|---|---|
| *k't (keht-, kehte-, kit-)* | Root word for principal, greatest, chief person, place or thing (e.g., *k't kunk* ="principal stream") |
| kuhkuhhunk | boundary or marking out (as of land) |
| *kuhkuhqueu* (see *k', uhq*) (cf. *quennuckque*) | he goes upwards, ascends progressively |
| *kuht-* (see *kehte*) | principal, greatest, large (e.g., *Kuhtuhquetnet* = "at the great place on the island") |
| *-kuk-* (see *kuski*) | difficult |
| *kunckq(a), kunuck(u)* (see *qunnuckque*) | high |
| *kup- kuppo-* (see *kup* (2)) | covered up, closed up, refuge place, thick (e.g., *Kuppikomuk* = "closed place") |
| *kuppadt (kuppad, capat)* (see *kuppi, -ohteau*) | ice ("when it is covered", "closed up") |
| *kuppi* (see *kup*(2)) | closed, narrow; "the woods", (a grove) |
| *kuppikomuk, cuppacommock* (see *kup*(2), *-komuk*) | closed place or secure enlcosure, denoting a refuge or hiding place, thick |
| *kuppomachaug* (see same) | thick wood, densely wooded place or swamp |
| *kushkai (kishki* (see *kussuhkoe*) | it is wide |
| *kuss-* (see *kussuhkoe*) | high, high land |

| | |
|---|---|
| *kussa-* (1), *kusse-* (see *kusse-*) | very much, fully, completly (a modifier) (e.g., *kussuhkoe* = "high", "high land") |
| *kussa-*(2), (*kusso-*) (see *kesu*) | hot, warm (used in composition) (e.g., *mohkusse* = "a burning coal") |
| *kussuhkoe* (see *kusse-*, *ohke*) | high, high land |
| *kutche* (*k∞che*) (*k'+ ∞che* ) (see *wutche*) | it begins, originates |
| *kutt-* (*kut*) (see *kehte*) | principal, greatest, large (e.g., *Kuttutuck* = "great river") |
| *kutto-* (see *kehte*) | principal, greatest, large |
| *-kw-* (see *quinni*) | long |
| *-kwana-* , *-kwene-* (see *quinni*) | long |
| *-kwel-* (see *kenugke*) ("*l*" dialect) | mixed |
| *kwen-* (see *quinni*) | long |
| *-kwil-* (see *kenugke*) ("*l*" dialect) | mixed |
| *-kwin-* (see *kenugke*) or (see *quinni*) | mixed (or) long |

(Footnotes)

1          See  Place Names section

| Algonquian Fragment/Root | Translation |
|---|---|
| | |
| **L** | |
| *lasha-* (see *nashawe*) ("*l*" dialect") | midway, fork (e.g., *Lashaway* = "place between") |
| *lashaway* (see *nashawe*) ("*l*" dialect") | midway, fork (e.g., *Lashaway* = "place between") |

181

| lou- (see *moue*, or "*l*" dialect equivalent ?) ? | meeting, meeting place (e.g., *Lou-isquissett* = "at the meeting place") |
|---|---|

| Algonquian Fragment/Root | Translation |
|---|---|
| | |
| **M** | |
| *maan-* (see *maï*) | path, a way, road, trail (e.g., *Maanexit* = "place where the path is") |
| *mach-* (1) , *mache-* (see *mache*) | bad, useless (e.g., *Machmucket* = "bad fish here") |
| *mach-* (2) , *mache-* (see *mishe, mish, miss, mash, mass, missi*) | big, large, great (e.g., *Machaquamagansett* = "place of big beach wells (hollow logs that fill up with fresh water at low tide)") |
| *mache moodus* (see *mache*) | bad noise (e.g., *Machemoodus* = "there is a bad noise") |
| *machipscat* (see *mayi, -ipsk-, át*) | a stone path |
| *mad, madd-* (see *mache*) | bad, useless (e.g., *Maddock* = "bad land place") |
| *mag-, mang-* (see *mogke*) | great, huge (e.g., *Magonck* = "a great tree"); (e.g., *Mangunck-akuck* = "place of great trees" (Trumbull, 1881, p. 18)) |
| *magke* (see *missi*) | great, big (plural) |
| *magou* (*mag∞* ) (see root, *m-g*) | of giving, gift ("he gives, offers, presents"); e.g., *mag∞ mag∞ónk* = "he gives offerings"; e.g., *num-mag* = "I offer". |
| *magun-* (see *m-g*) | gift, giving (e.g., *Magunco* = "gift or grant") |
| *mah-* (see *maï*) | |

182

| | |
|---|---|
| *mahan(t)-* (from *mahantick, manantik* = "cedar swamp"? or *manatuck*= "a lookout or place of observation") | cedar swamp (Trumbull, 1881, *Willimantic*)? a lookout, place of observation, a high point |
| *mahchagq* (*machaug*) (see *mahchi*) | swamp; cf. *kuppomachaug* |
| *maï-, may-* (see *may*) | a way, path or trail |
| *make-, maka-* (see *mache*) | bad, useless |
| *man-* (1), *mana-, mang-, mia-* (see *miaeog*) | collection or gathering (e.g., *Manexit* = "he gathers them together") |
| *man-* (2), *mani-* (see *man* (2)) | island (e.g., *Manhan* = "an island") |
| *mana-* (see *mawnantuck*) | lookout, highpoint place(e.g., *Mananduk* = "lookout place") |
| *manch-* (see *manchagq* or *manchaug*) | swamp (e.g., *Manchaug* = "where the rushes grow (swamp)") |
| *man(e)-, mon(e)-, mon(o)-* (see *m∞i*) | black, dark |
| *mang-* (see *mogke*) | great, huge (cf. *mag-*, above) |
| *mangun-* (see *mangai*) | collection or gathering |
| *manha-* (see *munnoh*) | island (e.g., *Manhan* = "island") |
| *mani-, manit-* (see *manit, manitt∞*) | God, of God or Spirit (e.g., *Manitook* = "God's [The Spirit's] country") |
| *manna-, mana-* (see *maï*) | carry, carrying place (a path) (e.g., *Manamoyik* = "carrying place") |
| *manshk* (see *manshk*) | a fort, stronghold |

183

| | |
|---|---|
| *-mant-* (see *mawnantuck*) | lookout, highpoint (e.g., *Willia-mantic* = "a good lookout") (one possible meaning) |
| *many-* (see *maï*) | path, a way, road, trail |
| *maq-* (see *mecq*) | beaver (e.g., *Maquam* = "a beaver") |
| *mas-* (see *missi*) | big, large, great  (e.g., *Massaco* "the great outlet") |
| *masca-, mascak-* (see *moskeht, muskechuge*) | grass, meadow, place where rushes grow, a plain (e.g., *Mascachowage* = "place of long rushes (cat tails?)")" |
| *mash-* (1), *masha-, mashe-* (see *missi*) | big, large, great (e.g., *Mashantucket* = "well-forested place") |
| *mash-* (2), *masha* (see *matche*) | bad, useless  (e.g., *Masheet* = "bad place") |
| *mashe-* (see *missi*) | big, large, great  (e.g., *Mashepogoche* = "land near great pond") |
| *mashentuck,* (from *mishuntugk* = "much wood") | well wooded (e.g., *Mashentucket* = "well wooded place") |
| *mashantacktuck* (from *mishuntugk* = "much wood") | |
| *mashi-* (see *missi*) | big, large, great  (e.g., *Mashipaug* = "great pond") |
| *mask-, maska- , maskataq-* (see *moskeht, muskechuge*) | grass, meadow, place where rushes grow  (e.g., *Maskataquatt* = "place of rushes; grassy place")" |

| | |
|---|---|
| *maskataq-* (see *moskeht, muskechuge*) | grass, meadow, place where rushes grow (e.g., *Maskataquatt* = "place of rushes; grassy place") |
| *masqua-* (1), *masquachowa* (see *moskeht, muskechuge*) | grass, meadow, place where rushes grow (e.g., *Masquachow-awaug* = "place where rushes grow? (one meaning)) |
| *masqua-* (2) (see *msqui , muski*) | red (e.g., *Masquachowawaug* = "salmon fishing place?" (one meaning)) |
| *mass-* , *massa-*, *massha-* (see *missi*) | big, large, great (e.g., *Massa-chusetts* = "at or near the great hills") |
| *Massasoit* (see *massa, sohk*) | The Massasoit was the Grand Sachem ("Chief") of the Wampanoag Nation; first to befriend the Mayflower Pilgrims of Plymouth Plantation in 1621. His Indian name has been recorded as *Ousa Mequin* = "Yellow Feather"; Massasoit means "great commander, or Leader" |
| *massadchu* (see *massa, wadchu*) | great mountain |
| *massapaug* (see *missi-, paug*(1)) | large/great pond |
| *massequock* (from *mukkoshqut* = "a plain or meadow") | |
| *mat-* (1), *matt-, matta-, mata-* (see *mat*) | bad, useless, negative, not (e.g., *Matachuset* = "the place without hills") |
| *mat-* (2), -, *matta-* (see *mat*) | old, worn out, bad, useless (e.g., *Mattacheese* = "old fields") |

| | |
|---|---|
| *match-* (see *mache*) | bad, useless, negative, not (e.g., "*Matchuk* = "bad lands") |
| *matha-* (see *matta* (1)) | big, large, great |
| *mato-* (see *mawnantuck*) | lookout place (e.g., *Matomy* = "lookout place; observation height") |
| *matta-*(1), (see *missi*) | big, large, great |
| *matta-*(2), *matte-* (see *mat*) | bad, useless, negative, not (e.g., "*Mattatuck* = "place of no trees") |
| *mattap-, mattapp, mattapo-, mattapoi-* (see *maï, áppu, mattappu*) | path + rest, end of portage for canoes &c (where we rest along the path) (e.g., *Mattapoiset* = "(small?) resting place on portage, " one possible meaning) |
| *mattoon* (see *mawnantuck*) | lookout place (e.g., *Mattoonuc* = "lookout hill place") |
| *matun* (see *mawnantuck*) | lookout place (e.g., *Matunuck* = "high or observation place") |
| *-mau-* (see *may, maï*) | path, a way, road, trail |
| *maush-, mash-* (see *missi*) | big, large, great |
| *maut-* (see *mache*) | bad, useless, negative, not |
| *mauthquo-* (see *musqui, muski*) | red |
| *mawn-, mown-, mon-* (see *mawnantuck, montup*) | lookout place (e.g., *Montauk* = "high land fort place") |
| *may-*(1) (see *-âm,namaus*) | fish |
| *may-* (2), *mayi-* (see *maï*) | path, a way, road, trail (e.g., *Mayannoes* = "where the road (trail) lies"); plural = *mayash* |
| *me-, mett-, metta-* (see *m∞i* ) | black (e.g., *Mettaubscot* ="black rocks place") |

| | |
|---|---|
| *mech-* , *mench-* (see *meech*) | food, of food, eating, eat it (e.g., *Menchoiset* = "much food here"?) |
| *mecq* , *mec* (see *meech*) | water being or monster |
| *mehtug* (*mehtukq*, *mehtug*) (see *m'tugk*) | tree (*meh* ="the"); plural= *mehtugquath* |
| *melw-* (cf. *wunni*) ("*l*" dialect) | good, beautiful, pleasant |
| *mem-* (see *munnoh*) | island (e.g., *Memeeneessitt* = "little islands everywhere") |
| *men-* (1) (see *agu*) | concealing, hiding, haven, refuge, bog, swamp (e.g., *Menikuk* = "shelter for canoes") |
| *men-* (2) (see *munnoh*) | island (e.g., *Menikoe* = "shelter islands") |
| *men-* (3) (from *man* ∞ *t*="basket") | |
| *menuh* (see *menuhki*) | firm, hard, congealed, strong(e.g., *méquin* = "a feather") |
| *menuhkog* (see *menuh*) | strong, strongly (e.g., *menuhkonog* = "a stronghold") |
| *menuk-* (see *menuhki*) | strong, strongly (e.g., *Menunketesuck* = "strong-flowing stream") |
| *méquin* (see *menuh, quin*) | feather (e.g., *Ousa Méquin* = "Yellow Feather") |
| *mer-* , *merr-*, *merri-* ("*r*" dialect) (see *moonaeu*) | deep (valley or steam) (e.g., *Merrimack* = "deep river") |
| *mesh-* (see *missi*) | big, large, great (e.g., *Meshanticut* = "place of many big trees") |

187

| | |
|---|---|
| *metaûhock* (see *-hog; mehtauog* = "ear") (Narr.) | the periwinkle used for white wampum beads (cf. *suckaúhock*); "ear-shaped shell" |
| *mete-* (see *metweis*) | black earth , graphite |
| *mi-* (from *maiwene* = "a gathering of people, court, assembly") | collection or gathering (e.g., *Miamogue* = "where we come together to fish") translation: *maiwene-am-ag* |
| *miáe* (*miyáe, moeu, mowee*) | together (e.g., *moáe pas∞tshakg* = "you (plural)--draw near together") |
| *miantonemi, miantonomi* (see R. Williams, *A Key*, p. 137) | he wages war, he gathers together for war. *Miantonomi* was the Narragansett Tribe "War Chief" in historic times. |
| *mich-* , *michi-* (see *missi*) | big, large, great (e.g., *Michigan* = "big lake") |
| *micúckaskeete* (see *mishe, ask* (1), *-et*) (Narr.) | a meadow |
| mihtuck | tree |
| *-min-* (see *min*) | berry, fruit, corn, fruit (e.g., *Minnechaug* = "berry mountain") |
| *minis-* (see *munnohes*) | little island |
| *mina-* , *minna-* (see *munnoh*) | island[1] (e.g., *Minamok* = "islands place") |
| *-minna-* (see *min*) | berry, corn (e.g., *Minnabaug* = "berry pond") (one possible meaning) |
| *-minne-* (see *min*) | berry, corn (e.g., *Minnechaug* = "berry-land") |
| *mis-* (1), *mys-* (see *missi*) | big, large, great (e.g. *Mystic* (*Mystik*)= "great tidal river") |

| | |
|---|---|
| mis- (2), misa-, mish- , misha- misqu- (see *msqui* ) (Narr.) | red  (e.g., *Misquamicut* = "red-fish  (salmon place") |
| -*mis* (3), -*mish, mus-*  (see *min, -ash*) | of a tree, tree nuts; cf. Narragan-sett, *wómpimish* = "a chesnut tree" (white tree nuts) |
| *mis-* (4) (see –*es*) | little |
| *misadchu* (see same) | a great mountain |
| *mish-* (1) , *mishi-, mishe-* (see *missi*) | big, large, great   (cf. *misha*) |
| -*mish* (2), -*muck, -misk, -uck* | of a tree; e.g., *wómpimish* = "chesnut tree" (white nut-tree); may also imply "nuts" |
| *misha-* (see *missi*) | big, large, great   (e.g., *Misha-wamut* = "at the great spring") |
| *mishā̄ nnek* (see *mishe, n-k*) (Narr.) | squirrel ("big scratcher") |
| *mishimmayaget* (see *mishe, mayi, -et*) | a great way |
| *mishoon* (see same) | a canoe, dugout, biat, or ferry |
| *mishuntugk*  (see *mishe,  h'tugk*) | much wood in a forest, etc. (basis for modern *Mashantucket* = "well-wooded place") |
| *misqu-, misqua-, misque-, misqui-, mihqua-* (see *msqui, muski*) | red (see *Misquamicut*) |
| *misquámaug* (see *misqua, -âmaug*) (Narr.) | red fish (salmon) place |
| *misquáshim* (see *misquá, -shim*) (Narr.) | red fox ("red animal") |
| *míshquock*  (see *misqui, -ock*) (Narr.) | red earth |
| *mishquochuck* (see *míshquock, -uck*) | copper, red earth or red kettle |
| *misqushkon* (see *misquá, suckete*) | trout |

189

| | |
|---|---|
| *miss-, missi-* , *missa-* , *mass-, massa-, mish-, mash-,* *misu-* (see *missi, mishe*) | big, large, great (*miss-, &c* is a very common root) (e.g., *Mississippi* ="great river" (not in New England!); e.g., *Mashantucket* = "well -forested place"; *Massapog* ="great lake"; *Massachusetts* = "near the great hills" |
| *missúckeke*(Narr.) | bass ; plural = *missúckekequock* |
| *mist-, mista-, miste-* (see *missi*) | big, large, great (e.g., *Mistassini* = "big rocks") |
| *miyac* (*mine, mueu*, etc.) (see *miáe*) | together (used in composition) (see *miyáeog*) |
| *moan-* (see *miáe , maiwene* ) | collection or gathering |
| *móaskug* (see *m∞ , skug*) (Narr.) | black snake |
| *mocissinass* (*mokus, mokis, mohkussin* ) (see *mohw*) (root is *m-k*) | shoes (mocassins) (e.g., *ummokis* = "his shoe") |
| *móeu* (*moáe, miyáe, maywe*) | jointly, together (e.g., *moeonk* = "meeting") |
| *mog-, moge-* , *mogke-* (see *mogke*) | great, huge (e.g., *Mogewetu* = "big house") |
| *mogkeóaas* (see *mogk, ôâas*) (cf. *muhquoshim*) | wolf ("great animal") (there are many names for wolves such as white wolf, black wolf, gray wolf, etc.; the black was most respected) |
| *mogkam* (see *mogke, -âm*) | a great (large) fish (maybe a sturgeon) |
| *mogkunk* (see *mogk, -unk* (2)) | a great tree |

| | |
|---|---|
| *Mohegan* (see *muhkoas*) | wolf (e.g., The tribal nation, the Mohegans = *Muhhekannêuck* = "wolf people"); some spell "Mohican" as in the movie , "The Last of the Mohicans"(1992). Note: many other variant spellings inLaFantasie, vol. 1. |
| *mohw-* , *mokw-*, *moowk-* (see *móhwhaü* = "he eats him") | eat, chew (cf. Mohawk Indians —lit. "they eat live flesh.") |
| *-moi-* (see *-âmaug* ) | water (fresh), fish (e.g., *Huttmoiden²* = "of the principal fishing-place") |
| *mol-*, *molli-*   (see *moonaeu, moonoi*) ("*l*" dialect) | deep (valley or steam) (e.g.,  *Molligwasset* = "valley place") |
| *mola-* (see *moonaeu, moonoï*) ("*l*" dialect) | deep (valley or steam) (cf. *mol*) |
| *mon-* (1), *mona-, mono-, monh-, mon(t), monoh-*(see *munnoh*) | island (e.g.,  *Monhiggan*  = " island" place) |
| *mon-* (2), *mano, mono*  (see *mawnantuck, montup*) | lookout (e.g.,  *Monomonack* = "lookout point") |
| *mon-* (3), *mona-,  mono-, manhon-* (see *moonaea, moonoï*) | deep (valley or steam) |
| *mónáe* | there is much, abundance |
| *monát* | abundance ("there is much") |
| *mon(e)-, man(e)-, mon(o)-* (see *m ∞i* ) | black, dark |
| *monoo-* (see *moonaea, moonoi*) | deep (valley or steam) |
| *mont-* (1) (see *montup*) | of the head, top (e.g., *Montup* = "the head or summit") (one possible meaning) |
| *mont-* (2) (see *manit*) | spirit, supernatural being |
| *-moo* | "it being divided, separated" |

| | |
|---|---|
| moon- (1) (see *moonai*) | deep (valley or steam) (e.g., *Moonassachuet* = "deep reversing current") |
| moon- (2) (see *nquitteconnaúog*) | eel (e.g., *Moonkeek* = "place of eels"?) |
| m∞noi (see *m∞naea*) | deep (as a stream or valley) |
| moonokoiyeu, oonoukoi (from same, Trumbull, 1903) | valley |
| moos- , moosi- (see *m∞s*) | A moose |
| moose- (see *missi*) | big, large, great (e.g., *Moose-hausic* = "at the great marsh") |
| -moosi- (see *m∞s*) | bare, smooth |
| m∞wk (*mosk*) | bear (animal) (black ?) ("he devours or licks his paw") |
| mosh- , mosha-, moshe- (see *missi*) | big, large, great (e.g., *Moshas-suck* = "great brook in the marshy meadow") |
| moshennips (see *missi, nip*) | great pond |
| m∞shipsk (see *m∞si, -ompsk-*) | smooth stone |
| mosk-(1), moskit-, muk-, musch- (see *moskeht*, *muskechuge*) | grass, meadow, place where rushes grow (e.g., *Moskituash* = "a meadow") |
| mosk (2) (see *m∞wk, mosq, paukún-nawwaw*) | (black?) bear (animal) (from root "to lick") |
| moskeht (*maskeht*) (see *mos, ask* (1)) | grass or herb (e.g., *nummoskeh-teum* = "my herb"; *nummoskeh-teumash* = "my herbs") |
| mosketu (cf. *moskeht*) | medicine (*iyanaskehtuash* = "many kinds of medicines") |

| | |
|---|---|
| *mosson-* (see *mish∞n*) | boat, Indian canoe, dugout |
| *mosq*(see *mosk*) | A bear; plural = *mosquog* |
| *mous-* (see *moskeht, muskechuge*) | grass, meadow, place where rushes grow (e.g., *Mouscokhuck* = "place of rushes and reeds") |
| *mowáshuck* (see *mowesu, -uck*) (Narr.) | iron-metal ("black metal") |
| *-mpsk-* (see *-ompsk*) | rock, of rocks, standing or upright rock (e.g., *Swampscott* = "at the red rock") |
| *-ms-* (see *-ompsk*) | rock, of rocks, standing or upright rock (e.g., *Quahmsit* = "at the rock") |
| *-msk-* , *-msh-* (see *-ompsk*) | rock, of rocks, standing or upright rock (e.g., *Babaquamshk* = "split rock") |
| *mskik* (see *ask* (1), *sk*) | grass |
| *mskq-* (see *msqui* , *muski*) | red |
| *-msq-* (1) (see *-ompsk*) | rock, of rocks, standing or upright rock |
| *msq-* (2) (see *msqui* , *muski*) | red or salmon |
| *-muc, -mac* (see *acawmuck*) | water (fresh) |
| *muchqua-* (see *msqui, muski*) | red |
| *-muck* (1) (see *-âmaug* ) (cf. *amuck*) | water (fresh), fish (e.g., *Nip-muck* (*Neepmuck*) = "fresh-water fishing place") |
| *-muck* (2), *-muk* (see *-âmaug* ) (cf. *amuck*) | water or fish (e.g., *Congamuck* = " long fishing place") |

| | |
|---|---|
| *-muck-* (see *muckquashim*) | wolf |
| *muckquétu* (Narr.) | swift, as a river (e.g., *kummum-muckquete* = "you are very swift") |
| *-mug* (see *-âmaug*) | fishing-place, fish-curing place |
| *muhhóg* (see *m', -hogk*) | the body (e.g., *wuh*hog = "his body") |
| *muhhuk-* (see *muhkoas*) | wolf (e.g., *Muhhekaneew* = "wolf people"?) |
| *múhkoas* (see *m∞wk, ôâas*) | wolf ("hungry animal") |
| *múhkos* (see *mukqs, -unq*) | a nail, talon, claw, hoof |
| *-muit , -muet* (see *maï , -ut*) | place where path is, carrying place (e.g., *Kickamuit* = "place where otters pass"; from *nkeke* = "otter") |
| *muk-* (see *moskeht, muskechuge*) | grass, meadow, place where rushes grow |
| *-muk-* (see *muckquashim*) | wolf |
| *mukukki* (see *mukki* ?) | bald, smooth |
| *mun-* (see *munnoh*) | island (e.g., *Munnanock* = name of the sun or moon (from *anogqs* = "star" or *munnóh* = "island")) |
| *munhan* (see *munnoh*) | island (e.g., *Munhan* = "an island") |
| *munna-, munnaw-, munnáh* (see *munnóh* (1) (see *munnoh*) | island (e.g., *Munnacommuck* = "island place or plantation" (other possible meanings)) |
| *munna-* (2) (from *munnawhateaug* = "menhaden (a fish)") | menhaden (e.g., *Munnatawkit* = "menhaden country") |
| *munnataukit* (see *munnoh, aûke, -ut*) | in the island country, country of the islanders |
| *munnises* (see *munnoh, -es*) | small island |
| *munnohhan, munnohanne,* (see *munnoh*) | of an island, esp. small |

| | |
|---|---|
| *munnohhanit, munnohhannit, munnah-hanit* (see *munnoh, -it*) | on, to of an island |
| *munnóhkōmuk* (see *munnóh,* , *kōmuk* ) | island place |
| *musc-* , *musqua-, mux* (see *moskeht, muskechuge*) | place where rushes grow (a meadow) (e.g., *Muscoota* = "meadow") |
| *musch-, muscho-* (see *missi, mishe*) | big, large, great (e.g., *Muscho-paug* = "wide pond") |
| *muscho-* (see *msqui , ôâos*) | muskrat |
| *muske-, muski-* (see *msqui , muski*) | red (e.g., *muski-ompsk-ut* = *Swampscott*[3] = "at the red rock") |
| *muskechuge* (see *moskeht, -ge*) | place where rushes grow (rushes are used for mats to cover the *wétu*). |
| *musqua-* (see *msqui , ôâos*) | muskrat (e.g., *Musquashcut* = "abode of muskrats") |
| *musquampskut* (see *musqui, -ompsk, -ut*) | at the red rock |
| *musque-* (see *muski*) | red (e.g., *Musquebaug* = "red pond") |
| *mussh-, museh-* (see *missi*) | big, large , great |
| *mussi* (cf. *missi*) | whole (e.g., *mámusse* = "all," "whole," "wholly") |
| *musta-* (from *mishon* = "wide") | |
| *mut(t)* (see *missi*) | big, large, great |
| *mux-* , *mus-* (2) (see *moskeht, muske-chuge*) | grass, meadow, place where rushes grow |
| *mys-* (see *missi-*) | big, large, great (e.g., *Mystic* = "great tidal river") |

(Footnotes)

1        Two words for "island" were translated and are seen in place names: *ahquidne* & *munnoh* (see Goddard, 2002);  munnoh may imply any dry place or refuge like an island (perhaps derived from  *m'nunnu* = "dry place") ; *ahquidne* may imply a floating or suspended mass, as related to other Algonquian words for "canoe".

2        From Morton, 1669, page 67.

3        Shows loss of initial "m" in muski ("it is red") as this letter  was not heard in translation.

| Algonquian Fragment/Root | Translation |
|---|---|
| | |
| **N** | |
| n | as seen in Trumbull's writing, written as superscript or exponent to denote a nasal *n* sound; e.g. *pau$^n$tuck* , 1881, p. ix) |
| *na-* (see *nai*) | a point of land, angular, pointed, corner, jutting out |
| *naam-* (see *–âm, nâmaus*) | fish |
| *nab-* , *nob-, nabna-* (see *nunobpe* , *nnapi*) | dry (as land) (e.g.,  *Nabnasset* = "near the dry land") |
| *nachick* (*nashik* ) (see *nái, -îk*) | a corner , angle, boundary place |
| *nag-, nagunt-* (see *nagunt*) | bank, dune, sand bank |
| *nagi-*   (see *naiag*) | point of land, angular, pointed, corner, jutting out |
| *nagga-* (see *agu*) | concealing, hiding, haven, refuge, bog, swamp |
| *nah-*  (see *nai*) | a point of land, angular, pointed, corner, jutting out (e.g., *Nahicans* is one old name for *Narragansett* Indians, q.v.). |
| *nahig-*  (see *naiag*) | a point of land, angular, pointed, corner, jutting out (e.g., *Narragansett,* see below) |
| *nagihanet* (see *naiag, -es, -et*) | the country about the point (cf. Narragansett) |

| | |
|---|---|
| *nai-* (see *nayu*) | a point (like a point of land) (e.g., *Naiag* = "a point") |
| *naiwa-* , *naiank-* (see *naiag*) | a point of land, angular, pointed, corner, jutting out (e.g., *Naiwayouk* = "crooked point") |
| *nal-, nalt-* (see *neut*) | narrow, slender, scanty, tight |
| *nam-, nama-, namas(s)-, nams-, naum-* , *name-* (see *–âm, nâmaus*) | fish (usu. a small one) (e.g., *Namacook* = "at the fishing-place") (e.g., *Namasket* = "at the fish place") |
| *nâmans* (*namohs*) (see *-âm*) | fish |
| *nan* (1) (see *nnin*) | denoting sameness, same likeness as, identity, native, indigenous |
| *nan-* (2) (see *neut*) | narrow, slender, scanty, tight |
| *nan-, nana-* (3) (see *nnapi*) | dry (e.g., *Nanakumas* = "dry land (the shore)") |
| *nan-* (4) (see *nashaue*) | midway, fork (e.g., *Nanaquonset* = "confluence of two streams") |
| *nanepash-* (see *nepauzshad*) | month, moon (e.g., *Nanepashemet* = "he who walks the night (i.e., the moon)") |
| *naneswe* (see *nashawe, nees*) | both |
| *nanhig-, nanhigg-, nanihg-* (see *naiag*) | a point of land, angular, pointed, corner, jutting out (cf. *naiag*) |
| *nanó* | it increases more and more (e.g., *nano missi* = "it becomes greater") |
| *nânumiyeu* (see *nannumit, -iyeu*) | northward, the north |
| *napache* (see *na, pache*) | as far as |

197

| | |
|---|---|
| *-napp-* (see *nippi*) | drinking water; pond or body of fresh water (drinking water) |
| *-naq-, -naqu-* (see *naiag*) | a point of land, angular, pointed, corner, jutting out |
| *narrag-, narag-, narig-, narrig-, naryg-* (see *naiag*) | a point of land, angular, pointed, corner, jutting out (literally , "a point of land jutting between waters") (cf. *Narragansett*). Note: many other variant spellings in LaFantasie, vol. 1. |
| *Narragansett* (see *naiag, -es, -et*) | at or about the small point . (The people are named *Nanhigganêuck* = "people of the point"). In historic times, the largest and most powerful Indian Nation in southeastern New England, sometimes called The Nahicans, &c. |
| *nas- , nasa-, naw-* (see *nashaue* ) | midway, fork (e.g., *Nashua* = "between streams") |
| *nashaukomuk* (see *nashaue, -komuk* ) | half-way house |
| *nashaw-* (see *nashaue*) | midway, fork (e.g., *Nashaway* = "a place in the middle") |
| *nashawauke-, nashaueaûke* (see *nashaue, aûke*) | the half-way place |
| *nashaue-* (see *nashaue*) | midway, fork (e.g., *Nashua* = "the land between") |
| *nashaui* (*nashaue, nahshowe* ) (see *noeu, nees, -shau*) | midway, between (see *nashaueaûke*) |
| *nashaway* (see *nashaue*) | midway, fork (e.g., *Nashaway* = "a place in the middle") |

| | |
|---|---|
| *nashik* (see *nái*, *-îk*) | at the corner  (e.g., *yau ut naskik ohke* = "the four corners of the earth") |
| *nashin* (*nái*) | it makes an angle |
| *nat-, natt-* (see *nittauke*) | land, place of (e.g., *Natick* = "my land") |
| *natchau* (see *nau* (1), *nauwut*) | far away, too difficult to visit frequently |
| *natchau-* (see *nashaue*) | midway, fork (e.g., *Natchaug* = "between rivers") |
| *nau-* (1) (see *nauwut* , *nôadt*) | far away  (e.g., *Nauwot* = "a great way, far away") |
| *nau* (2) | clam |
| *-naug*  (see *aug* (2)) | place of (e.g., *Apponaug* = "shell fishing-place") |
| *nauga-*  (see *naukot*) | one (of something) (e.g., *Naugatuck* = "one tree") |
| *naukh-, nauk-* (from *nooki* = "soft") | |
| *naum-*  (see *-âm*) | eel or fish (e.g., *Naumkeag* = "eel place") |
| naumoquok | a heap, pile |
| *naush-*  (see *nashaue*) | midway, fork (e.g., *Naushon* = "middle"?) |
| *naüt* (see *na*, *ut*) | thereon, thereat, threat, therein |
| *nauwoh-* (see *yaw*) | four |
| *nauwut* (*nôadt*) (see *nau* (1), *w'*) | far off, away |
| *naw-* (cf. *nas*, above) | midway, fork or a point of land (from *nai*) |
| *nawayack-*  (see *naiag*, *ac* (2)) | a point of land, angular, pointed, corner, jutting out (cf. *naiwa*) |

| | |
|---|---|
| *-nawbes* (see *nuppis*) | small pond or bay (e.g., *Nawbe-setuc* = "land of the pond") |
| *nay-* , *naya-*, *nayu-* (see *nia*) | a point of land, angular, pointed, corner, jutting out (e.g., *Nayaug* = "point of land") |
| *nayaug* (see *naiag*) | a point of land, angular, pointed, corner, jutting out (e.g., *Nayaug* = "point or angle") |
| *-ne-* (1) (see *wunni*) | good, beautiful, pleasing (e.g., *Nepaug* = "good pond"); Trumbull, 1881 |
| *-ne-* (2) (from *nunni* = "fresh") | good, beautiful, pleasing, fresh (e.g., *Nepaug* = "fresh pond"); Trumbull, 1881 |
| *necáwme* (*negone*) (see *nequt*) | first, original, before |
| *-neck* (see *naiag*) | a point of land, angular, pointed, corner, jutting out |
| *neechi-* (see *-etu, -ittu*) | give birth to, newborn |
| *neep-* (see *nippe*) | drinking water; pond or body of fresh water (drinking water) (e.g., *Neepmuck* (*Nipmuck*) = "fresh-water fishing place") |
| *nees-* , *neese-*, *neesh-*, *nesh-* (see *neese*) | two, double (e.g., *Neeshapaug* = "place of two ponds") |
| *neeshaúog* (see *neese, -og*(2)) (Narr.) | eels ("they go in pairs") (other terms for and types of eels; *sas-samaúquock*, *nquittéconnaúog*, which have the roots "single, straight, long, fish") |

| neg-, neca- (see *negone*) | first, original (e.g., *Negan Odanak* = "the original town (village)") |
| -negk, -neghk (see *neg, hk*?) | peaked (as a rock, of rocks) (e.g., *Hassunegk* = Horseneck= "a rock shelter") |
| neh- (see *nai*) | a point (such as of land) |
| nehum(k)- (see *neeshaûog*) | eel (several types of) |
| neimpaûog (see *-pauog*) (Narr.) | thunder |
| -nem, -nemos (see *-âm*) | fish (taken by hook) (e.g., *Amoskeag* = "place of fish traps") |
| nep- (see *nippi*) | drinking water; pond or body of fresh water (drinking water) (e.g., *Neponset* = "a good water-fall") |
| nepattau (*quentau*) | it stands there (e.g., *neepau* = "he stands, rises") |
| nepauzshad (*nanepauzshad*) (see n', *paspishau*, *pomushau*) | moon (root means "night walker", "night traveler") |
| nepon- (see *winne, pon* (1)) | good, full (e.g., *Neponset* = "a good water-fall") |
| nepun (cf. *sequan, papone*) | summer (latter part of), harvest time |
| nesâhteag (see *ne* (2), *sahke, teag*) | its length |
| netop (see n ē *top*) | friend (e.g., *Netop* = "my friend") |
| neuh (see *na*) | there |
| neuqui- (from *nekoshag* = "the breadth of" | broad, wide |

| | |
|---|---|
| *neut-* , *neuta-*, *not-*, *nuta-* (from *neuta* = "scant, short, deficient in, lacking") | narrow, slender, scanty, tight, deficient in, lacking (e.g., *Neu-taconkanut* = "at the short (scant) boundary") |
| *neyhom* (see same) | turkey |
| *nia-* , *nya-* (see *naiag*) | a point of land, angular, pointed, corner, jutting out (cf. *nai*) (e.g. *Niantic* = "point of land at the tidal river") |
| *niack-* , *nyac-* (see *naiag*) | a point of land, angular, pointed, corner, jutting out (e.g., *Nyac* = "a point") |
| *niantic* (from *naïtukq* = "a point of land on the (tidal) river or estuary") | a point of land on the (tidal) river or estuary (e.g., *Nianticut* = "at a point of land on the (tidal) river or estuary") |
| *niche, nitche-* (see *nashaue*) | midway, fork |
| *nikk-* , *nukk-* | - one (in number)<br>- easy |
| *nini-* (1) (see *nun* ? or from *nunáe* = dry<br>or<br>or *nunni* = "fresh") | dry ? or fresh? |
| *nini* (2) (see *nippe*) | drinking water; pond or body of fresh water (drinking water) dry ? |
| *nip-, nipp-* (see *nippe*) | drinking water; pond or body of fresh water (drinking water) (e.g., *Nipmuck* = "fresh-water fishing place") (sometimes given as *Neepmuck*, among other spellings) |
| *nipeash* (*nipsach*) (see *nippe, -ash*) | water (plural of *nippe*) |

202

| | |
|---|---|
| *nipi-* (see *nippe*) | drinking water; pond or body of fresh water (drinking water) (cf. *nip*) |
| *nippawus* (*nepáuz*) (Narr.) | the sun |
| *nippekontu* (see *nippe*, *-kontu* (2))) | where much water is |
| *nippi-* (see *nippe*) | drinking water; pond or body of fresh water (drinking water) (e.g., *Assinippi* = "rocky water") |
| *nis-* , *niss-*, *nees-* (see *neese*) | two, double (e.g., *Nissitisset* = "near the two small rivers") |
| *nis(w)-* (see *missi*) | big, large, great |
| *n-k* (see *n-g*) | Root word for "he scratches, tears things" (onomatopoetic root for "otter or other fur bearing animals") |
| *nkèke*(see *-quock*) (Narr.) | an otter (from *n'g* or *n'k* = "he scratches, tears things" (imitative)); plural = *nkèkekéquock* |
| *nnáppi* (see *n'*, *áppu*) | dry ("no water") |
| *no-*(1) (see *nau* (1)) | far away (e.g., *Nockum* = "land can be seen far off") |
| *no-* (2), *noa-* (see *nashawe*, *nashaui*) | middle of, narrow, thin (e.g., *Nowesit* ="middle place") |
| *no-* (3) (see *nai*) | a point of land, angular, pointed, corner, jutting out (e.g., *Noag* = "a point of land") |
| *nôadt* (see *nô* (1), *adt*, *nauwut*) | afar off |
| *-noag* (see *-noag* , *nnin*) | people, folk of an area (e.g., *Wampanoag* = "The people of the first light" or "dawnlanders", among other translations) |

| | |
|---|---|
| *nóahtuk* (see *noeu*, *-tuk* ) | in the middle of the river |
| *noank-* (see *naiag*) | a point of land, angular, pointed, corner, jutting out (e.g., *Noank* = "it is a point") |
| *nob-* ( see *nnapi*) | dry ?, rock, of standing rocks (e.g., *Nobska* = "rock place") |
| *nock-* (see *nôadt*) | far away (e.g., *Nockum* = "land can be seen far off") |
| *nôeu* (*noe*) | in the middle of |
| *nohham* (*nohh∞m*) (see *noh* (2), ∞*m*) | he (or I ?) goes by water |
| *nokuskau* (*nockuskaw*) | to meet |
| *none-, nona-, nonne-, nonnew* (see *nun* (2)) | dry (e.g., *Nonnewaug* = "dry land") |
| *noi-* (see *nai*) | a point of land, angular, pointed, corner, jutting out (e.g., *Noag* = "a point of land") |
| *nono-* (1) , *nanow-, noone-* (see *noeu*) | middle of, narrow, thin (e.g., *Nonotuck* = "in the middle of the river") (one poss. meaning) |
| *nono-* (2) , *nanow-* (see *neut*) | narrow, slender, scant, tight (e.g., *Nonotuck* = "narrow river") (one poss. meaning) |
| *nonquit-* (from *nannogkuit* = "south-west", R. Williams, *A Key*) | |
| *nóóhteau* (see *nô* (1), *-ohteau*) | it is far off |
| *nook-, nock-* (from *nooki* = "soft") | |
| *n∞keu* (see *n', nukon*) | he goes downward, descends |
| *noos-* , *-noose,* (see *n∞sup*) | beaver (e.g., *Nooseneck* = "the beaver- place") |

| | |
|---|---|
| n∞tau (n∞teau) (see *yot* | fire, devouring element (e.g., *nnanótissu* = "I am on fire"(I have a fever)) |
| -noot- (from *manoot* = "basket" ) | lift up (e.g., *Nootash* = "carry loads in them, take it on your back " ; i.e., baskets) |
| nooze- (see *n∞sup*) | beaver (e.g., *Noozapoge* = "beaver- pond") |
| nop- (1) (see *nôadt*) | far away (e.g., *Nopque* = "utmost, furtherest place" ) (one possible meaning) |
| nop (2) (see *p*) | |
| nópadtinayeu (see *-iyeu*) | towards the southwest |
| not- ( see *neut*) | narrow, slender, scant, tight (cf. *neut*) |
| nor-(1) , norw- (see *naiag*) | a point of land, angular, pointed, corner, jutting out (e.g., *Norwalk* = "a point of land") |
| nor-(2) , norw- (see *noeu*) | middle of, narrow, thin |
| note , yote, chickot, squatta, nootau, oot (see *note , yote, chickot, squatta, nootau*) | fire, several different types/meanings of "fire" |
| now- (1) (see *nashawe, nashaui*) | middle of (e.g., *Nowesit* = "middle place") |
| now- (2) (see *nnapi*) | dry (e.g., *Nowpaug* = "dry pond") (one possible meaning) |
| noy- (see *nai*) | a point of land, angular, pointed, corner, jutting out |
| npeshwog (see *nuppoh, psuk, pt∞wu, -og* (2)) (Narr.) | wild fowl in general (imitative of flock at "take-off") |

| | |
|---|---|
| *-nte-* (see *tn, dn*) | mountain |
| *nuhkehk-, nukkek-* (from *nickquenum* = "I am returning home to my family" [very solemn words]) | desired home, my beloved family |
| *nuk- , nukkon-* (see *psg*) | darkly, by night |
| *nukkon-* (see *nukkone*) | old, ancient, very first |
| *-num-* (*-um-, -un-, -am-, -n-*) | action by the hand ;*tohqunn*um = "he takes (by hand)") |
| *numma-* (see *-âm*) | eel or fish |
| *nun-, nunn-* (see *nnappi*) | dry (cf. *nunna*) |
| *nungee* (from *nunnukkushau* = "he trembles) | quaking, trembling |
| *nunk-, nunka-* (see *-wonk-*) | crooked, bent, oxbow, back turn in stream, sudden turning or twisting (e.g., *Nunkertunk* = "bent river") |
| *nunkane* (*nonkane*) | light in weight (e.g., *nunkomp* = *nunkane* + *omp* = "a young man (a man light in weight)") |
| *nunna- , nunnaw-* (see *nnapi*) | dry (e.g.,  *Nunnawauk*  = "dry-land") |
| *nunnapaug* (from *nunni* = "fresh, *-paug*(1)) | fresh pond |
| *nunni-* (see *neut*) | slender, narrow |
| *nunnohaûke* (see *nun, aûke*) | dry land |
| *nunnukque* (see *uhq*) | dangerous |
| *nup, nip* (see *nup∞onk*) | die (e.g., *mosnunnop* = "I must die") |
| *nuppe-, nups-* (see *nippi*) | water |
| *nuppis* (see *nippe, -is*) | small body of fresh water (diminutive of *nip*) |

| | |
|---|---|
| *nyac-, nyack-, niack-* (see *naiag*) | a point of land, angular, pointed, corner, jutting out (e.g., *Nyac* = "a point") |

| Algonquian Fragment/Root | Translation |
|---|---|
| | |
| **O** | |
| *ôâas* (*oaus, howaas*) (in comp., *-as-*, *-us*) (cf. *–ashim*) | animal, wild beast, living creature (e.g., *mogkéoas*) |
| *-oag* (1)  (see *-og* (2)) | pluralization stem for "animate" forms, nouns. Sometimes includes a preceding "glide" *w* or *u* or *y* or *l*, etc. |
| *-oag* (2)  (see *og* (3)) | at, near, place of. Sometimes includes a preceding "glide" *w* or *u* or *y* or *l*, etc. |
| *-ob-* (1)  (see *wompi*) | white, the light, dawn, the East |
| *-ob-* (2)  (see *-ompsk*) | rock, of rocks, standing or upright rock (e.g., *Canob* = "long rock") (e.g., *Cos Cob* = "high rock") |
| *-oba-, -obah-*  ( see *ohké*) | land, place of. Sometimes includes a preceding "glide" *w* or *u* or *y* or *l*, etc. |
| *-obsc-*  (see *-ompsk*) | rock, of rocks, standing or upright rock (e.g.,  the tribe *Penobscot* = "place where the  rocks widen") |
| *-obsk-*  (see *-ompsk*) | rock, of rocks, standing or upright rock |
| *obwe-*  (from *ocque* = "end of summit") | tall, high, elevated (e.g., *Obwe-betuck* = "top of a tree") |

| | |
|---|---|
| *-oc-* (see *aûke*) | land, place land, ground, place, country (not enclosed or limited). (e.g., *Occupasstuxet* = "place of small cove on tidal creek") |
| *occ-* (see *aucùp*) | cove (e.g., *Occupaspatucket* = "near the cove on the shallow tidal creek") |
| *occa-* (see *ogkome*) | other side of, over against |
| *occape, onkuppe* (see ∞*t, menuh, kup* (1)) | strong liquor ("fire water") |
| *occo-* (see *weque*) | at the end/head of |
| *occu-* (see ogguhse) | small, little (e.g., *oggusepaug* ' "little pond") |
| *-ochi* (see *–tch-, -ch-, -tchuan*) (see *ooche*) | from, issuing from, flowing out |
| *-ock* (1), *uhq-, -og* (see *uhquan*) | hook, so shaped, at end of (e.g., *Hockamock* = "hook shaped place" or "land formation like a hook"). Sometimes includes a preceding "glide" *w* or *u* or *y* or *l*, etc. |
| *-ock* (2) (see *–og* (2)) | pluralization stem for "animate" forms, nouns. Sometimes includes a preceding "glide" *w* or *u* or *y* or *l*, etc. |
| *-ock* (3) (see *aûke*) | land, ground, place, country (not enclosed or limited). (e.g., *Hassunock* = "stony place"). Sometimes includes a preceding "glide" *w* or *u* or *y* or *l*, etc. |
| *-ock* (4) (see *–hogk*) | body, shell |
| *-ocke* (see *aûke*) | land, ground, place, country (not enclosed or limited). Sometimes includes a preceding "glide" *w* or *u* or *y* or *l*, etc. |

| | |
|---|---|
| *-ockoo* (see *ogkome*) | other side of, over against |
| *ocque-* (see *ukque*) | at the end of. Sometimes includes a preceding "glide" *w* or *u* or *y* or *l*, etc. |
| *ocqui-* (see *agwe*) | under, underneath, below |
| *ocsech-* (see *wonkqŭssis*) | fox (e.g., *Ocsechoxit* = "[little] fox country") |
| *-oct* (see *aûke*) | land, ground, place, country (not enclosed or limited). Sometimes includes a preceding "glide" *w* or *u* or *y* or *l*, etc. |
| *-octe* (see *aûke*) | land, place of. Sometimes includes a preceding "glide" *w* or *u* or *y* or *l*, etc. |
| *-og* (1) (see *aûke*) | land, ground, place, country (not enclosed or limited). Sometimes includes a preceding "glide" *w* or *u* or *y* or *l*, etc. |
| *-og* (2) (see *-og* (2)) | pluralization stem for "animate" forms, nouns. Sometimes includes a preceding "glide" *w* or *u* or *y* or *l*, etc. |
| *ogan-* (see *-hegan*) | instrument of, agent, tool for |
| *-oge* (see (see *aûke*) | land, ground, place, country (not enclosed or limited). Sometimes includes a preceding "glide" *w* or *u* or *y* or *l*, etc. |
| *-ogg* (1) (see *aûke*) | land, ground, place, country (not enclosed or limited). Sometimes includes a preceding "glide" *w* or *u* or *y* or *l*, etc. |
| *ogguhse* (*oggus*) | small, little in quantity (e.g., *og-gusepaug* = "small pond") |

209

| | |
|---|---|
| *ogguhsemese* (see *ogguhse*, *-emes*)) | least of an amount, smallest of (e.g, *oggusemse nippe* = "very little water") |
| *oggusepaug* (see *ogguhse*, *-paug* (1)) | small pond |
| *-ogue* (see *aûke*) | land, ground, place, country (not enclosed or limited). Sometimes includes a preceding "glide" *w* or *u* or *y* or *l*, etc. |
| *ogkome* (see *ongkome*) | on the other side of, over against |
| *ogkosse* (see *ogguhse*) | small, little in quantity |
| *-ogw* (see *agwe*) | under, underneath, below |
| *ohka-* (from *ohkuk*, *ohkuhk*, *ahkuhk*, *aúcuck* = "a kettle") | kettle, earthen pot (e.g., *Ohkakquiset* = "at the small hollow (kettle-hole)?") |
| *ohkee* (see *ohke*, *-e*) | earthen, of earth |
| *-ohki-* , *-ohko-* , *-oke-* (see *aûke*) | land, ground, place, country (not enclosed or limited). (e.g., *Ohkonkumme* = "village on the other side"). Sometimes includes a preceding "glide" *w* or *u* or *y* or *l*, etc. |
| *ohkon-* (from *oton* = "village, town") | village, town |
| *ohkomm-* (see *ongkome*) | on the other side of, over against |
| *ohmo-*, *ohmow-* (from *tattagoskituash* = "trembling, wet, grassy") | bog, swamp, wet place, refuge (e.g., *Ohmowauke* = "owl's place") (Indian refuge place) |
| *oho-* (1) (see *∞h∞maus*) | owl (e.g., *Ohomowauke* = "at the abode of owls") |
| *oho-* (2) (see *agu*) | concealing, hiding, haven, refuge, bog, swamp (e.g., *Ohomowauke* = "at the abode of owls") |

| | |
|---|---|
| *-oke-* (see *aûke*) | land, ground, place, country (not enclosed or limited). |
| *ohteuhkonat* (see *ohke, át*) | to plant |
| *okom-, okomma-* (see *ogkome*) | other side of, over against (e.g., *Okommakemsit* = "at the field on the other side") |
| *-om* (1) , *-on* (see *át*) | at, in, on |
| *-om-* (2), *-am-* (see *ôm*) | a fish hook and line (e.g., *Absalon-omiscut* = "place of the fish trap; where fish are caught in a weir") |
| *-omp-,-omps-* (see *-ompsk*) | rock, of rocks, standing or upright rock (e.g., *Ascocompamache* = "small place closed in by boulders") |
| *-omscut-* (see *ompskut*) | place of rock, of rocks, standing or upright rock |
| *-ompsk-, -ompsq-,-ompsc-, -ipsk-, -aumsc-,* etc, | rock, of rocks,a standing, upright hard rock (e.g., *kehtompskut* = "at the great rock"; e.g., modern place name, Sw<u>ampsc</u>ott; also "stone" in Narragansett. whetstone, flint (e.g., *cauómpsk* = "a whetstone , stone, millstone, grinding stone for corn and other uses") |
| *ompskut* (see *-ompsk-, -ut*) | at the rock |
| *-omsk-* (see *-ompsk*) | rock, of rocks, standing or upright rock (e.g., *Gotomska* = "big rock") |
| *-on , -om* (see *át*) | at, in, on |
| *-ong , -oag* (see *-og* (2)) | at, near, place of. Sometimes includes a preceding "glide" *w* or *u* or *y* or *l*, etc. |

| | |
|---|---|
| *ongkome* (see *ogkome*) (cf. *acawmen*) | on the other side (e.g., *ogko-mutsepu*ut = "beyond the river") |
| ongkoue | beyond, end-place |
| *-onck* (see below, *-onk* (2)) | tree, wood |
| *-onk* (1) (see *honck*) | goose, geese (e.g., *Seekonk* = "place of black geese" (one possible meaning)) |
| *-onk* (2), *-anck, -onck, -unck* (see *unk* (2)) | tree, wood (e.g., *Agwonk* = "under a tree). Sometimes includes a preceding "glide" *w* or *u* or *y* or *l* as in *−wonk.* |
| *-onk* (3), *-uck, ick, -it, -eg* (also Narr.) | at, in, place of |
| *-onom-* (see *annem*) | paint, pigment (e.g., *Tonomy* = "red paint hill"?) |
| *-ont-* (see *-ut*) | at, in, by near, (popularly, "place of") Sometimes includes a preceding "glide" *w* or *u* or *y* or *l*, etc. |
| *-ontop, -ontup* (see *antep*) | head (e.g., *Montup* = "the summit or look-out place") |
| ontseu | he descends, comes from |
| *-oo, -oo* (see − ∞ ,∞ ) | particles of negation (when before a root) or affirmation (when a suffix); see Trumbull, 1903, p. 111. |
| *-ooc* (see *-ag* (1)) | land, place of. Sometimes includes a preceding "glide" *w* or *u* or *y* or *l*, etc. |
| *-ooch , -ootch* (see *wutche* or from ∞ *oochaus* = "a fly") | out of, from (or) flies (insects) |

| | |
|---|---|
| *-oock* (see *-ag* (1)) | people, folk of an area. Sometimes includes a preceding "glide" *w* or *u* or *y* or *l*, etc. |
| *-oog* (1), *-oag* (see *êuck* ,*-og* (3)) | people, folk of an area Sometimes includes a preceding "glide" *w* or *u* or *y* or *l*, etc. |
| *-oog* (2) (see *-ag* (1)) | land, place of (e.g., *Watchoog* = "hill country"). Sometimes includes a preceding "glide" *w* or *u* or *y* or *l*, etc. |
| *-oogk-* (1) (see *oonk*) | dish, plate, bowl (so shaped) |
| *-oogk* (2) (see *-ag* (1)) | land, place of. Sometimes includes a preceding " glide" *w* or *u* or *y* or *l*, etc. |
| ∞*h∞maus* (see *ôâas*) | owl ("animal that says *oohoo*") |
| ∞*hk*, ∞*nk* (see *askug*) | worm |
| ∞*hqui* (see *ohkee*) | section of land, a neck of land |
| *-oohk-* (see *–ukq, -uhk-*) | of permanence, continuation |
| *-ook* (see *-ag* (1)) | land, place of (e.g., *Suncook* = "rocky point of land"). Sometimes includes a preceding " glide" *w* or *u* or *y* or *l*, etc. |
| ∞*m∞∞* (see *omm∞* ) | it goes from |
| *-oon-, -oom-* (see *mish∞n*) | boat, Indian canoe, dugout (cf. *mishoon*) |
| ∞*ne* (see *wunni*) | good, pleasing, favorable |
| *-oonk-* (see *oonk*) | dish, plate, bowl (so shaped) |
| *-oonoi-,-ooni- oonou-* (see *mooneau, moonoi*) | deep (as a valley or stream) |
| ∞*noi* (see *peshaui*) (Narr.) | blue or deep |

| | |
|---|---|
| *oonoukoi, moonokoiyeu* (from same, Trumbull, 1903) | valley |
| *-oot* (see *-ut*) | at, in, by near, (popularly, "place of") (e.g., *Aucoot* = "at the cove") |
| *opponenaûhock* (see *apwonat* , *-hock*) (Narr.) | oysters |
| *ora-, ore-* (see *wunni,* "r" dialect) | good, beautiful, pleasant |
| *osa, ousa* (*wesaui*) | (it is) yellow;e.g., Ousa Mequin= "Yellow Feather" was The Massasoit who met the Pilgrims at Plymouth, 1620 |
| *-oshim* (see *–ashim*) | of animals |
| *oss-* , *ossi-* (see *hassen*) | rock, of rocks, standing or upright rock (e.g., *Ossipee* = "rocky river") |
| *-ot* (see *-ut, aûke*) | land, ground, place, country (not enclosed or limited). (e.g., *Nauwot* = "a great way, faroff"). Sometimes includes a preceding "glide" *w* or *u* or *y* or *l*, etc. |
| *-otan-* , *-uten-* (see *otan-nash*) | village, principal town |
| *-ott* (see *-ut*) | at, in, by near, (popularly, "place of") (e.g., *Masscomscott* = "place of large (or red?) rock") |
| *-otong* (see *utic*) | at, near, place of |
| *-ous* (see *wussi*) | other side of, beyond (cf. *hous*) (e.g., *Housatonic* = "beyond the mountain") |
| *ouwán* | mist |

214

| | |
|---|---|
| *oxe-* (see *ogguhse*) | little in quantity, small (e.g., *Oxecoset* = "place of small pine trees") |
| *oxo-* (see *ogguhse*) | little in quantity, small (e.g., *Oxoboxo* = "a small pond") |
| *oxy-* (see *ogguhse*) | little in quantity, small (e.g., *Oxyboxy* = "very little water") |

| Algonquian Fragment/Root | Translation |
|---|---|
| | |
| **P** | |
| *pa-* (see *pau*) | falls in the stream, water falls, rapids |
| *pab-* (see *pohsh*) | between-two, half, part of, divided, split (e.g., *Pabaquamske* = "split rock") |
| *-pac* , *-pack* (see *-paug* (1)) | watery open area, lake, pond, bay still-water (e.g., *Pacatuck* = "open, clear river") |
| *paca-*, *pach-* , *pack-* (see *pohque*) | clear, open, bare, shallow (e.g., *Pacanaukett* = *Pokanoket* = "place of the cleared land") |
| *pacassett* (see *pohk, ,-es, -et*) | small separating, dividing, opening place (e.g., *Chachapacassett* = "at the great widening") |
| *pach-*, *pack-* (see *pauchau*) | turn, deviate, change (e.g., *Pachaug* = "a turning place") |
| *pache* (see *pummeu, paáme*) | up to, as far as, until |
| *pacheshin* (see *pache*) | it comes to, extends as far as |

215

| | |
|---|---|
| *pachqu-* , *pohque-* (see *pohque*) | clear, open, bare, shallow (e.g., *Pachquadnack* = "place of clear mountain") |
| *pacum-, pocum, paucom-* (see *pohqu'un*) | clear, open, bare, shallow |
| *pădkodche* (*pogkodche*) (see *pohshane*) | thoroughly, completely |
| *-pag* (see *-paug* (1)) | watery open area, lake, pond, bay still-water (e.g., *Pagassett* = "place where the river widens") |
| *-pague* (see *-paug* (1)) | watery open area, lake, pond, bay still-water |
| *pagwa-* (see *pohque*) | clear, open, bare, shallow (e.g., *Pagwonk* = "cleared land") |
| *pahcu-* (see *pohque*) | clear, open, bare, shallow (e.g., *Pahcupog* = "clear water pond") |
| *pahqui-* (see *pohque)* | clear, open, bare, shallow |
| *pahtatunniu* (*puhtadtuniyeu*) (see *pâ-*, *-iyeu*) | westward, towards the west |
| *paht∞* (see *pă*, *∞ch*) | run, flow as a stream, river &c |
| *pak-* , *pack-* (see *pohque*) | clear, open, bare, shallow (e.g., *Packwacke* = "open place") |
| *paka-, pack-,packach-* (see *pachau*) | turn, divide, change |
| *pakepaug* (see *pahke*, *-paug*(1)) | clear or pure water pond |
| *pamooso* (fom *pam∞s∞* = "he swims") | |
| *pam-* (from *penneu* = "he falls down"), or (see *-pau* (1)) | descending, falling, sloping (e.g., *Pamaquesicke* = "at the ledges") |
| *pamishik* (see *paáme*, *-ik*) | where it extends |

216

| | |
|---|---|
| *pamushau* (*pahmushau, pomushau*) (see *pà , musset, -shau*) | walk, walking ("he who goes on foot, walks, passes by") |
| *pan-* (from *penneu* = "he falls down"), or (see *-pau* (1)) | falls in the stream, water falls, rapids (e.g., *Pantoosuck* = "at the falls in the brook") |
| *pana-* (see *panna*) | open, spread out land, materials |
| *panna-* (see *panna*) | open, spread out land, materials (e.g., *Pannaheconnok* = "extended country") |
| *panne* (see *pă, panneaü*) | away, another way, off of, persistently (from *penouwe* = strange") |
| *pap-* (1) , *pohsh-, paup-* (see *pohsh*) | between-two, half, part of, divided, split (e.g., *Pappacontucksquash* = "gorge") |
| *pap-* (2) (*papone*) (Narr.) | of northland, winter (e.g., *paponaumsúog* = "winter fish") |
| *papan-* , *papon-* (see *pap, papone*) | winter, northland (e.g., *Papanomscutt* = "placewhere we get winterfish—tomcod, frostfish)," one possible meaning) |
| *papaquantuck* (see *pohque, -uck*) | broken [many times] land |
| *papóne* (see *pap, -e*) (Narr.) | winter (e.g., *papanaumsuog* = "winter fishes") |
| *pap∞s* (see *pă, pewe*) (Narr.) | a young child (papoose) |
| *paqua-, paqui-* (see *pohque*) | clear, open, bare, shallow (e.g., *Paqua* = "open or clear pond") |
| *-paquan-* (see *pohqu' un*) | cleared, opened (such as land) (e.g., *Papaquantuck* = "clear or shallow river") |

217

| | |
|---|---|
| *pas-* (1) (cf. *pasc*) | bloom, blossom, burst forth |
| *pas-* (2), *pass-*  (see *pissagk*) | muddy, miry (e.g., *Pasquesit* = "miry place") |
| *pasc-* , *pask-* (see *pohq*) | forking, splitting, dividing, turning, opening (e.g., *Pascoag* = "where the way turns") |
| *pash-* (see *pohsh*) | between-two, half, part of, divided, split  (e.g., *Pashebesauke* = "near the outlet of a river mouth") |
| *pashk* (*paashk*) (see *pohq*) | burst out |
| *paso-* (see *pâs∞*) | near, nearby, proximity |
| *pasq-*  (see *pohq*) | forking, splitting, dividing, turning, opening (related to *pas-sohtham* = "he digs a ditch") |
| *pass-*, *pas-* (see *pissagk*) | muddy or miry (e.g., *Passanoke* = "muddy place") |
| *passa-* (see *posh*) | between-two, half, part of, divided, split |
| *pâs∞* (*pâhsu, pausaw* (Narr.)) | near, nearby, proximity, neighborhood |
| *pâs∞che* (see *pâs∞*) | a little way, away |
| *pas∞tshau* (see *passo, -shau, ∞m*) | he goes or comes near |
| *passcat-*  (see *-pisk* (2)) | at the branch or fork in river |
| *pata-, pataag-*  (see *p'etùk'qui*) | round (e.g., *Patagumskocte* = "place of round rock") |
| *patack-, pataag-*  (see *pautuk*) | falls in the stream, water falls, rapids |
| *patopu-* (see *pohk* or *paut*)? | separating, dividing, opening or jut out |

| | |
|---|---|
| *patta-*, *pattaquo-*  (see p'etùk'qui) | round (e.g., *Pattagussis* = "little oxbow") |
| *pattag-*  (see p'etùk'qui) | round (cf. *patta-*, above entry) |
| *patan-* (see p'etùk'qui) | round |
| *patuck* (see *pautuk*) | falls in the stream, water falls, rapids |
| *pau-* (1) (see *paw* , *pau* (1)) | falls in the stream, water falls, rapids (e.g., *Pautuxet* = "at the little falls") |
| *pauchag-*  (see *pauchau*) | turn, deviate, change (e.g., *Pauchaug* = "at the turning place") |
| *pauchau-*  (see *pauchautaqua*) | branch-branches (cf. *Pauchag*, above) |
| *paucutun-*  (see *pohquettahun*) | broken up, cultivated |
| *-paug-*, *-paugh-* , *-pauk-*  (see *-paug* (1)) | watery open area, lake, pond, bay still-water (e.g., *Massapaug* = "great pond") |
| *pauga-*  (see *pohk*) | separating, dividing, opening (e.g., *Paugasset* or *Pocasset* = "place where a strait widens") |
| *paugan-* (from *pauquanna* = "there is a slaughter, of destruction in war") | |
| *paugas(s)* (above *pauga-* & diminutive *–s-* ("little")) | *see* Trumbull, 1970, p. 40 |

| | |
|---|---|
| *-pauge-* (see *-paug* (1)) | watery open area, lake, pond, bay still-water (e.g., *Paugeamapauge* = "divided pond; shallow fishing place at pond") |
| *-paugeset* (see *paug* (1), *-es, -et*) | at the little pond |
| *-paugh-* , *-paug-*, *-pauk-* (see *-paug* (1)) | watery open area, lake, pond, bay still-water |
| *-pauk-* (see *-paug* (1)) | watery open area, lake, pond, bay still-water (e.g., *Aquapauksit* = "at the end of a small pond") |
| *-pauk-* (1) (see *pauchau*) | turn, deviate, change |
| *-pauk-*(2), *-paukoh-* (see *paukúnaw-waw*) | a bear (Narr. Lang.) |
| *paupak-*, *paupog* (see *–pau* (2), *-paug*(1)) | little pond |
| *paupukqua-*, *paupogqu* (see *pohque*, *-paug*(1)) | clear pond |
| *pauqua-* (see *pohque*) | clear, open, bare, shallow (e.g., *Pauquapaug* = "clear water pond") |
| *pauque-* (see *pohque*) | clear, open, bare, shallow |
| *pauqu'unaûkeet* ( or *pauqu'unohkeit*) | at the place of the cleared land (translation of name of the place of Pokanokets and the name of historic tribe/nation *Poka*noket (Wampanoag presently)) |
| *paut-* (from = *p∞tôae,* "bulging or jutting out") | jut out (e.g., *Pautapaug* = "the jutting cove or pond") |

| | |
|---|---|
| *pautuk, pawtuck* (see *pau-, -tuk*) | falls in a tidal river (e.g., Pautuxet = "at the little falls") |
| *pau wau* (see *waw, tau puwau*) | an Indian priest or Holy Man (cf. "Powwas" (spiritual leader), "powwow") |
| *paw-* (1) (*-pau* (1)) | falls in the stream, water falls, rapids (e.g., *Pawtucket* = "waterfalls place") |
| *paw-* (2) (see *-pau* (2)) | little (e.g., *Pawawget* = "small clear meadow") |
| *pawca-* (see *pohq*) | divided, separated, opened (e.g., *Pawcatuck* = "divided stream") |
| *-pawog-* (see *-paug* (1)) | watery open area, lake, pond, bay still-water |
| *payqua-* (see *pohque*) | clear, open, bare, shallow (e.g., *Payquage* = "cleared land") |
| *pe-* (1), *pee-, pea-* (see *pewe, pe* (1)) | small, tight (e.g., *Peamecha* = "small river near the hill") |
| *-pe-* (2) (see *nippe, pe* (2)) | drinking water; pond or body of fresh water (drinking water) |
| *-peag-* (see *peauke*) | water-place |
| *peakō̄ muk* (see *pewe, kō̄ muk*) | a little enclosure, shelter |
| *pecon-* (see *pohqu' un*) | cleared, opened (such as land) |
| *-pee-* (see *nippe, pe* (2)) | drinking water; pond or body of fresh water (drinking water) (e.g., *Sunapee* = "rocky pond") |

| | |
|---|---|
| *peeg* - (see *–paug* (1)) | watery open area, lake, pond, bay still-water (e.g., *Peegwon* = "tear drop" ?) |
| *peemayagat* (see *pewe*, *mayi,át*) | a little way |
| *-pege-* (see *-paug*(1)) | watery open area, lake, pond, bay still-water |
| *pem-* (1) (from *penneu* = "he falls down") | descending, falling, sloping (e.g., *Pemtegwatook* = "extended descending river current") |
| *pem-* (2), *pom-* (see *pom -*) | journey, travel, passing by (e.g., *Pomachaug* = "over the hill") |
| *pem* - (3) (see *peemayagyat*) | narrow, slender, scanty, tight (e.g., *Pemonos* = "narrow trial") |
| *pemi-*, *pumm-* (see *pemisuâi*) | sloping, aslant, twisted, awry (e.g., *Pumpisset* = "at the crooked place," one meaning |
| *pemsquam-* (see *pemsquamku* ) | hardwoods (birch) (e.g., *Pemsquamkutook* = "hardwoods near river") |
| *pen-*, *penn-*, *penna-*, *pena-*, *pene-* (see *pă* or from *peónogog* = "of a path or way") | bending, sloping, curving, bending backwards, all about in some direction or a path, way (e.g., *Pennacook* = "sloping-down place") |
| *penk-* (from ponquag = "a fording or shallow place") | |
| *penugque* (from punukquékontu = "on the bank of the river") | on the bank of the river |
| *pequa-* (see *pohque*) | clear, open, bare, shallow (cf. *pequon*) |

| | |
|---|---|
| *pequan-* (1)  (see *pohqu' un*) | clear, open, bare, shallow (e.g., *Pequag* = "cleared land") |
| *pequan* (2) (see *pequawas*) | grey fox  (for Pequot Tribe) ("circler") |
| *pequann-* (from *paúquana* = "there is a slaughter, of destruction, in war") | |
| *pequon -* (see *pohqu' un*) | cleared, opened  (such as land) (e.g., *Pequonnock* = "a small plantation") |
| *Pequot* (see *pequan*) | the destroyers (name of several New England tribes or nations: Mashantucket Pequots, Paucatuck Pequots, Eastern Pequots, in Connecticut). Note: many other variant spellings in LaFantasie, vol. 1. |
| *pesh-*  (see *peshaui*) | blue colored, bluish, violet  (see *oonoi*) |
| *pesi* (*pisi, puk*) (see *pohq*) (Narr.) | fog, smoke, dense enough to hinder eyesight |
| *pesk-, peska-* (see *peskatuk*) | divided, split, forked as a river (e.g., *Pesketuk* = "river fork") |
| *pesuponck* (see *pésuponck*) | sweat lodge (e.g., *Pesuponck* = "sweat lodge") |
| *pete-* , *pette-, petti-*  (see p'etùk'qui) | round (e.g., *Quonset* (*Petequonset* ?) = "round shallow cove") |
| *peth-* (from *pehteau* = "it foams") | |
| *petta-, putta-, puttu-*   (see p'etùk'qui) | round (e.g., *Pettaquamscutt* = "at the round rock") |
| *pettiq-* (see p'etùk'qui) | round (e.g., *Pittaquamscut* = "at the round rock") |
| *petuk-* , *petuck-* (see p'etùk'qui) | round (cf. *petuckqua*, below) |

| | |
|---|---|
| *petuckqua-* (see p'etùk'qui) | round (e.g., *Petuckquapaug* = "round pond") |
| *petuckquampskut* (see p'etùk'qui, *-ompsk, -ut*) | at the round rock |
| *-pi-* (1) (see *p* ) | water (e.g., *Picosick* = "river opens out" ?) |
| *-pi-* (2), *pee, pea*   (see *pe* (1)) | small |
| *-piac* (see *peauke*) | water-place (e.g., *Quinnipiac* = "long water land") |
| *-piak*  (see *peauke*) | water-place  (cf. *piac* above) |
| *pis-, piss-, pissa-* (see *pissagk*) | muddy or miry (e.g., *Pissoups* = "murky place") |
| *pisc-, pisca-* (see *peskatuk*) | at the branch or fork in river or stream (e.g., *Piscatook* = "at the river branch") |
| *piscata-* (see *peskatuk*) | at the branch or fork in river or stream   (e.g., *Piscatook* = "at the river branch") |
| *pisg-* (see *pissag*) | muddy (e.g., *Pisgah* = "muddy") (one possible meaning) |
| *pish-* (1) (see *peskatuk*) | at the branch or fork in river  or stream (e.g., *Pishgachtigok* = "where the stream branches") |
| *pish-* (2) (see *pissagk*) | muddy or  miry (e.g., *Pishatipaug* = "muddy river") |
| *pishagqua* (see *pissagk*) | it is muddy or miry |
| *-pisk-* (see *-ompsk*) | rock, of rocks, standing or upright rock |
| *pisq-* (see *peskatuk*) | at the branch or fork in river or stream (e.g., *Pisquataquis* = "at the river fork") |

| | |
|---|---|
| *pisqu-* (see *pissagk*) | muddy or miry (e.g., *Pisquasent* = "muddy or slippery rocks place") |
| *piss-* (see *pissagk*) | muddy or miry |
| *-pittae, -petae* | hot action by fire (adjective or adverb) |
| *p-k* (see *peauke*) | water (root word) |
| *-poag-* (see *-paug* (1)) | watery open area, lake, pond, bay still-water (e.g., *Massapoag* = "great pond") |
| *poapu* (*pohpu*) (see *puhqui*) | he plays, is playing |
| *poca-, poco-, pocum-* (see *pohq*) | separating, dividing, opening |
| *pocas-, pocass-, pacass-* (see *pohk, -es*) | little separating, dividing, opening place (e.g., *Pocasset* = "place where a strait widens") |
| *poch-* (see *pohk* (or) *pauchau*) | separating, dividing, , opening (or) turn, deviate, change |
| *pochaak* (see *p∞tsai*) | corner |
| *-pock* (see *-paug* (1)) | watery open area, lake, pond, bay still-water (e.g., *Betuckquapock* = "round pond") |
| *pock-* (see *pauchau*) | turn, deviate, change |
| *poekqua* (see *pohqu'un*) | cleared, divided, opened (as land) |
| *pok-, poka-, pock-, pak-, pykwa-* (see *pohque*) | clear, open, bare, shallow (cf. *Pokanoket*) |
| *pocon-* (see *pohqu'un*) | cleared, divided (such as land) |
| *pocoto-* (see *pohquettahun*) | divided (e.g., *Pocotopaug* = "divided pond") |
| *pocotan-* (see *pohquettahun*) | divided |

| | |
|---|---|
| *pocum-* (from *pemayog* = "small-path place"; see *pe-*, *may*, *-og*( 2)) | narrow, small path (e.g., *Pocumtuck* = "narrow swift river" (one possible meaning)) |
| *podunk* (see *pōdunk*) | where you sink in mud (*podunk* is the sound) |
| *-pog* , *-pag*, *-paug* (see *-paug* (1)) | watery open area, lake, pond, bay still-water (e.g., *Massapog* = "great lake") |
| *pogatan-* (see *pohquettahun*) | broken up, cultivated |
| *-poge-* (see *-paug* (1), (2)) | - watery open area, lake, pond, bay still-water (e.g., *Pogue* = "pond")<br>- flat, level, still (as a pond) |
| *-pogset* , *-paugset*[1] (see *-pauges*, *-et*) | little pond place (e.g., *Wequapaugset* = "at the end of the small pond") |
| *-pogue* (see *-paug* (1)) | watery open area, lake, pond, bay still-water (e.g., *Wequepogue* = "end of the pond") |
| *poh-* (see *pauchau*) | turn, deviate, change |
| *poho-*, *pohag-* (see *pohque* or *pohq*) | shallow, narrow or opened, divided (e.g., *Pohoganut* = "shallow, sandy pond") |
| *pohq-*, *pohqua-* (see *pohque*) | clear, open, bare, shallow (e.g., *Pohqui* = "open, clear, shallow") |
| *pohquag* (see *pohque*, *-ag* (1)?) | a hole (as in a bead) |
| *pohquáshinne* (see *pohque*, *pohshane*) | open (as land) |
| *pohsh-* (see *pohsh*) | dividing, broken up |
| *pok-* , *pock-*, *pocka-*, *poka-* (see *pohque*) | clear, open, bare, shallow (cf. *Pokanoket*) |

226

| | |
|---|---|
| *Pokanoket*  (see *pauqu'unaukeet*) | "place of the cleared land"  In historic times, a large nation/ confederacy in southeastern New England whose leader  (the *Massasoit*, called *Ousa Mequin* = "Yellow  Feather") befriended the Pilgrims in Plymouth Colony. Original British  spelling from 1600s was  *Pawkunnawkutt, inter alia,*; today,  called Wampanoags. |
| *polap-, polyp-* (see *app ∞ au*) | shellfish (oysters) |
| *pom-* (see *pom-*) | journey, travel (e.g., *Pomham* ="He journeys by sea") |
| *pommeu* (see *pomushau* | it crosses, goes across (used in composition) |
| *pomp-* (1), *pump-* (see *pomperaug*, Trumbull,1881, p. 53, who says "place of offering", from *pummunum* = "he offers is to a superior, such asA Sachem) | See Trumbull, 1903, p. 135, |
| *(p)omp-* (2) (see *–ompsk* with a preceding "p" Perhaps elided) | rock, of rocks, standing or upright rock |
| *pomp-, pompo-* (3) (from *pompu* = "he plays) | |
| *pon-* (1) , *pan-, -paw-, pown-*  (see *-pau* (1)) | falls in the stream, water falls, rapids (e.g., *Ponset* = "at the falls") |
| *pon-* (2) (see *panna*) | open, spread out (e.g., *Mashqua- ponitib* = "where the big nets are spread") |

| | |
|---|---|
| *-pona-, -penhu-* (see *appooau*) | shellfish (oysters) (e.g. *Ponagan-sett* = "oyster place"; cf. *Ap-ponaug*) |
| *ponaqua* (from *ponquag* = "a fording place") | a fording (shallow) place; the dot in *n* is a nasal sound used by some Colonial translators; see entry *n,* above |
| *-ponik (see ponquag)* | A fording (shallow) place; the dot in *n* is a nasal sound used by some Colonial translators; see entry *n,* above |
| *-ponk-* (see *pohk*) | cleared, divided, opened |
| *ponquag-* , *ponk-* (see *pohque*) | clear, open, bare, shallow (e.g., *Ponkapog* = clear, open pond") |
| *-pons-* (see *paug* (1), *-es*) | little pond place (e.g., *Neeseponset* = "near the two little ponds") |
| *pood-* (see *paut)* | corner, recess, jutting |
| *poohoo-, pookoo-, poohpohs-* (from *poopohs* = "cat" (European import) | cat, where cats are |
| *pookpoawkqua* (see *pohquodche ?)* | open country? |
| *-p∞n* | cease (in composition of modern fragments) |
| *poot-* , *poot-* (see *paut*) | corner, recess (e.g., *Pootatugock* = "at the place of the cove in the river" or "at the shallow cove in the river") |
| *p∞tau* (*p∞taeụ*) | he blows (whales, whaling) |
| *p∞tsai* (*p∞chóag, p∞chag*) (see *pă, -ag* (1)) | corner, recess |
| *pootuppog, p∞tuppag* (from *p∞tuppog* = "a bay") | a bay |

| | |
|---|---|
| *p∞untuck* (see *pautuk*, above) | |
| *pop-* (see *pohsh*) | between-two, half, part of, divided, split split (e.g., *Popanumpscut* = "double-boulder place") |
| *popp-, poppa-* (see *pohsh*) | between-two, half, part of, divided, split (e.g., *Poppasquash* = "broken rocks" ?) |
| *poqua-, poquo-* (see *pohque*) | clear, open, bare, shallow (or) related to *pauquan*, below; see Trumbull, 1870, p. 40 (e.g., *Poquannuc* = "cleared lands") |
| *pauquan-* (from *pauquanna* = "there is a slaughter, of destruction in war") | see Trumbull, 1870, p. 40 (e.g., *Poquannuc* = "cleared lands") |
| *poquaûhock* (Narr.) (see *pohq, -hogk*) | a round clam (the modern-day "quahog" from word *pohk*eni meaning "closed") |
| *poquetan-* (see *pohquettahun*) | broken up, cultivated (e.g., *Poquetanuck* = "land broken up as plowed for crops") |
| *poquon-* (see *pohqu' un*) | cleared, opened (such as land) (e.g., *Poquannuc* = "cleared lands") |
| *porcha-* (see *pauchau*) | turn, divide, change |
| *pot-, pott-, poot-* (see *pootau*) | blow (whaling) (e.g., *Pottanumacutt* = "whale-fishing-place") |
| *pota-, powta-* (see *-pau* (1)) | falls in stream, water falls, rapids (e.g., *Potatuck* = "land near the falls") |
| *pote-, potta-* (see *paut*) | jut out |

| *pouq-* (see *paug* (1)) | watery open area, lake, pond, bay still-water |
|---|---|
| *pow-, pown-, paw-, pau-, powta-* (see -*pau*(1)) | falls in stream, water falls, rapids (e.g., *Powtatuck* = "land near the falls") |
| *pown-* (see –*pau* (1)) | falls in stream, water falls, rapids |
| *powt-* (see *pau* (1)) | falls in stream, water falls, rapids |
| *powntuck* (see *pautuk*) | falls in a tidal river (e.g., *Powntuck* = "river-falls") |
| -*powset* (see –*paug* (1), -*es*, -*et*) | place of little pond (e.g., *Seepowset* = "place of little salt water pond") |
| -*poxet* (see -*pauges*, -*et*) | place of little pond |
| -*psg-* (see *nukon*) | darkly, by night |
| -*psc-* (see -*ompsk*) | rock, of rocks, standing or upright rock (e.g., *Sheepscot* = "many rock channel") |
| *p-t* (see *pĕtŭ'kqui*) | round, round about (root word with intermediate letters) |
| *pt∞eu* (see *pt∞wu*, *∞m*) | he goes by flying (imitative of an arrow being released?) |
| *puck-* (1) , *puckwa-* (see *pohque*) | clear, open, bare, shallow (e.g., *Puckhunk* = "clear stream") |
| *puck* (2) (see -*paug*(2)) | flat (e.g., *pucksun* = "flat stone") |

| | |
|---|---|
| *-pug-* (see *-paug* (1)) | watery open area, lake, pond, bay still-water<br>(e.g., *Pug* = "lake") |
| *pughquo-* (see *pohque*) | clear, open, bare, shallow (e.g., *Pughquonnack* = "cleared lands") |
| *puhpúkki* (see *pukqui*) | it is hollow (e.g., *puhkuk* = a head) |
| *pukcha-* (see *pauchau*) | turn, divide, change |
| *pum-*(1), *pumm-* (see *pemisquâi*) | sloping, aslant, twisted, awry |
| *pum-* (2) (see same) | sea, open sea |
| *pumm* (see *pummu*) | shoot (an arrow, etc.) |
| *pummeu* (see same) | it crosses, goes across |
| *pumukau* (from *pumukau* = "he dances" | |
| *pumupsk* (see same*)* | a rock in the sea |
| *punnuck* (see *-uck*) (cf. *nágunt*) | bank, dune, sand bank (dune) |
| *punnuckquékontu* (see *punnuck, que-, -kontu*(1)) | on the bank of the river |
| *puppossi* (from *puppossi*) | dust, dirt |
| *puppuh*(*k*) (from *puhpúhki* = "it is hollow") | a cave |
| *pusc-* (see *pissagk*) | muddy or miry (e.g., *Puscommatas* = "muddy pond") |
| *pussoúgh* (Narr.) | wild-cat ("he scents an animal") |
| *put-* (see p'etùk'qui) | round (e.g., *Puttawuamscut* = "at the round rock") |
| *puttacaw-* (see p'etùk'qui) | round |
| *-putten-* (see *adene*) | mountain |
| *pyqua-* (see *pohque*) | clear, open, bare, shallow<br>(e.g., *Pyquiag* = "open land") |

| | |
|---|---|
| *pwa-, pwo-, pwoa-* (see *pau-* (1) above) | |

(Footnotes)
1         Combination of three elements: pond + little + place of.

| Algonquian Fragment/Root | Translation |
|---|---|
| | |
| **Q** | |
| *qu-* (see *kowaw*) | fir-tree |
| *-qua-* (1) (see *pohque*) | clear, open, bare, shallow |
| *-qua-* (2) (see *pohquettahun*) | broken up, cultivated |
| *-qua-*(3), *-que-*, *-quo-* (see *aquabe*) | before, on this side of |
| *-quad-* (see *pohque*) | clear, open, bare, shallow |
| *quag-* (see *quequan*) | shake, tremble (e.g., *Quag* = "where land shakes and trembles") |
| *quahog* (see *poquaûhock*) (Narr.) | dark colored shell used for *wampam* (wampum); a clam |
| *-quam-*, (see *-pissag-*) | mud, mire, sticky stuff |
| *quan-*, *quana-* (see *quinni*) | long (e.g., *Quanabog* = "long pond") |
| *quana-* (see *quinni*) | long (e.g., *Quanatuck* = "long stream") |
| *quaquish* (see '*sh*) | run (as water) |
| *quassa-* (1) (see *qussuk*) | stones (e.g., *Quassapaug* = "stones in the pond") |
| *quassa-* (2) (see *k'che*) | big, large, great, principle (see *Quassapaug*, Trumbull, *Ind. Names*, p. 59) |

| | |
|---|---|
| *qusasa-* (see *qussuk*) | rock, cave, ledge |
| *que-* (1) (see *quinni* ? ) | high, up above, elevated (e.g., *Quenaumett* ="look out place") |
| *que-* (2) (from *ques* = "fast") | fast (e.g., *Quechee* = "quick, whirling falls") |
| *quechau-* (see *–ch, -tchuan*) | swift running water, current |
| *quehpee* (see *que-, pee*) | up from the water |
| *quenappu* (see *api*) | he sits on (it), rests on it |
| *quequan* | it shakes, trembles (such as an earthquake) (e.g., *quequanne* = "shaking marsh") |
| *queque-* (from *ques* = "fast") | very fast (e.g., *Quequecham* = "very swift current") |
| *quequécham* (see *queshau*) | it leaps and bounds |
| quequécum | a duck; plural = *quequécummâuog* (from *quéqussu* = "he quacks") |
| *-ques-* (see *muckquétu* ? ) | fast, swift (e.g., *Keesequechan* = "place of swift water") |
| *queshau* (*quehshau*) (see *-esh, -shau*) | he leaps, jumps |
| *-quitch-* (see *uhquae*) | at the end of (e.g., *Mattaquicham* = "edge of the rocks") |
| *-quid-, -quidd-* (see *aquedn*) | island (e.g., *Quidnesset* = "at the small island") |
| *quil-* (see *kenugke*, "*l*' dialect) | mixed (e.g., *Quillicksq* = "mixed water and earth" (mud)) |
| *quilli-* (see *quinni*, "*l*" dialect") | long |
| *quillp(i)* (see below, *qunnipi-*) | |

233

| | |
|---|---|
| *quin-* , *quine-* (see *quinni*) | long (e.g., *Quinebog* = "long pond") |
| *quinn(e)-* (see *quinni*) | long (e.g., *Quinnamaug* = "long fish lamprey place") |
| *quinnapaug* (see *quinni*, *-paug*(1)) | long pond |
| *quinne* (from *koneu* = "he sleeps") | few, many (used with numbers & time) (e.g., *ogguhse quinne* = "a few days") |
| *quinnip(i)-* (see *quinnuppinuh*) | where we change our route (e.g., *Quinnipiac* = "place where we change our route") |
| *quinsig-*, *quonsig-* (from *qunôsog* = "pickerel (a fish)) | |
| *quinnuppinuk* (see *quinnuppu*, *-uk*) | *quinnuppinuk* (see *quinnuppu*, *-uk*) |
| *qunnuckque* (see *qunni*, *uhquáe*) | it is high |
| *qunnuhquitugk* | tall tree |
| *qunnuppe* (*quaquinnippe*) | around about |
| *quirri-* (see *quinni*, "r" dialect) | long |
| *quit-* (1) (see *quinni*) | long (e.g., *Quittacus* = "long brook"?) |
| *-quit-* (2) (see *quttukqshau*) | turning |
| *quit-* (3), *quitt-* (3) (see *kehte*) | large, great, principal (e.g., *Quittuwashett* = "at the great hill") |
| *-quit-* (4), *-quet-* (see *misque*, *miske*) | red |
| *-quit-* (5), *-aquet-* (see *ahquedne*) | island |
| *Quitemug* or *Quitamug* (name of an Indian man who lived in Dudley, Mass.) | |

| | |
|---|---|
| -*quog* (see same) | a pluralization stem (animate form) with glides |
| -*quon*- (see *qunnuhqui*) | tall, high, elevated |
| *qun*- (see *quinni*) | long |
| -*qunkan*-, -*qunkkan*- (from *kuhkuhheg* = "a (land)-mark, boundary, limit") | land boundary (e.g., *Neutaqunka-nut* = "At the short (scant) boundary mark"); other variant spellings in RI Place Names section. |
| *qunna*- (see *quinni*) | long |
| *qunnamaug* (see *quinni* , -*âmaug*) | lamprey (fish) fishing-place |
| -*quoag*- (see same) | a pluralization stem (animate form) with glides |
| -*quon*- (1) (see *qunnuhqui*) | tall, high, elevated (e.g., *Quonack-quk* = "high place") |
| -*quon*- (2) (see p'etùk'qui) | round (e.g., *Quonset* = "shallow round cove" ?) (one possible meaning) |
| *quon*- (3) (see *quinni*) | long (e.g., *Quonopaug* = "long pond") |
| *quon kō muk* (see *quon*, -*komuk*) | long house, long enclosed place |
| *quonkqu*- (see *qunnuckque* ) | high |
| *quons*- (see *quons*) | long (with diminutive "little"? "a little long") |
| *qunosuogamaug* (from *qunôsuog* = "pickerel, -*âmaug*) | the pickerel-fishing place |
| -*qush* (see *misqushkon*) | trout |
| -*qus*-, -*quss*-    (see *qussuck*) | rock, cave, ledge |
| *qussockomineawug* (see *qussuck*, *min*, -*aug* (1)) | cherry tree ("tree with stone fruit") |

| | |
|---|---|
| qut | long (e.g., *Quttonckanitnuing* = "wide (long) planted place") |
| -*qut-* (2) (see *quttukqshau*) | turning |
| *quttukqsheau* (*quttukqshau*) ( see *qut-chikque*) | turns, makes an angle (of a border) |
| -*quuh-* (2) (see *quinni*) | long |
| -*quunk-* (2) (see *qunnuckque*) | high (e.g., *Quunkwatchu* "high mountain") |

| Algonquian Fragment/Root | Translation |
|---|---|
| | |
| R | "R" is not found in Algonquian dialects of RI. See RI Place Names section for examples. |

| Algonquian Fragment/Root | Translation |
|---|---|
| | |
| S | |
| -*s-* (cf. –*es, -ese, -ash*) | - plural ending for "inanimate" forms, nouns - in middle of word, could indicate something less in quality, degraded, inferior plural marker ; e.g., in *Massachusetts*, the next to last *s* stands for plural marker of hill/mountain (see Figure 5) |
| *sa-, sau-* (2) (see *sauk*) | outlet of river or brook, stream, flowing of a pond or lake (cf. *sauch*) |
| *saak- , sak-* (see *sauk*) | protrude, emerge |

236

| | |
|---|---|
| *sachem* (see *sâchim*) | sachem, "King," tribal/village leader, "chief" |
| *sach-* (see *sauk*) | outlet of river or brook, stream, flowing of a pond or lake (e.g., *Sachuset* = "little place of outlet by little hills") |
| *saco-* (1), *sako-* (see *sauk*) | outlet of river or brook, stream, flowing of a pond or lake (e.g., *Massaco* = "the great outlet") |
| *saco-* (2) (see *sucki*) | black, dark colored, purple (e.g., *Sakonnet* (*Saconet*) = "place of black geese") (one possible meaning) |
| *saconk-* (see *sauk*) | outlet of river or brook, stream, flowing of a pond or lake |
| -saë | action by heat (animate form) |
| *sag-* (1), *saga -, sago-, sagat -* (see *siogke*) | firm, hard, congealed liquid (ice, tallow, &c) |
| *sag –(2), sak- (see sauk)* | outlet of river or brook, stream, flowing of a pond or lake (e.g., *Sagadahoc* = "outflowing of a swift current as it nears the sea") |
| *sak-* (see *sohk* ?) | seize hold |
| *sako-* (see *sucki*) | black, dark colored, purple |
| *sammau* (from *assaumaü* = "he feeds him, gives him nourishment") | |
| *sampwi* (see *saumpwi*) | it is right, just, straight |
| *sanak-* (see *siogke*) | difficult (related to *see* = "sour, bitter") |
| *sanq-* (see *sauk*) | outlet of river or brook, stream, flowing of a pond or lake |

| | |
|---|---|
| *-sape-* , *-sapo-* | stream |
| *sa-* (see *sauk*) | outlet of river or brook, stream, flowing of a pond or lake |
| *sapose* (*sepose*) | stream |
| *saqu-* (see *siogke*) | firm, hard, congealed liquid |
| *sasa-* (from *sassamaúquock* = "eels") | eels (e.g., *Sasagacha* = "black slippery fish"; feels (one possible meaning)) |
| *sasag-, sasagook(a)-* (see *sesékq* (*ses-ikw*)) | ratlesnake or "adder"[1] |
| *sasak -* (see *sesékq*) | rattlesnake (e.g., *Sasaketasick* = "rattle snake place" ?) |
| *sasco-, sasq-, sesq-* (Trumbull, *Ind. Names*, p. 63) | marshy land, swamp |
| *sasémin* (see *min* ) (Narr.) | a cranberry Plural = *aséminneash* |
| *sassa -, saso -, sassemin -* (see *sasémin-neash* ) | cranberry |
| *sat-* (see *sauk*) | outlet of river or brook, stream, flowing of a pond or lake |
| *sauc-, sauch-* (see *sauk*) | outlet of river or brook, stream, flowing of a pond or lake |
| *saug-* (see *sauk*) | outlet of river or brook, stream, flowing of a pond or lake (e.g., *Saugatuck* = "tidal river outlet") |
| *sauga-, sauge-* (see *sauk*) | outlet of river or brook, stream, flowing of a pond or lake (e.g., *Saugatuck* = "tidal river outlet") |
| *saugatuck* (see *sauk, -tuk*) | at the outlet of the river |
| *saugh* (see *sauk*) | outlet of river or brook, stream, flowing of a pond or lake |
| *saugo-* (see *sauk*) | outlet of river or brook, stream, flowing of a pond or lake |

| | |
|---|---|
| *sauk-* (see *sauk*) | outlet of river or brook, stream, flowing of a pond or lake (cf. *saco*) |
| *sauki-* (1) (see *sauk*) | outlet of river or brook, stream, flowing of a pond or lake |
| *sauki-* (2) (see *sucki*) | black earth, black ground, it is dark colored (e.g., *Saukiog* = "black ground") |
| *saumpwi* (*samwpi*) | straight, right, just |
| *sawca-* , *sawka-* (see *sauk*) | outlet of river or brook, stream, flowing ofa pond or lake (e.g., *Sawkatucket* = "at the outlet of the tidal river") |
| *sawka-* (see *sauk*) | outlet of river or brook, stream, flowing of a pond or lake (cf. *sawca*) |
| *-scak-*, *-skate-* (see *squtta*) | of fire |
| *scan-* (see *peskatuk*) | at the branch or fork in river or stream (e.g., *Scantic* = "where the river branches") |
| *scat-* (see *peskatuk*) | at the branch or fork in river or stream (e.g., *Schaghticoke* = "where the river divides") |
| *schag-* ,*sch -* (see *peskatuk*) | at the branch or fork in river or stream (e.g., *Schaghticoke* = "place where the rivers meet") |
| *scho -*, *schoo-* (see *squtta* under *yòte*) | fire (e.g., *Schooset* = "fire place" ) |
| *-sci-*, *-scit-* (see *ochi*) | issuing from, flowing from |
| *-scit-* (see *peskatuk*) | at the branch or fork in river or stream |

| | |
|---|---|
| *scitu-* (see *sonki*) | cool to touch taste (e.g., *Scitu-ate* = "at the cool spring, or cold brook") (one possible meaning) |
| *scok-* (1) (see *qussuck*) | rock, cave, ledge |
| *scok-* (2) (see *askug*) | snake |
| *-scuc-* (see *askug*) | snake (e.g., *Scucurra* = "Snake Hill") |
| *se-* (see *missi*) | big, large, great  (e.g., *Sebago* = "Big Lake") |
| *seap -*, *seapu* (see *séip*) | river, stream, current (e.g., *Seapuit* = "in the current") |
| *-seb-* (see *séip*) | running water |
| *-sebese-* (see *sepues*) | a short river, stream |
| *-sebethe-* (see *sepues*) | a short river, stream |
| *-sebo-*, *-sibo-* (see *séip*) | river, stream   (cf. *sib*, below) |
| *sec-* (see *sucki*) | black (e.g. *Seconnet* = "Rocky outlet; at the outlet; black goose abode") |
| *see* (see *séë*, *séog*) | salt water (e.g., *Seepowset* = "place of small salt water pond") |
| *seek-*, *ceac-* (see *sucki*) | black (e.g., *Seekonk* = "place of the black goose" (one possible meaning)) |
| *seep -* (see *seogee*) | outlet of a river or brook, stream, flowing of a pond or lake |
| *segre-* (see *siogke*) | hard (as stone), difficult (e.g., *Segreganset* = "place of little hard stones") |

| | |
|---|---|
| *seip-* (see *sepa-* below) | river, stream |
| *seki-* (see *sucki*) | black, dark colored, purple (e.g., *Seketegansett* = "dark colored spring place") |
| *-sem-* (see *-ashim*) | of animals |
| *-sen-* (see *assen, hassen*) | rock, stone, of rocks or stones, ledge, cave, den (e.g. *Sennebec* = "rocks in the pond") |
| *seogee-* (see *sauk*) | outlet of river or brook, stream, flowing of a pond or lake |
| *senep-* (see *missi, nippe*) | large pond |
| *-se-* | running water |
| *sepa-, sepi-* (see *séip*) | river, stream , usually a long one |
| *-sepos-* (see *sepues*) | a short river, stream (e.g., *Tuncksesapose* = "fast flowing and winding stream") |
| *-sepoese-* (see *sepues*) | a short river, stream |
| *sepu-* (see *séip*) | river, stream , usually a long one |
| *seq-* (see *sequin* ?) | dry (cf. *sequan-*, below) |
| *sequan* (see same) | Spring season |
| *ses-, sess-* (*-es* (1)) | little (e.g., *Manisses* = "Little island spirit") |
| *sesek, sesegk, sesekq , sesikw* (see *s-s-k*) | rattlesnake |
| *sequan -* (see *sequan*) | springtime ("when ice melts") (e.g., *Sequankit* = "place of summer dwellings"?) |
| *-set , -sett* (see *es , -et*) | place of small (something) (e.g., *Oxecoset* = "place of small fir trees") |

241

| | |
|---|---|
| *-sh-* (see *'sh*) | of swift or violent motion (perhaps in waterways) |
| *shan-,shann-* (see *nashaue* or from *shawwunk* = "a place where two streams meet"; Trumbull, 1881, p. 66) | midway, fork (or) a place where two streams meet |
| *-shau-* (1) (see *-shau*) | end of, distance |
| *-shau-* (2) (see *nashaue*) | midway, fork (cf. *nas*) (e.g., *Nashua* = between streams") |
| *-shau-* (3) (see *shau*) | a lessening of something (in motion verbs) |
| *shaum(e)-* (see *ashim*) | spring of water |
| *-shaw-, -shaww-* (1) (see *nashaue*) | midway, fork (e.g., *Shawwunk* = "at the place between") |
| *shaw-* (2), *show-* (see *mishoon*) | of boats (canoes) (e.g., *Shawomet* = "a place where canoes go"; an ancient Wampanoag village). *Shawomet* may come from "*mishawomet*" |
| *-she-* (1) (see *nashaue*) | midway, fork (e.g., *Shetucket* = "land between rivers") |
| *she-* (2), *shee-* (see *k'che, missi, mishe*) | big, large, great (e.g., *Shepaug* = "great pond") |
| *-shem-, -shim-* (see *shim*) | animal |
| *shen-* (see *ask*(1)) | Green, raw (e.g., *Shennunganock* ="green field") |
| *-shew-* (see *nashaue*) | midway, fork (e.g., *Shewatucket* = "at the place between tidal streams") |

| | |
|---|---|
| *shick-* (see *chick-* (2) above) | big, large, great (e.g., *Shick-asheen* = "Great spring") |
| *-shimmo-* (see *ashim*) | water-spring (e.g., *Shimmoah* = "a spring") |
| *-shk* (see *-shk*) | violence, disaster, explosion |
| *shock-* (see *chock-* above with 3 meanings) | |
| *shoon -* (from *sassamaúquock* = "eels") | eels (e.g. *Shoonkeek* = "abode of straight fish; eels") |
| *-showa-* (see *nashaue*) | midway, fork (e.g., *Showatucket* = "where the river forks") |
| *shum-* (see *ashim*) | spring of water |
| *si-* (see *sucki*) | black, dark colored, purple |
| *-sib-* , *-sibo-* (see *séip*) | river, stream (e.g. *Sippewisset*= "at the little river") |
| *sic-, sici-* (see *sucki*) | black, dark colored, purple (e.g., *Sicaog* = "black ground") |
| *sick-, sickc-* (see *suck, sucki*) | black, very dark color (e.g. *Sick-compsqu* = "black rocks" or "hard rocks") |
| *sickíssuog* (see *sohkissu, -og* (2)) (cf. *poquaûhock*) | the long black clam ("spittler", imitative of spitting sound); plural = *sikkissuogquah*og |
| *-sin* (see same) | of lying down (on the ground), extended body |
| *siogke* (see *seog*) | it is hard (as stone), difficult (e.g., *ne siogkok* = "a difficult matter") |
| *-sip-, -sipi-, -sipp-, -sippi-* (see *séip*) | river, stream (e.g., *Sippican* = "the muddy river") cf. Missis<u>sippi</u>) |

| | |
|---|---|
| *-sit* (see *-es*, *-et*) | place of small (something) (e.g., *Aquapauksit* = "at the end of the small pond") |
| *si(u)*(see *kóüs*) | thorn, briar, sharp thing |
| *-sk-* (1) (see *ask* (1), *ascoscoi*) | green or raw (e.g., *Skenunganuck* = "green field") |
| *-sk-* (2) | broken up, plowed, cultivated (as land) |
| *-skat* (1) | tide ebb |
| *-skat* (2) | dry (such as beach sand at low tide) |
| *skat-* (3), *schat-*, *scat-* (see *peskatuk*) | at the branch or fork in river or stream (e.g., *Schaghticoke* = "where the river divides") |
| *skat-* (4), *skate-*, *skata-* (see *squtta*) | fire (e.g., *Skatehook* = "fire place"?) |
| *ske-*, *sken-* (see *-sk-*) | green, grass-like (e.g., *Skenunganock* = "green field") |
| *-skug-* (see *askug*) | snake, monster, serpent (e.g., *Skug* = "a snake") |
| *skook-* (1) (see *qussuck*) | rock, stone, of rocks or stones, ledge, cave, den |
| *skook-* (2) (see *askug*) | snake |
| *skug* (see *ask∞k*) | snake |
| *snip-* (see *missi*, *nippe*) | large + pond e.g., *Snipsic* = "great-pond outlet") |

| | |
|---|---|
| soak- (see *sauk*) | outlet of river or brook, stream, flowing of a pond or lake (e.g., *Soakatuck* = "outlet of the tidal river") |
| -sock-  (see *sucki*) | black, dark colored, purple  (e.g., *Sockanosset* = "dark-colored land") |
| *sohkissu* (*suhkissu*) (see *soh-*) | it pours out |
| *songi-*  (see *sonki*) | cool to touch, taste  (e.g., *Songo* = "cold water") |
| *sonk-, sonki-*  (see *sonki*) | cool to touch, taste (e.g., *Sonkipog* = "cool pond") |
| *sonkipaug*  (see *sonki,-paug*(1))) | cool pond |
| *sohkunkquodt* (from *sonkin*) ? | height, elevation (e.g., *sohkonkeg* = "the height of it") |
| *sohteau* (see *soh-, -ohteau*) | it is so long, it extends |
| *sonki-, soonki-*   (see *sonki*) | cool to touch, taste (e.g., *sonkippog* = "cool water") |
| *sowan* (see same) | south |
| *sowanauke*  (see *aûke, sowan*) | south counry |
| *sowans-*  (see *sowan*) | land of the south (e.g., *Sowanamsett* = "in the south country") |
| *sq- , squi-*  (*see msqui , muski*) | red[2] (e.g., *Squamcut*  = "red earth" or "red fish  (salmon)") |
| *squa-* (from *askuhum* = "lookout, observation point") | lookout, observation point (e.g., *Squakheag* = "watching (lookout) place" |
| *squam-*(1) (see *msqui, -âm*) | salmon (red fish) (e.g., *Squamicuck*  = "salmon fishing place") |

245

| | |
|---|---|
| *squam*-(2) (see –*ompsk*) | rock, of rocks, standing or upright rock |
| *squi*- (see *msqui* , *muski*) | red (cf. *sq*) |
| -*squo*- (from *aséquam* = "he sews it") | door flap of wigwam (*wétu* = *wigwam*) or possibly a skunk (e.g., *Squontam* = "door or gateway") |
| squtta | fire (domestic, lit tobacco, related to Fire Spirit) |
| -*sset* (see *es*-, *et*) | little place of (something) |
| -*ssk*- (see -*s-sk*-) | rattling, sticky, muddy |
| *s-s-k* (see *s-s-k*) | rattlesnake (imitative sound of tail) |
| -*s-sk*- | sticky (like mud) (cf. *pissagk*) (root word) |
| -'*ssum* | action by fire ("makes the stone hot") |
| *suc*-, *succ*-, *succo*-   (see *sucki*) | black, dark colored, purple (e.g., *Suckiaug* = "black earth") (e.g., *Succanesset* = "where the dark shells are (for wampum making)) |
| *suck*- (1) (see *sauk*) | outlet of river or brook, stream, flowing of a pond or lake |
| -*suck* (2), -*sucks* (see same) | pluralization stem for "animate" forms, nouns |
| *sucka*- , *sucki*- (see *sucki*) | black, dark colored, purple (e.g., *Suckiaug* = "dark colored earth") |
| *suckaúhock* (see *sucki*, -*hock*) (Narr.) (cf. *metaûhock*) | dark (purple) shells (see *wampum*) |
| *suckete* (see *soh*-) | a mist |
| *suckiaug* (see *sucki*, *aûke* ) | black earth |

| | |
|---|---|
| *-sum* (see *-sem*) | animal, beast; root for "action by heat" (e.g., *chickosum* = "he burns it") |
| *sump-* (from *súmhup* = "beaver") | beaver (e.g., *Sumphauge* = "place of male beaver") (one possible meaning) |
| *-sun-* (see *assen* ) | rock, stone, of rocks or stones, ledge, cave, den (e.g., *Suncook* = "rocky point") |
| *-suna-* (see *assen* ) | rock, stone, of rocks or stones, ledge, cave, den (e.g., *Sunapee* = "rocks in the water") |
| *sunki-* (see *sonki*) | cool to touch, taste (e.g., *Sunkip-aug* = "cool pond or brook") |
| *sunnattunniyeu* (cf. *nâmummiyeu* ) | northwards, towards the north |
| *sw-* (see *msqui, muski*) | red (e.g., *Swampscott* = "at the red rock") |
| *swan-* (see *sowan*) | south, south country, of the south, in southerly direction |

(Footnotes)
1          Any of several North American snakes ... that are harmless but are popularly believed to be venomous—*Merrian-Webster* online dictionary.
2          Shows that letter "m" was often not heard as an Algonquian sound.

| **Algonquian Fragment/Root** | **Translation** |
|---|---|
| | |
| T | |
| *-t-* (see *t', aûke*) | The "accommodating t" some-times inserted between a vowel-vowel sequence for phonetic reasons. Also see O'Brien, *Indian Grammar Dictionary* (Appendix). |

| | |
|---|---|
| *tab-* , *taba-*, *tap-*, *taub-*  (cf. *wame* (1))  (see *tapi*) | - enough, sufficient (e.g., *Tabamapaug* = "this pond is sufficient") - giving thanks (e.g., *Tabusimtac* = "he gives thanks") |
| *tac-*, *tack* (see *tuk-*) | a tidal river, broad river, an estuary |
| *tag-*(1) (see *t -g*) | repeated strokes (e.g., *Tagwonk* = "a stone mortar") |
| *tag-*(2), *-tage* (see *tuk-*) | a tidal river, broad river, an estuary |
| *tahk-*, *teik-*  (see *t-k*) | cold, cool |
| *-tak-*, *-tac-*  (see *'tugk*) | wood, tree, forest  (e.g., *Taconic* = "place of wilderness") |
| *take-*  (1) (see *takekum*) | spring, water place (e.g., *Takemuit* = "place of the spring") |
| *take-* (2) (see *t -g*) | repeated strokes |
| *takekum* (see *tahki*, *t-k*) (Narr.) | cold spring (implying  drinking water) |
| *takone* (see *'tugk*, *-e*) | wild lands, forest (the  woods) |
| *tam-* (from *tomógkon* = a  water flood) | |
| *taq-* (see *tuk-*) | a tidal river, broad river, an estuary |
| *taquatsha* ( see *t-p*) (Narr.) | frozen |
| *-tasia*  (see *tuk-*) | a tidal river, broad river, an estuary (possibly small) (e.g., *Quaquetasia* = "very long tidal river") |
| tatackom | a porpoise (fish); plural = *tatack-ommâúog* |

| | |
|---|---|
| *tath*  (see *ta*) | there |
| *taub-* (see above *tab-*) | |
| *-taug-* (1) (see *'tugk*) | wood, tree |
| *-taug-* (2) ((see *'tugk, aûke*) | place of wood, tree |
| *taupoo* (see *tau pauwau)* | wise man, counselor |
| *-tch-* (see   *-ch,- ,-tchuan*) | running water  or issuing from, flowing from |
| *te-, tet-, ti-*   (see *kehte*) | large, great, principal |
| *-teawa-* (from *touwag* = "a gap or space left open") | |
| *-teaonk* (*see –onk* (3)) | of teaching, instruction |
| *tegh-, teigh-* (see *kehte*) | large, great, principal |
| *teik-, tahk-*   (see *t-k*) | water  spring (e.g., *Teikiming* = "a fountain" or "cool springs place") |
| *terrapin* ("r" dialect ?) | turtle ("walks to water" ?) |
| *t-g* | Root word for repeated strokes (root word) (cf. *togk*u) |
| *-tic , -(c)tic* (see *tuk*) | a tidal river, broad river  (e.g., *Niantic*  = "point of land  at tidal estuary") |
| *-tick*  (1) (see *tuk*) | a tidal river, broad river |
| *-tick*  (2) (see *tughk*) | wood, tree (e.g., *Woodtick* = "boughs, branches or limbs" ; "piece of wood") |
| *-tin-*  (see *adene*) | mountain |
| *tion-*  (from *tannag* = " a crane (bird)) | |
| *-tippoc-, -tuppoc-* | of night |

| | |
|---|---|
| *tiq-* (see *tuk-*) | a tidal river, broad river (e.g., *Monatiquot* = "at the tidal stream" or "lookout place") |
| *tish-, tishco-* (see *touohpen*) | bridge or ford in stream (e.g., *Tishcottic* = "at the wading place or ford") |
| *tit-, titt-, titi-* (see *kehte*) | large, great, principal (e.g., *Titicutt* = "at the great tidal river"; *Taunton* also comes from this root) |
| *t-k* (see *takekum*) | root word for spring of water (root word) |
| *t'makwa* (cf. *nóosup, tummûnk, amisk*) (Abenaki language) | beaver ("ugly teeth") (cf. The *Tomaquag* Museum in Exeter, RI) |
| *-tn-* (see *adene*) | mountain |
| *tock-* (see *t-g*) | repeated strokes or a mill (grinding) stone |
| *togwonkanompsk* (see *togkonk, -ompsk-*) | a mill (pounding) stone |
| *tokekommuit* (see *takekum, -it*) | at the spring or water source |
| *tommany, tonomy, tonemy* (see *tn (dn)*) | of a hill, lookout, mountain |
| *tomaq-* (see *tummòck*) | beaver (e.g., *Tomaquag* = "beaver place") |
| *-tomq-*, (see *-ompsk*) | rock, of rocks, standing or upright rock |
| *-took-* , *-tuck-*, *-tug-* (see *-tuck* (1)) | water in motion such as a stream or river (e.g., *Aroostook* = "shining river") |

250

| | |
|---|---|
| *t∞n (tor)* | turtle, tortoise (basic root) (see *t∞nuppasog*) |
| *t∞nuppasog* (see *ta, nuppe, toueu, áppu*) | turtle/tortoises ("he is near water" or "he remains solitary on land") |
| *t∞p* (see *t-p*) | dew |
| *tor-* (see *torupe*) | turtle (e.g., *Torup* = "snapping-turtle") |
| *torube, torup* ("r"dialect ?) | snapping or sea turtle ( from *tor*, *t∞n* roots) |
| *tou-, touis-* (see *eataw*) | worn out, old, deserted (such as land (e.g., *Touiscet* = "at the old fields") |
| *toueu (towew)* | deserted, solitary, unoccupied (e.g., *touohkpmuk* = "the forest" (literally, "a solitary place")) |
| *touohpen (tiusk, toyusk)* | a bridge |
| *toy- , tuo-* (see *touohpen*) | bridge, ford in stream (e.g., *Toyusk* = "a bridge") |
| *t-p* (see *montup*) | head (root word) |
| *t-p ( q-p, t-k)* | freezes (root word); e.g., *taquáttin* = "frost" |
| *tseppi-¹, cheppi-* (see *tseppi*) | separated (e.g., *Chappaquidick* = "separated island land") |
| *-tu-, -tuhc-* (see *'tugk*) | wood, tree |
| *-tuc (-tuch, -tuk, -tug)* | water in motion such as a river or stream (in compound words) |

| | |
|---|---|
| *-tuck-* (1) (see *-tuck* (1)) (cf. *-took-*) | water in motion such as a stream or river (e.g., *Pawcatuck* = "narrow river") |
| *-tuck-* (2) (see *–uck, -ick, -eck*) | locatives meaning "in, at, near, place of" and the "accommodating t" before vowel, which see above |
| *-tuck-* (3) (see *'tugk*) | wood, tree (e.g., *Naugatuck* = "one tree") |
| *tucker-* (see *petuqqunneg*) | bread (e.g., *Tuckernuck* = "a round loaf of bread") (one possible meaning) |
| *-tucket* (1) (see *tuck* (1), *-et*) | place of or at the water (e.g., *Pawtucket* = "water-falls place") |
| *-tucket* (2) (see *'tugk, -et*) | place of trees (e.g., *Mashantucket* = "well-forested place") |
| *-tug-* (1) (see *-tuck* (1)) | water in motion such as a stream or river |
| *-tug-* (2) (see *'tugk*) | wood, tree (e.g., *Tug* = "a tree"). |
| *'tugk* (*tugq*) (see *m'tugk*) | wood, tree (*taug, tawk* or *h'tugk* is imitative of tree-struck sound) |
| *-tuk-* (1) (see *'tugk*) | wood, tree (e.g., *Mashantucket* = "well-forested place") |
| *-tuk-* (2) (see *-tuck* (1)) | a tidal river, broad river, an estuary (e.g., *Mystuk* = "great tidal river") |
| *tul-* (see *troupe*, "*l*" dialect) | turtle |
| *tummòck* (cf. *tummûnk*) (see *tummussum*) (Narr.) | beaver ("he cuts off trees");plural = *tummòckquaog* |
| *tun-, tunup-* (see *troupe, t∞ nuppasog*) | turtle(s) (e.g., *Tunipus* = "little turtle") |

| | |
|---|---|
| -tunck-, -tunk-, -tunx-, -tux- (see *tuck* (1), -es)) | water in motion (e.g., *Tunxis* = "fast flowing little stream") |
| -tunk- (see *'tugk*) | wood, tree (e.g., *Tunk* = "wood, tree" ?); also seen for *tuck-* = "river) |
| *tuppa-* (see *tuppuhqueu* ) | twist, turn, roll |
| tuppuhqueu | it turns or rolls (e.g., *tuppuhqua-mash* = "beans") |
| *turupe* (see *t∞nuppasog*) | turtle |
| *tusco-* (from *t∞skeonk* = "a ford or wading place") | |
| -tux- (1) (se -*tuk* -*es*) | a tidal river, a broad river, an estuary, a brook (used in composition; e.g., *Massatux*et = "At the great brook") |
| -tux- (2) (see *tukes*) | narrow river (e.g., *Tuxis* = "little steam") |
| -tux*et* (see -*tuk* -*es*, -*et*) | place of small tidal river, place of small broad river, place of small tidal estuary, placevof small brook (e.g., *Massatux*et = "At the great brook") |
| -tux*ot* (see -*tuk* -*es*, -*et*) | place of small (tidal) river, place of small road river, place of small tidal estuary, place of small brook (e.g., *Mattatux*ot = "At the worthless little river?") (one meaning) |

(Footnotes)
1        Dialectal form from The Islands.

| Algonquian Fragment/Root | Translation |
|---|---|
| | |
| **U** | |
| *u* (see *u*) | A "glide" sometimes preceding a vowel as in −*uash* = *u* +-*ash* |
| *-uash* (see −*ash, u*) | pluralization stem −*ash* with a "glide" *u* |
| *-uatchu-* (see *wadchu*) | mountain, hill |
| *-ubq-* (see *-ompsk*) | rock, of rocks, standing or upright rock |
| *-uc* (see −*uck, -ick, -eck*) | at, near, place of (e.g., *Alamoosuc* = "little dog place"). Sometimes includes a preceding " glide" *w* or *u* or *y* or *l*, etc. |
| *-uck* (1) , *-unk* (see −*uck, -ick, -eck*) | land, place of (e.g., *Ashpatuck* = "high place"). Sometimes includes a preceding "glide" *w* or *u* or *y* or l, etc. |
| *-uck* (2) , *-unk* (see −*og* (2)) | pluralization stem for "animate" forms, nouns |
| *-uck* (3) (see *'tugk*) | tree, wood (e.g., *Mattatuck* = "without trees, or poorly, sparsely wooded") |
| *-ud, -ude* (see *-et*) | at, in, by, near |
| *-ug* (see *-og*(2)) | common pluralization stem for animate forms (e.g., *mukkiog* = "boys") (many variants esp. w/ preceding double consonants and connective inserts) (cf. *-ash*) |
| *-uhku* | floating, appearance of |

| | |
|---|---|
| *-uhq* (1), *-uhk*, *-ukq* | of permanence, continuation |
| *uhq* (2) (*uhk*) (*uhquan*, *uhquon*) (cf. *kous*) | a point or sharp extremity (enters into many words) (e.g., *uhquan* = "a hook, fish hook") |
| *-uhquae* (see *ukque*) | end of |
| *uhquan* (*uhquon*) (see *uhq*) | hook, so shaped |
| *úhque* (*ukque*) (see *uhq*, *weque*) | at extremity |
| *-uhquetn* (see *ahquidne*) | island (e.g., *Kuhtuhquetnet* = "at the great place in the island") |
| *-uhtug* (see *-unk* (2)) | tree, wood (in compound words) (e.g., *mishuntugk* = "much wood") |
| *-uk* (see *–uck*, *-ick*, *-eck*) | at, near, place of (e.g., *Matchuk* = "bad lands") |
| *ukque* (*uhque*) (see *weque*) | at extremity, end of suffix for adverbs or adjectives (e.g., *touko-mukukque* = "of the forest or wilderness") |
| *ukwe-* (see *ukque*) | at the end of |
| *-um-* (see *-ompsk*) | rock, of rocks, standing or up-right rock (e.g., *Cawsumsett* = "Sharp rock place; whetstone rock place") |
| *-umb-* (see *-ompsk*) | rock, of rocks, standing or upright rock (e.g., *Catumb* = "at the place of the great rock") |
| *-umoonk*, *-umoowonk* | a separation of living things (a tribe) |
| *-umps-* (see *-ompsk*) | rock, of rocks, standing or upright rock (e.g., *Matumpseck* = "bad rock place") |

| | |
|---|---|
| *-umpsk-* (see *-ompsk*) | rock, of rocks, standing or upright rock |
| *-ums-* (see *-ompsk*) | rock, of rocks, standing or upright rock (e.g., *Cowsumscutt* = "place of sharp rock") |
| *-un* , (see *-un* (1)) | at, near, place of |
| *-unamaug* | Where there is a body of water (see Goddard,1990) |
| *-unak-* (see *un* (1), *ahke*) or possibly (*munnoh*, *-ag* (1)) | island, where there is an island[1] (e.g., *Chaubunakungamaug* = "a divided- island-lake") |
| *unca-* (see *ukque*) | at the end of (e.g., *Uncawannuck* "fishing-place at the furthest place") |
| *uncawa-* (see *ongkoue*) | beyond, end-place (e.g. *Uncawannuck* = "fishing place at the furthest place") |
| *uncoa-* (see *ongkoue*) | beyond, end-place (e.g., *Uncoa* = "yonder place") |
| *uncoway-* (see *ongkoue*) | beyond, end-place |
| *uncu-* (see *ukque*) | at the end of (e.g., *Uncushnet* = "at the end of the rapid stream") |
| *-ung* (see *-og*(2)) | pluralization stem for "animate" forms, nouns (or) land, country, place |
| *-unk* (1) (see *-ut*) | at, in, by near, (popularly, "place of") |
| *-unk* (2), *-anck*, *-onk*, *-onck*, *-unck* (see 'tugk) | tree, wood |

| | |
|---|---|
| *-unk* (3)(see *-uck*) | of land (in composition) (seen in many modern place names) |
| *unnogque* (see *un* (2), *ogque*) | towards |
| *unnome* | within |
| *unqua-* (see *ongkoue* or *ukque*) | beyond, end-place (e.g., *Unqua-monk* = "at the end place") |
| *unsatu* (from *tomogkon* = flood)? | of flooding ? |
| *-unsk-* (see *-ompsk*) | rock, of rocks, standing or upright rock |
| *-untsat-* (from *tomogkon* = flood) ? | of flooding ? |
| *-unum* (cf. *–num-*) | denotes (in composition) action by the hand or physical activity (e.g., *pohqunn*um = "he breaks it with his hands") |
| *-uock* (see *êuck* (1)) | people, folk of an area |
| *-uog* (see *-og* (2)) | pluralization stem for "animate" forms, nouns |
| *uppaquóntup* (see *-ontop*) (Narr.) | the head |
| *uppeshau* (see *pashk*) | a flower ("it bursts forth") e.g., *peshaónash* = "flowers" |
| *-uppo-* (see *-antep*) | head |
| *-uppoo-* (see *-uppoo*) | eat, chew (e.g., *Uppooquantup* = "eat bass head") |
| *-upsk-* (see *-ompsk*) | rock, of rocks, standing or upright rock |
| *-us* (see *us* (1)) | little (e.g., *Saugus* = "little out-let") |

257

| | |
|---|---|
| *uspunneaûke* (see *uspunnumun, aûke*) | high land |
| *uspunnumun* (see *un*) | elevated, high, lift (ashp is also a root) |
| *usque-* (see *ukque*) | at the end of (e.g., *Usquepaugh* = "at the end of the pond") |
| *-ussett* (see *–eset, esett*) | place of something small |
| *ussishau* (see *ussē'nát, -shau, aü*) | he goes quickly, runs to (cf. *quaquish*) |
| *ussosu* (cf. *tummussum*) | to cut (e.g., *nē kussôsu* = "he cuts or gashes") |
| *ut sepuunt* (see *-ut, sepi*) | at or near the river |
| *-ut, -utt* (see *-ut*) | the term *-ut* is a common suffix meaning: at, in, on, where something is, place of, near (e.g., *kehtompskut* = "at the great rock"). Also used as a preposition (e.g., *ut ohkeit* = "on the earth") |
| *-uten-* (see *otan*) | principal town (e.g., *Keetuteny* = "principal town") |
| *-utic* (see *-ut, -ick*) | at, in, on, by near, (popularly, "place of") Sometimes includes a preceding "glide" *w* or *y* or *l*, etc. |
| *-utick* (cf. *utic*) | at, in, on, by near, (popularly, "place of"). Appears to be a double locative, here is the approximate location where something is |

| | |
|---|---|
| *-uting*  (cf. *utic*) | at, in, on, by near, (popularly, "place of"). Appears to be a double locative, here is the approximate location where something is |
| *-utock*  (cf. *utic*) | at, in, on, by near, (popularly, "place of"). Appears to be a double locative, here is the approximate location where something is |
| *-utook*  (cf. *utic*) | at, in, on, by near, (popularly, "place of"). Appears to be a double locative, here isthe approximate location where something is |
| *-utn*  (see *adene*) | mountain |
| *-utt*  (see *-ut*) | at, in, on, by near, (popularly, "place of") |
| *-utta*  (see *-ut*, *utta*) | at, in, on, by near, (popularly, "place of") |
| *-utten-*  (see *adene*) | mountain |
| *-uwock*  (see *êuck* (1)) | people, folk of an area (with "glide" *u*) |
| *-uwog*  (see *êuck* (1)) | people, folk of an area (with "glide" *u*) |

(Footnotes)
1          See Goddard, NY Times, 1990, who provided this new translation vice Trumbull's rendition (1881/1974) based on a similar Algonquian language and knowledge of geographic reference.

| Algonquian Fragment/Root | Translation |
|---|---|
| **W** | |
| *w* (see *w'*) | a "glide" sometimes preceding a vowel as in *-wash* = *w* +*-ash* |

| | |
|---|---|
| *-wa* (see (*aug*) | land, country, place; elided with a g-glide |
| *waápu* (*waápeu, waábeu*) (see *waábe, ∞m*) | he goes up, rises (related to "wind") |
| *wab-* , *waba-* (see *wompi*) | white, the light, dawn, the East (e.g., *Wabanaki* = "people of first (white) light" or "Dawnlanders") |
| *waban* (*waupi*) (see *waapu*) | the wind ("it is above") |
| *-wach-*, *-wachu-* (1) (see *wadchu*) | mountain, hill (cf. *wachu*) |
| *wach-* (2), *wacha-* (see *weque*) (cf. *watche*) | at the end of (e.g., *Wachuset* = "place of little hills") |
| *-wachu-*, *-wadchu-* (see *wadch*) | mountain, hill (e.g., *Wachuset* = "place of little hills") |
| *wadchùash* (see *wadchu*, *-ash*) | plural of *wadchu* (hill, mountain) |
| *wádchumes* (see *wadchu*, *-emes*) | small mountain, hill |
| *wadchue kontu* (see *wadchu*, *-kontu* (2)) | in the hill country |
| *wachue ohkeit* (see *ohkeit*, *wadchu*) | the hill country |
| *-wadjo-* (see *wadchu* ) | mountain, hill |
| *-wadsh-* (*wadtch*) | nest, especially a birds' ("born", "proceeds from") |
| *-wal-* (see *wewen*, *-wonk-*) | crooked, bent, oxbow, back turn in stream, sudden turning or twisting |
| *walk-* (see *aûke*) | land, ground, place, country (not enclosed orlimited). |
| *wallum-* , *wol-, woll-, wallom-* (see *wunni*) | good, beautiful, pleasant (e.g., *Wallum Lake* = "beautiful lake") |

260

| | |
|---|---|
| *wam-*, *wamb-*  (see *wompi*) | white, the light, dawn, the East (cf. *wamp*) |
| *wamp-*, *wampa-* (see *wompi*) | white, the light, dawn, the East (cf. *Wampanoag*) |
| *Wampanoag*  (see *Pokanoket, wamp, noag*) | Dawnlanders; Easterners,  people of early light. (In historic times, a federation of confederacy of about 41 tribes (loosely a Nation) in southeastern New England, and initially called  *Pokanoket* by colonists). Note:many variant spellings in LaFantasie, vol. 1 |
| *wamsu-* (see *woomussu*) | down hill |
| *wan-*(1) (see  *ouwán* ) | disappear; fog, mist, vapor |
| *wan-*(2) (see *wunni*) | good, beautiful, pleasant |
| *wana-* , *wanash-*  (see *wanasq*) | top, summit, end place  (e.g., *Wanacottaquet*  = "land at the end of the tidal river") |
| *wanash-* , *wanasq-* (see *wanasq*) | top, summit, end place  (e.g., *Wanasquatomska* = "rock summit") |
| *wanask* (cf. *kodtukoag*)  (see *wanasq*) | summit, top place, end of,  end-place |
| *wanashquompsqut* (see *wanasq*, *-ompsk, -ut*) | at the top of the rock |
| *wanasquatucket* (see *wanasq, -tuck*(1), *-et*) | at the end of the tidal river (name for *Providence* *River*) |
| *wanasq, wanaski* (*wanashque, wa-nasque*) | upon the top, end of, end-place |
| *wang-* (1) (see *wonkqŭssis*) | fox |

| | |
|---|---|
| *wang-* (2), *wonk-*, *wonck-*, *wal-* , *wank-* , *wong-* (see *wewen, -wonk-*) | crooked, bent, oxbow, back turn in stream, sudden turning or twisting (e.g., *Wangam* = "bend") |
| *wangungatuck, wongagatuck* (see *–wonk-, tuk*) | bent river |
| *-wangom-* (see *wewen, -wonk-*) | crooked, bent, oxbow, back turn in stream, sudden turning or twisting |
| *-wana-, -woon-* (*wonki* = "it is bent, crooked") | crooked, bent, oxbow, back turn in stream, sudden turning or twisting |
| *wann-* , *wanna* (see *wunni*) | good, beautiful, pleasant (e.g., *Wannamoiset* = "at the good fishing place") |
| *wannume, waname, wannem* (see *wunni*) | a good lookout place, observation post |
| *wanonk-* (see *–wonk-*) | crooked, bent, oxbow, back turn in stream, sudden turning or twisting |
| *wap-* , *wapa-, wappa-, wape(n), wappo-* (see *wompi* ) | white, the light, dawn, the East (e.g., *Wapping* = "dawn place") |
| *wapasem* (see *wap, -sum*) | opossum ("white animal") |
| *wapwa-* , *wapper* (see *waubos*) | strait, narrow (e.g., *Wappewassick* = "at the narrow straits") |
| *wapway* (see *wapwa*) | narrow passage, crossing place |
| *war-* (1) , *warw-* (see *waûk,* "r" dialect) | bending, sloping, curving, bending backwards |
| *war-* (2) , *warw-, waure-* (see *wuuni,* "r" dialect) | good, beautiful, pleasant |
| *was-* (1), *wass-, wassa-* (see *wohsi*) | shining or slippery |

| | |
|---|---|
| was- (2) (see *wadsh*) | nest, bird's nest (e.g., *Mabsw-aschi* = "bird's nest" (one possible meaning)) |
| -waas- (see *washe* [dialect?]) | river (imitative) (e.g., *Nowass* = "between rivers") |
| wassa- , was-, wass- (see *wohsi*) | shining or slippery |
| wash- (1), (see *wanasq* & *wana*- above) | top, summit, end place (e.g., *Washukquatom* = "Summit of hill") |
| -wash (2) (see *w', -ash*) | pluralization stem –*ash* with a "glide" *w* |
| washe | river |
| -washim- (see -*ashim*) | of animals (with "w" glide) |
| wat-, -wata-,watu- (from *wadchabüke* = "roots, spruce roots") | sewing thread, made of roots (e.g., *Wataba* = "roots") |
| -watch-, watchu- (see *wadchu*) | mountain, hill (e.g., *Watchoog* = "hill country") |
| watch- watche- , wach-, watcha- (see *weque*) | at the end of (e.g., *Wauchemo-quit* = "at the end of the fishing place or cove") |
| waubos | crossing, passage, fording (cf. *Weybosset*) |
| wauchùash (see *wadchu, -ash*) | plural of *wadchu* = mountain, hill |
| -waug (see *aûke*) | land, ground, place, country (not enclosed or limited). (e.g., *Nounewaug* = "dry land") |
| -wauk-, -wauki- (see *wauki*) | crooked, bent |

263

| | |
|---|---|
| *waum-* (see *waumsu*) | downhill, winding down (e.g., *Waumpanickseepoot* = "place of white foamy waterfall in the river") |
| *waupa-, wauphan-* (see *wómpi*) | light of day, dawn, daybreak, white |
| *wauqu-* (*wonki* = "it is bent, crooked") | bent, crooked |
| *waure-* (see wunni) | good, beautiful, pleasant (e.g., *Wauregan* = "a handsome thing") |
| *-waw* (*-quaw*) (Narr.) | state of, condition, status; e.g., *Segousquaw* = "widow" (i.e., "woman left behind") |
| *wa –wa., wayway-, wewea-* (*wonki* = "it is bent, crooked") | round about, winding (e.g., *Wawaytick* = "winding tidal creek") |
| *-wawya-* (*wonki* = "it is bent, crooked") | crooked, bent, oxbow, back turn in stream, sudden turning or twisting |
| *-way-* (*wonki* = "it is bent, crooked") | crooked, bent, oxbow, back turn in stream, sudden turning or twisting (e.g., *Waymessick* = "winding brook") |
| *waybos-* (see *waubos*) | strait, narow (e.g., *Waypoiiset* = "at the narrow place or strait") |
| *wayway-* (*wonki* = "it is bent, crooked") | crooked, bent, oxbow, back turn in stream, sudden turning or twisting (e.g. , *Waywaypounshag* = "twisting outlet") |
| *-weak-* (see *weque, ukque*) | at the end of |

| | |
|---|---|
| -wean- (see *wewen*, -wonk-) | crooked, bent, oxbow, back turn in stream, sudden turning or twisting |
| weat- (see *wétu*) | dwelling (wigwam) (e.g., *Weataug* = "at the village") |
| weatchimín (see *ewachimineash*, *min*, *weatchimíneash*) (cf. *meech*) | corn (Corn is the miracle food of the Indians in New England; literally, "the plant growing in the field") |
| weca-, wece- (see *weque* , *ukque*) | at the end of (e.g., *Wecapaug* = "at the end of the pond") |
| wechekum (see *weque*, -*ke* (2) *un* (1)) (cf. *kehtoh*) | the sea shore ("great land beyond the earth") |
| weck- (see *weque* , *ukque*) | at the end of (e.g., *Weckwannuck* = "at the end of the hill") |
| weco- (see *weque* , *ukque*) | at the end of (e.g., *Wecoachett* = "at the end of the hill") |
| wecq (*wesq*) (see *weque*) | end of, furthest away |
| -wee- (see *peewe*) | small (e.g., *Weepoiset* = "at the small pond") |
| week- ,weeka- (see *weque* , *ukque*) | at the end of (e.g., *Weekapaug* = "at the end of the pond") |
| ween- (1), weena (see *wewen*, -wonk-) | crooked, bent, oxbow, back turn in stream, sudden turning or twisting (e.g., *Weenachasett* = "At the divided, winding place (or hills)?") |
| ween- (2) (see *wuuni*) | good, beautiful, pleasant |
| weenwas (*win∞s*) (see *ween*) | onion, wild shallot |

265

| | |
|---|---|
| *weep-* , *weepi-* (see *weque* , *ukque*) | begin, end |
| *weepo-* (see *waubos*) | strait, narrow (e.g., *Weepowaug* = "narrow crossing") |
| *weequ-* (see *weque* , *ukque*) | at the end of (e.g., *Weequakut* = "at the end") |
| *weet-* (see *wétu*) | dwelling (wigwam) (cf. *weat*) |
| *-weewe-* (see *wewen, -wonk-*) | crooked, bent, oxbow, back turn in stream, sudden turning or twisting |
| *wehquohke* (see *wehque, ohke*) | end of the earth |
| *wehqshi* (*weekshik*) (see *weque, -shik*) | it extends to, goes as far as, at the end of |
| *wehque* (see *weque*) | at the end of(e.g., *wehque paugeset* ="at the end of the small pond") |
| *weka-,* (see *weque*) | crooked, bent, oxbow, back turn in stream, sudden turning or twisting |
| *w'ekonne (-wek-, -week-)* | it is sweet |
| *wene* (see *wunni*) | good, beautiful, pleasant |
| *wenómin* (see *ween, min*) (?) | grape; plural = *wenóminneash* |
| *wenphen -* (see *wómpi*) | light of day, dawn, daybreak, white |
| *wenshik* (see *ween, -shik*) | where is curves, bends |
| *went-* (see *weque* , *ukque*) | from here, therefore |
| *wepo-, wepi-, wipi-, webi-, wepu-* (see *waubos*) | strait, narrow |
| *wepu-* , *weepwoi-* (see *waubos*) | strait, narrow |
| *weqa-* (see *weque* , *ukque*) | at the end of |

266

| | |
|---|---|
| *weqau-* ( see *weqaui*) | light in color (e.g., *wequash* = "swans") |
| *wequ-* (1) , *wequa-* (see *weqaui*) | torch, flaming stick, a light (e.g., *Wequaque* = "torch light place ") (one possible meaning) |
| *wequ-* (2) , *wequa-* (see *wohsi*) | shining, glistening, slippery (e.g., *Wequaquet* = "shining place") (one meaning) |
| *wequa-, weque-* (1) (see *weque , ukque*) | at the end of (e.g., *Wequadnack* = "at the end of the mountain") |
| *weqaui* | light in color (e.g., *wequash* = "swans") |
| *wequa-* (2) (see *weque , ukque*) | at the end of (e.g., *Wequadnack* = "at the end of the mountain") |
| *weque-* (see *weque , ukque*) | at the end of (e.g., *Wequepogue* = "end of the pond") |
| *wequishin* (*weekshin, wehqshik*) (see *weque*) | it ends |
| *wera-* (see *wunni*, "*r*" dialect) | good, beautiful, pleasant (e.g., *Weraumaug* = "good fishing place") |
| *wesaui* (*osa, ousa*) (Narr.) | yellow |
| *-wese* (see *-ese*) | little, small (e.g., *Montowese* = "little God") |
| *-wesq* (see *weque*) | at the end of |
| *wesa-, wissa, wissi-* (see *wohsi*) | shining or slippery or glistening |
| *wessa-* (see *wesq*) | furtherst away, end of (e.g., *Wessagusset* = "edge of the rock" ?) |

267

| | |
|---|---|
| *-wet-, -weat-* (see *weet, wetu*) | dwelling (wigwam) (cf. *weat*) |
| *-weta-* | the woods (forest) ? |
| *wétuaûke* (see *wétu, aûke*) | wétu place (a village, camp) |
| *-wewe-* (see *wewen, -wonk-*) | crooked, bent, oxbow, back turn in stream, sudden turning or twisting (e.g., *Weweeder* = "winding about") |
| *weybos-* (see *waubos*) | strait, narrow (e.g., *Weybosset* = "at the narrow passage") |
| *wica-* (see *weque , ukque*) | at the end of (cf. *wico*) |
| *wichci* (see *weche*) | together with,along, with; e.g., *wéche peyau keemat* = "he is coming with your brother" |
| *wick-, wicka -, wicker-* (see *weque, ukque*) | at the end of (e.g., (e.g., *Wickaboxet* = "at the end of the little pond") |
| *wico-, wick-, wicker-* (see *weque , ukque*) | at the end of (e.g., *Wickerboxet* = "at the end of the small pond") |
| *wik-* (1) (see *wik* (1)) | dwelling (wigwam) |
| *wik* (2) | end of, end-place |
| *willi-* (see *wunni*, "*l*" dialect) | good, beautiful, pleasant (e.g., *Willimantic* = "good cedar swamp") (one possible translation) |
| *win-, wine-* (see *wunni*) | good, beautiful, pleasant (e.g., *Wintucket* = "at the good tidal creek") |
| *winna-,winne-, winni-, winny-* (see *wunni*) | good, beautiful, pleasant (e.g., *Winnemaug* = "good fishing place") |

268

| | |
|---|---|
| *winoos-* (See *win∞ski* = "onions, onion country") | |
| *wipo-* (see *waubos*) | strait, narrow |
| *wirri-* (see *wunni*, "r" dialect) | good, beautiful, pleasant |
| *wnog-* (*wonki* = "it is bent, crooked") | crooked, bent, oxbow, back turn in stream, sudden turning or twisting (e.g., *Wnogquetookoke* = "place of bending of the river") |
| *-wock* (see *w, −og* (2)) | pluralization stem for "animate" forms |
| *-wog, -woag* (see *aûke*) | land, ground, place, country (not enclosed or limited). Sometimes includes a preceding "glide" *u* or *y* or *l*, etc. |
| *wohkon∞s* (*wohkon∞ssin*) (see *hassen*) | fort |
| *wookoonos, wonkunk* | wall, fence, sometimes a weird (e.g. *Wonocomaug* = "fishing fence or weir |
| *wohsi-* (see *wohsi*) | shining or slippery or glistening |
| *wol-* , *woll-* (see *wallum*, "l" dialect) | good, beautiful, pleasant |
| *woll-* (see *wol*, "l" dialect) | good, beautiful, pleasant (e.g., *Wollumnuppoag* ="place of the beautiful lake") |
| *wom-* , *woom-* (see *waumsu*) | downhill, winding down |
| *women-* (see *waumsu* ) | descending, falling, sloping (e.g., *Womenshenick* = "place of steep rocks") |
| *womp-* (see *wómpi*) | light of day, dawn, daybreak, white (e.g., *Assawompset* = "white stone place") |

| | |
|---|---|
| *wompa-* (see *wómpi*) | light of day, dawn, daybreak, white (e.g., *Wampanoag* = "people of the early dawn, Dawnlanders, Easterners" or "people of the first light") |
| *womapsq-* (see *wompasq*) | swamp, marsh, bay |
| *wonamma-* (see *wunni, montop*) | a good lookout place |
| *wonasqua* (see *wanashque*) | end of, end-place, summit, upon the top (e.g., *Wonasquatucket* = "at the end of the tidal river") |
| *wong-, wongan-* (*wonki* = "it is bent, crooked") | crooked, bent, oxbow, back turn in stream, sudden turning or twisting |
| *wongunpaug* (see *wongun, -paug(1)*) | crooked or bent pond |
| *-wongum-* (*wonki* = "it is bent, crooked") | crooked, bent, oxbow, back turn in stream, sudden turning or twisting |
| *-wongun-* (*wonki* = "it is bent, crooked") | crooked, bent, oxbow, back turn in stream, sudden turning or twisting (e.g., *Wongun* = "at the bend") |
| *-wonk-* , *-wonck-* (*wonki* = "it is bent, crooked") | crooked, bent, oxbow, back turn in stream, sudden turning or twisting (e.g., *Wonkituck* = "crooked river") |
| *wonq-* (see *wewen, -wonk*) | crooked, bent, oxbow, back turn in stream, sudden turning or twisting |
| *wonqùssis* (see *wonk, w∞nki*) | a fox ("bend, circle about"), or other small fur-like animal |
| *woom-, woon-* (see *woomussu*) | steep descent (e.g., *Woonsocket* = "place of steep descent") |

| | |
|---|---|
| -woon-, -wana- (wonki = "it is bent, crooked") | crooked, bent, oxbow, back turn in stream, sudden turning or twisting (e.g., *Woonachasset* = "crooked little hill") |
| woonk-, woonks- (see *wonqùssis*) | fox (e.g., *Woonksechocksett* = "fox country") |
| -woonki- (wonki = "it is bent, crooked") | crooked, bent, oxbow, back turn in stream, sudden turning or twisting |
| wopo- (see *waubos*) | strait, narrow (e.g., *Wopowage* = "at the narrows") |
| wor- (wonki = "it is bent, crooked") | crooked, bent, oxbow, back turn in stream, sudden turning or twisting (e.g., *Woronoco* = "winding about") |
| wos-, wososh- (see *wososki*) | marshy, muddy, of a swamp |
| wososki (wososhki) (cf. *pissagk*) | marshy, muddy |
| wuchípoquamin (see *w'*, *chippe* ?, *min*) | pear-pears; plural = *wuchípoquaminneash* |
| wugche (see *wuche* , *wutche*) | from, because of, on behalf of, therefore, it proceeds from |
| wunn- (from *wonugs* = "cavity, hollow") | dish, bowl, plate (e.g., *Wunnegunset* = "bowl shaped country") |
| wunna-, wunne- wunn-, wunne- (see *wunni*) | good, beautiful, pleasant (e.g., *Wunnamuktukoogk* ="good fishing place at the river") |
| wunnash (see same) | summit, top place, end of |
| wung- (see *wongum*) | crooked, bent, oxbow, back turn in stream, sudden turning or twisting |
| wunnàm (Narr.) (see *w'*, *wunni*) (cf. *msquì* ) | red paintings on Indian garments, faces, bodies, etc. from pine and red earth (red earth = *mishquock*) |

| | |
|---|---|
| *wunnàugun* (see *un* (1), *wewen*, *aûke*) | dish, bowl, plate, so shaped |
| *wunni* (*wunne*, *willi* (l-dialect), *wirri* (r-dialect), -∞ne-, -wune-, -unne-, -unna-, -tunna-, -wun- | pleasing, favorable, good, beautiful; (literally, "it is good") (e.g., *wunniyeu* = "he is happy") |
| *wunnohke* (see *wunni*, *ohke*) | good land |
| *wushówunan* (Narr.) | hawk (imitates sound of bird) |
| *wuskowhanan* (see *wuskowhan*) | pigeon (or dove) (e.g., *Wuskowhananaukit* = "at the abobe of pigeons") (a delicacy to Indians) |
| *wuske*, *wusk-*, *wask-* | young, new (e.g., *wuskenin* = "young man") |
| *wuskowhan* | pigeon or dove (imitates sound of bird) |
| *wuss-*, *wass-* (see *wussi-*) | other side of, beyond (cf. *hous*) |
| *wussoquat* (Narr.) | walnut tree (related to *sussequnut* = "to anoint with oils") |
| *wut-* (see *wut-*) | at, to, on |
| *wutche* (*w'* + ∞*che*) (*wutji*, ∞*tch*, ∞*ch*) | Important word with many meanings—from, because of, on behalf of, therefore, it proceeds from |
| -*wutt-* , -*wutten-* (see *wadchu*) | mountain (e.g., *Wuttounug* = "rocky place") |
| *wuttamâuog* (see *wuttatash*) (Narr.) | tobacco ("what they drink [smoke]") |
| *wuttohkohk∞minneinash* (see *wuttah*, *min*,-*ash*) | blackberries |

| | |
|---|---|
| *wya-, wawya-* (see *wewen, -wonk-*) | crooked, bent, oxbow, back turn in stream, sudden turning or twisting (e.g. *Wyantenug* = "where the water swirls around the hill") |
| *wyan-* , *wean-* (see *wewen, -wonk-*) | crooked, bent, oxbow, back turn in stream, sudden turning or twisting (e.g. *Wyantenug* = "where the water swirls around the hill") |
| *wyas-* (see *âshâp*) | flags, rushes, flax, &c (e.g., *Wyasup* = "place of flag, rushes") |

| Algonquian Fragment/Root | Translation |
|---|---|
| | |
| X | |
| *-xet* (see-*es* (1), -*et*) | place of small something (e.g., *Akoaxet* = "at the place of young or small pines?; "place of small fields?" (two possible meanings)) |

| Algonquian Fragment/Root | Translation |
|---|---|
| | |
| Y | |
| *y* (see –*y*-) | a "glide" sometimes preceding a vowel |
| *-yak*[1] (see *aûke*) | land, ground, place, country (not enclosed or limited). (e.g., *Namyak* = "fishing place"). Includes a preceding "glide" *y*. |

273

| | |
|---|---|
| *yan-* (see *yaueun*) | on one side, extending to (e.g., *Yantic* = "as far as the tide goes up this side of the river") |
| *yau-* (1), *yauuh* , *nauwoh* | four |
| *yau-* (2) (see *yo (yeu)* ) | on one side , extending to (e.g., *Yaubucks* = "on one side of the small pond") |
| *yaw-* (see *yo (yeu)* ) | on one side , extending to (e.g., *Yawgoog* = one side of the pond") |
| *yeanni-* (see *yowa, yeu* (2) ) | extending or far reaching (as a mountain or river) |
| *yeu* (see *yeu* (2)) | this place, at this place |
| *yew-, yewt-* (see *yote*) | fire (e.g., *Yewtack* = "fire place") |
| *yo* (see same) | here, there, thus far |
| *yoai-, yoaea-, yoae-* | on that side |
| *yo chippachâusin* (see *yo, chippu, -shik*) (Narr.) | where the way divides |
| *yo nmúnnatch* (see same) | at, on the left side |
| *yo mtúnnock* (see same) | at, on the right side |

(Footnotes)

1      "y" is probably a vowel "glide" interspersed between a stem ending in a consonant (*-nam*) and one beginning in a vowel (*auke*).

# Appendix I

---

## Linguist Sheds Some Light on Roots of Word 'Aquidneck'

Originally published in The Newport Daily News, July 6-7, 2002

To the Editor:

In a recent letter to your newspaper, Norman E. Champagne speculates that the meaning of the name "Acquidneck" may be "Peace Day," relying on the spelling "Aquiday" and the Narrangansett word "Aquene" that Roger Williams translates as "peace." The island was indeed named in the Narragansett language, a close relative of Massachusett (no s!) in the Algonquian family, but these languages adhere strictly to highly complex but orderly grammatical rules in forming their words, which cannot be chopped up and rearranged at will, as the writer proposes. It is not remotely plausible that an authentic, early Indian place name could be derived from part of a Narragansett word added to an English word.

The reliable early spellings, used by Williams and others, correspond to the name used today; they include "Aquedenick," "Acquednecke," "Aqueedneck," and "Aquidnecke." The interpretation of this name in Narragansett is obvious enough. It means "on (some kind of) island." The usual word for "island" in John Eliot's Massachusett Bible (1663) is "munnoh," but he also uses "ogquidnash" for "islands" (Isaiah 40:15; -ash is the plural ending) and "kishke ahquednet," literally "near the island," for "under (i.e., in the lee of) a certain island" (Acts 27:16).

In the Massachusett form "ahquednet," the ending "-et" marks it as locative ("in, on, at," etc.; the vowel is variably spelled). This corresponds exactly to the "-eck," "-ick," etc. in the spellings of "Aquidneck," which is the locative ending in Narragansett. For example, in his grammar, Eliot gives the Massachusett for "in my house" as "Neekit," while Williams has the same word in Narragansett as "Nékick." The dialectical difference between the "t" and "k" endings was real, but the other spelling variations in all these words (such as that between "t" and "d") were caused not by variability in pronunciation, but by the difficulties the English had in perceiving and writing unfamiliar sounds, compounded by the vagaries of English orthography.

Given that Eliot's usual way of translating "on the island" in Massachusett was munnohhannit (several spellings), we can only speculate on what difference in meaning there may have been between this and "ahquednet." But the etymological connections of the latter word are clear. It is the agent noun ("that which, the thing that") corresponding to a verb that is widespread in the Algonquian family meaning "it floats; it is in water." The prototypical subjects of this verb in narrative are islands and canoes. And in fact, the noun meaning "island" in southern New England is matched exactly by "ákwiten, canoe" in the Penobscot language of Maine. When then of the odd spelling "Aquiday"? Contrary to what the writer claims, this spelling does not appear in Williams' correspondence, sent or received (see the standard edition by Glenn W. LaFantasie, 1988). The letters by Williams cited by the writer as using this spelling in 1642 were actually written in 1638 and have only variants

276

of the familiar spelling, such as "Aquedenick." Rather, "Aquiday" is the spelling that appears in the journals of Gov. John Winthrop of the Massachusetts Bay Colony. And, in fact, the passage the writer quotes about Anne Hutchinson is not, as he claims, by Williams at all. It is from Winthrop's journal entry for March 16, 1639, and refers to the famous earthquake of June 1638.

To be precise, "Aquiday" can only be considered the best guess of Winthrop's editors as to what he wrote. As I am informed by Peter Drummey, the librarian of the Massachusetts Historical Society, where Winthrop's journal is kept, Winthrop's handwriting is one of the most difficult of that period, and even for specialists the exact spelling intended is often a guess. Whether re-examination of the parts of Winthrop's journal that survive will shed light on the matter is an open question, but in any event "Aquiday" is off the direct line of transmission of the name that is today Aquidneck.

Ives Goddard
Senior Linguist, Department of Anthropology
Smithsonian Institution
Washington, D.C.

# Appendix II

---

## Translation of Some Indian Place Names
in Southern New England

# List of Root Words

# A Note on Translations

## ☙❧

## The Glossary of Roots

The vast majority of regional Indian place names denote land or country, river and lake and bay and pond and stream &c, fishing-place, hill and mountain, stone and rock, natural or man-made enclosure, and island. To these elemental features are added modifiers of size, number, quality and locatives, and other grammatical features and of course, intertribal dialectical (phonetic & semantic) variations.

The following abridged topical list of common roots and combining elements from the Massachusett, Narragansett and similar languages can be used as a quick reference in deciphering some of the Indian place names in the book. The first column gives roots &c in the original Indian language, the second shows alternative corrupted spellings seen in the actual names, and lastly, the essential meaning of the Algonquian as seen in place names.

Keep in mind that sometimes the root or combining element in an Indian place name is not much corrupted. Several variant source spellings are given to assist in identification of degenerated roots which, through the corruption process, have become difficult to discriminate in modern Indian names. This observation applies to listings of the same corrupted spellings associated with different roots (especially for those roots relating to descriptions of division, separation, opening, clearing, widening, narrowing &c). Be sure to remember the common connective vowel-consonant and syllabic glides, and reduced vowels, which often separate roots and combining elements— a, e, i, l, m, n, o, p, q, qua, quo, r, t, u, w, y.

Note on the placement of the hyphen in roots. Under Land Names is listed -adene. The prefixed hyphen indicates that -adene is seen at word-end. No hyphen means root-word might possibly appear anywhere (beginning, middle or end of a place name) excepting the addition of the terminal locative, diminutive and pluralization stems, if included.

For more detailed explanations of typical place-name vocabulary terms, see Trumbull's classic, *Comp. Ind. Geog. Names*. His Natick Dictionary is also important.

Toponymic translations—on the linguistic level—begin by searching for the corrupted fragments. Examples are shown at end of the lists in App. II as well in the *Introduction*, Figures 1- 5.

***CAUTION***—It is important to reiterate that one is not likely to be able to translate many Indian place names in southern New    279

England simply by linguistic analysis of the poorly spelled roots and combining elements. Begin with the oldest spelling(s) in a deed or other official document. Gather as much available data on the possible meaning of the Indian place name. Corroborating evidence is important. No single item of information is in and of itself determinative.

# List of Common Roots
# and Combining Elements

Sources:  Trumbull (1870, 1881 & 1903), Huden (1962) & Author

## I.  Land Names

| Algonquian | Modern (Corrupted) Spelling | Meaning |
|---|---|---|
| -adene (*inseperable generic[1]*) | -ahdin, -ahd, -attiny--*etc.* | mountain (sometimes hill) |
| aquidne, ahquedne, ocquidne | acquidn-, aqu-, aqueduen-, -idn-, -edn-, quid(n)-, uh-quetn-, *etc.* | island[2] (one word for) see munnoh |
| auke (see ohke, auke) | | |
| hassun, ohsun, assin | asa-, ass-, assa-, ashin-, as-hun-, asn-, cassa-, casso-, osi-, hassa-, horse(n), hooshus-, sen(n)-, sun(a)-, *etc.* | stone, rock (some-times cave, ledge, den) |
| -komuk | -comuc, -commuck, -gomuck--*etc.* | natural or artificial enclosed or limited or appropriated place like a village, build-ing, garden, or long-house or sweatlodge (not a wigwam, usu.) |
| mukkoskqut, micuckkaskeete | mascak-, mascack, mukqua-, masque-, mux, muy-, *etc.* | meadow, a plain, flags or rushes, green grass place |

| | | |
|---|---|---|
| munnoh, munno-han | munna, manha, minna, men-han, munhan, *etc.* | island (second & more common word for) see aquidne |
| munnoh-es | munnisses, manises, minis-- *etc.* | little island |
| naïag | niack, nyack, nayaug, naway-ack, naïänk, nahig, nanhig, narrag--*etc.* | a point of land, cor-ner, angle |
| ohke, auke | ac, ack, aug, auc, ag, ic, ick, ik, ahki, ocke, ock, oc, ogue, oock, uc--*etc.* | land, ground, place, country (not enclosed or limited) |
| -ompsk (*insep. gen.*) | -ampsc, -ipsk, -ob, -obsk, -mpsk, -msk, -ms, -psk, -pisk, -umsk--*etc.* | a standing or upright rock (hard or flint-like) |
| qussuck | quassa-, quass-, qusasa-, *etc.* | stone, rock, cave, ledge |
| -'tugk, -tugk (*insep. gen.*) | -tuck, -tunk, -tak, -tuk--*etc.* | wood, tree, made of wood |
| -unk, -unck, -anck, -onk (*insep. gen.*) | -aunk, -onck--*etc.* | a standing tree |
| wadchu, wauchu, adchu (in composi-tion) | watchu, wachu, achu, choo, chu--*etc.* | hill, mountain |

(Footnotes)

1       Inseparable generic (insep. gen.) means term not used as an independent word, but as a generic noun-affix in place names.

2       There were two words for island. According to Trumbull (1870), this word was used for islands (perhaps large) near a main land or islands discussed with reference to the main land.

## II. Water Names[3]

| Algonquian | Modern (Corrupted) Spelling | Meaning |
|---|---|---|
| -amaug (*insep. gen.*) | -amag, -amock, -ameock,- ameugg, -amyock, -amareck, -amelake, -amuck, -amond-- *etc.* | fishing-place (fish taken by hook); cf. âshâp |
| hashab, âshâp, ashòp | asab-, ashappa-, *etc.* | fish-net, weir; cf. -amaug |
| namohs, nâmâs | -am-, -ama-, -ame-, -om-, -nam-, *etc.* | fish in general or eel |
| nippe, nipi (see pe) | | |
| nuppis, nips | nawbes--*etc.* | little water, lake or a small pond (nippe + es) |
| -paug, -pâg (*insep. gen.*) | -pack,-pog, -poge, -pogue, -pauk, -pawog, -baug, -bog, -pag, -pague, -bogue--*etc.* | pond, lake, body of fresh water (water at rest, non-tidal); pe + auke combined |
| -pauges, -paugeset | -paugset, -pogset, -poxet, -boxet, -boxy--*etc.* | little pond, lake, body of fresh water (paug+es) |
| pe (for nippe, nip) (*insep. gen.*) | pi, bi--*etc.* | fresh water for drinking; in composition for lake, pond, cove, bay &c |

3       There are many, sometimes confusing, terms relating to water: an estuary is an inlet or arm of the sea; a stream is a small river; a brook is a small stream; intermediate in size is a creek. Other well-known ones include—spring, pond, lake, cove, bay, inlet, harbor, strait, channel, falls, waterfall, current, tides and ocean, sea. Still others are—ford, narrows, portage, weir, fork or branch, bar, bank, beach, delta, lagoon, peninsula, isthmus, rapids, reef.

| -pe-auke | -peag, -piak, -piac,-bequi, -bec--*etc.* | water-land, water-place |
|---|---|---|
| pauntuck, pawtuck | pautuck, powntuck, pooun-tuck, patuck--*etc.* | water falls in a tidal river |
| pauntuk-ese | | small water falls in a tidal river |
| sauk | -suc, -suck, -sauga, -saco, -sag, -sague, -seogee--*etc.* | outlet of a river or lake, stream flowing out of a pond or lake or river |
| sepu, seip | sip-, sippi, sep, seppe--*etc.* | a river, stream |
| sepu-es | sepose, sepo, sebese, sebethe--*etc.* | a short river, brook or rivulet |
| -tuk (*insep. gen.*) | -tick, -tic, -(c)tic, *etc.* | a tidal or broad river, estuary |
| -tuk-es | -tucks, -tux, -tuxet--*etc.* | a small tidal river, estuary |
| -utchaun, -uwan | -tch-, -ch-, -iak-?, -ich-, -idge-?, -itch-?, *etc.* | a rapid stream, a current |

## III. Adjectives / Descriptives

| Algonquian | Modern (Corrupted) Spelling | Meaning |
|---|---|---|
| askáski | ask-, shen-, *etc* | green color |
| chab-, chepi- | chippi-, chabe-, chappa-, chaub-, *etc.* | separated, apart |

| cuppi, kuppi | capo-, copa-, cope-, kappo-, koppo-, kuppo- | closed up, shut in, hiding place, refuge/ haven, a thicket |
|---|---|---|
| kehti-, kehchi- | got-, keht-, kehte-, ket-, kit-, kt-, kut-, kutty-, cot-, cod-, cat-, che-, cutty-, te-, tit-, *etc.* | chief, main, principal, greatest |
| matchi-, mache- | mat-, maut-, matta-, *etc.* | bad, evil, unpleasant, unfavorable |
| mishqui-, misqui- | mus-, msq-, mis-, misa-, musque-, sw-,sq-, squi-, squam- , *etc.* | red color, or salmon (red-fish) |
| missi-, mishe-, massa-, mashe- | mis-, -mas-, matta-, matha-, moshe-, mus-, musch-, she- *etc.* | big, large (sometimes "great") |
| mogke, mogki, mukki | mag-, mog-, *etc.* | very great, huge, great of its kind or by comparison |
| mooi-, moowi- | me(tt)-, mana-, mona-, mane- -*etc.* | black color |
| nashaui | nashawe, nashaway, natchaw, naush, ashwa, show, showa, shew, she--*etc.* | midway, between |
| ogguhse-, ogkosse- | occu-, oxo-, oxy-, abscu-, *etc.* | small, little in quantity |
| ongkome, ogkome, acáwmé | accom-, agame-, *etc.* | on the other side of, over against, beyond |
| ongkoué | uncoa, uncawa, uncoway, unqua--*etc.* | beyond |
| pâchau-, pahchau | pauk-, pauch-, pahch-, pach- | turning, changing route, deviating |

285

| pahke, pâk, pôgh, pohk, pohq, pohki, pâuqui[1] | pahcu-, paque-, paqua, paqui-, pahqai-, pauga-, pawca-, pequa-, poca-, pok-, pock-, poka-, poco-, pock-, pok-, poqua-, *etc.* | "It is clear, clean, pure"; used to show division, separation, breaking, opening, widening |
|---|---|---|
| peské, pisk | pesk-, pasq-, pasq-, *etc.* | split, forked, branched |
| p'etùk'qui | patta-, petti-, petuk-, petuck-, petuckqua, *etc.* | round |
| pewe, peawe | pe-, pee-, pea-, *etc.* | small, tight |
| pŏhque, pohquaé | pahcu-, pahqui-, pohqua-, pauqua-, paqua-, payqua-, pequa-, poqua-, poco-, pock-, pok-, pyqua-, puckwa-, pahcu-, pughquo-, *etc.* | "it breaks, is broken"; cleared (as land) or opened (as waterway) [sometimes transferred as: bare, shallow] |
| pohqu'un | poquon-, pocon-, paquan-, pequon-, pecon-, pocum-, *etc.* | cleared, opened (as land), widened |
| pohquettah-un | poquetan-, paucutun-, pogatan-, pocotan-, coddan-, cuttyhun-, cotting-, *etc.* | broken-up, cultivated (as land) |
| quinni | can-, con-, cona-, conne-, connec-, coh-, coon-, ken-, quin-, qun-, quilli-, quirri-, quan-, *etc.* | long |
| qunnŭhqui | conaqua-, -quon-, *etc.* | tall, high, elevated |
| sonki | soonka, sunki, saunquo, songi--*etc.* | cool to touch, taste |
| sucki-, sicki- | saco-, sauki-, sako-, seek-, seki, sic-, sick(c), sock-, suc(c)-, sucka-, *etc.* | black or purple, dark colored |

| wampi- | wab-, wam-, wamb-, wamp(a)-,wap- , *etc.* | white, dawn, the East |
| wepu- | wepo-, weepo-, wipo-, way-bos, wayway-, *etc.* | a strait, narrow |
| weque-, wequa- | weca-, wico-, ukwe-, aquee-, aqua-, *etc.* | at the end of |
| wongun, wonkun | wongum-, wangom-, -woon-, -wonk-, *etc.* | crooked, bended, winding |
| wesaui-, weesoe- | azio-, osa-, ousa-, *etc.* | yellow color, spruce pitch (as a glue) |
| wunni-, winni- | wirri-, wera-, willi-, waure-, wun-, *etc.* | good, easy, pleasing, favorable |

(Footnotes)
1        The distinctions for pahke, etc. & pŏhque, etc. are subtle and not always clear to the translator of corrupted names. Suggest to read Trumbull, 1903, pages 127-128 [entry **pohki**, **pahki** & entry **pohqui**].

# IV. PLURALS, DIMINUTIVES & LOCATIVES
## (INSEPARABLE PARTICLES)

| Algonquian | Modern (Corrupted) Spelling | Meaning |
|---|---|---|
| -ash | -as, -ass,-s-, *etc.* | plural ending, inanimate[1] form |
| -emes | -eemes, -emis, *etc.* | least, smallest |
| -es, -is | -ese, -as, -us, *etc.* | little, small (ending of word) |
| -et, -ut, -it, -ik, -ick, -ing | -at, -chet, -eck, -itt, -ong, -ung, *etc.* | at, in, on, of, by, near, place of (word ending) |

287

| -og | -aog, -ug, -ag, -ig, *etc.* | plural ending, animate form |
|---|---|---|
| -set, -eset | -sett, -sets, -eset,-setts,-esets, -sset, -ssett, *etc.* | little place of (word ending) |

(Footnotes)

1        Inanimate and animate are Algonquian "gender" distinctions.  Animate refers to things that are alive and move, and inanimate refers to those things which are not alive and do not move (exceptions exist in each case).  See Eliot's *Indian Grammar* reprinted in *Understanding Algonquian Ind. Words* (Moondancer & Strong Woman).


NOTE:   Other regional Algonquian names for animals, fish & water, birds, trees &c are contained in the authors' work, *American Indian Studies in the Extinct Languages of Southeastern New England.*
http://www.docstoc.com/docs/3237496/American-Indian-Studies-in-the-Extinct-Languages-of-Southeastern-New-England

# PLACE NAME EXAMPLES

Aquidneck = aquidne + ick (on some kind of island); see Appendix I.

Massachusetts = massa + wadchu + ash + et (at or near the big hills)

Misquamicut = misquesu + am + ick + ut [where we get red fish (salmon) ]

Narragansett = naiag + es + et (place of narrow small point)

Warwick = NOT INDIAN NAME even though "war" & "ick" may appear to be Indian name fragments connected by a w-glide. People make this mistake often. That shows just how mangled the words are in the records.

# FOR OTHER EXAMPLES, SEE:

1. Trumbull (1870 & 1881)
2. Roger Williams (1643 & LaFantasie, 1988)
3. Huden (1962)
4. Masthay (1987)
5. Moondancer & Strong Woman (1996/2001)
6. O'Brien (2003 & *American Indian Studies,* 2005)
7. Kennicutt (1909, 1911)

# Historic Southern New England
## Nations ▪ Tribes ▪ Villages

The source for most of the translations is Huden (1962). Some names have been translated or re-translated by the author. Gookin (1674) provided some in Massachusetts, including Cape Cod and the Islands. A number of other tribal names (not translated) may be found in the book by Bragdon, 1996, pp. 20-25.

| Name | Translation |
|---|---|
| Accomack | on the other side |
| Accominta | beyond the little river |
| Agawam | low land; overflowed by water; an unloading place |
| Amagansett | --at the council place where we smoke -- at the fishing place, at the point |
| Amoskeag | fishing place |
| Aquidneck | at the island, suspended floating mass |
| Aquinnah (Gay Head) | peace camp |
| Ashquoash | green garden stuff |
| Assonet | at the rock place |
| Chabanakongkomun, Chabanakong-muk | divided island lake |
| Corchaug | long separated land |
| Coweset | place of young pine trees |
| Hammonesset | at place of small islands or sandbars |
| Hassanamesit | small stones place |
| Hoosic | kettle rim; writing house? |
| Housatonic | beyond the mountain |
| Kenunckapacoof, Kenuck Pacooke | where the body of the water bends or turns |
| Magunkaquog | place of the gift |
| Mahican, Mohican | wolf |
| Manchage | place of departure or marveling |
| Mashpee | land near the great cove; large pond |
| Massachuset | near the great hills |

290

| | |
|---|---|
| Massacoe, Massaco, Massaqua, Mussawco, Massacowe, Mushko | great land; outlet |
| Mattapoisett | little resting place |
| Menameset | at the place where fish abound |
| Menunkatuck, Menuckketuck, Menunquatuck, Menunketesuck | strong flowing stream |
| Mohegan | wolf people |
| Montauk, Munnawtawkit | at the fort; high land (fort place) |
| Montup, Montaup, Montop | lookout place (Massasoit's Village) |
| Narragansett | at the small narrow point (Nahicans = Narragansetts) |
| Nashoba | between waters |
| Natick | my home, my land (place where Massachusetts language recorded by Indians and missionary John Eliot) |
| Naugatuck | one tree |
| Naumkeag | eel place |
| Nauset, Nawset | at the place between (Cape Cod Bay and Atlantic Ocean); on the point |
| Nehantic, Niantic | point of land on a tidal river or estuary |
| Neponset | a good (or easy) waterfall |
| Niantic | people of the point |
| Nipmuck, Nipnet | fresh water fishermen |
| Nonotuck | narrow river; in the middle of the river |
| Nowass, Nawass | between rivers; at the point |
| Norwottuck | place far from us |
| Pamet, Pawmet, Paumet | wading place; at the shallow cove |
| Paquoag | open or clear place |
| Pascataway | where the river divides |
| Paugusset | -- swift current in the divided river<br>-- river widens out<br>-- where the fork joins<br>-- small pond place |
| Pawtucket | at the water falls |

| | |
|---|---|
| Pawtuxet, Pautuxet, Patuxet | at the little falls (first Plymouth Village of Pilgrims; an old Indian village destroyed by epidemic). [Pautuxet was called Ompaan by Indians in King Philip's War (see B. Church, 1716)] |
| Pennacook | at the foothills; sloping down place |
| Pequot | destroyers |
| Peskeompscut | at the split rocks |
| Pocasset | where the stream widens |
| Pocumtuck | narrow swift river |
| Podunk | where you sink in (imitative sound) |
| Pokanoket, Pawkunnawkutt | at the cleared land [a tribal territory of Massasoit Ousa Mequin's home; Pokanoket was used by English to mean all Wampanoag peoples] |
| Pomperaug | place to walk, play; rocky place |
| Poquonock | cleared land (for cultivation) |
| Potatuck, Powtatuck | land near the (water) falls |
| Punkapog | shallow fresh water pond |
| Quabaug | beyond the pond |
| Quinebaug | long pond |
| Quinnatukut (Connecticut) | long tidal river |
| Quinnipiac, Quillipeak, Quillipeag, Quillipiac, Quinopiock, Quinnypiock | place where the path changes direction, course |
| Quiripi | where we change our route |
| Sagkonet, Saconet, Sakonett | black goose abode; rock outlet; at the outlet |
| Schaghticoke, Scatacook, Scaticook, Skaticook, | where two rivers come together or divide |
| Seekonk, Seaconke | -- black goose place (Native American translation)<br>-- an outlet; mouth of the stream |
| Senecksig, Senexit | place of small stones |

| | |
|---|---|
| Shawmut (Boston and surroundings & Wampanoag village) | -- at the neck (where we pull up our canoes) <br> -- canoe landing place |
| Shinnecock | place of stone? |
| Sicaog (Hartford, CT) | dark earth; muddy place |
| Sickanames | black fish |
| Siwanog | south people (probably) |
| Siwanoy | south people |
| Sokonnesset, Sockanosset | place of dark colored earth |
| Sowams | the south country (Narragansett name for Pokanoket) |
| Sowheage, Sequin | southland, south Sachemdom |
| Squakheag | watching place; spearing fish |
| Swampscott | at the red rock |
| Tunxis | fast flowing and winding stream |
| Unquachog | ? |
| Wabaquasset | place where we make mats for house coverings |
| Wamesit | there is room for all |
| Wampanoag | people of the first light |
| Wangunk | crooked land ? |
| Wappinger | easterners |
| Waramaug, Werewaug | good fishing place |
| Wauchimoqut | end of fishing place |
| Weantinaug, Weantinoque, Weantinock, Weantinoque, Wiantenuck, Wyantenug | where the river swirls or tumbles around a hill |
| Weekapaug | at the end of the pond |
| Wepaweaug | narrows; crossing place |
| Weshakim | surface of sea |
| Wessagusset | at the edge of the rocks |
| Woronoco | winding about |
| Wuttapa, Watuppa | roots (for sewing); where we sit and talk |

# Reservations and Settlements and Other Places

## State of Massachusetts

### (excluding Cape Cod or Nauset)

Some names are repeated from other sections (e.g., Assonet) so that the reader will know the meaning of the name in different contexts and have flexibility in locating a name under different headings. Also, some names listed by State cross multiple States. Famous Wampanoag names like Mashpee are listed under **Nations, Tribes, Villages.**

| Name | Translation |
|---|---|
| Acushnet | at the cove |
| Annawomscutt | at the shell rock; Annawon's Rock |
| Annawon | commander or conqueror (name of Wampanoag missinnige or War Chief in King Phillip's war) |
| Assameskq | a cave |
| Assonet | at the rock place |
| Assowamsoo, Assowamset | halfway place |
| Chabanakongkomun Chabanakongmuk | Divided island lake |
| Chickatawbut | his wetu (house) is on fire |
| Coaxit, Coxit, Coquitt (Part of Dartmouth) | an arrow point; at the high point |
| Cokesit | pine place |
| Copicut | at the refuge place |
| Cotuhtikut | planting fields place |
| Hassanamesit | small stones place |
| Hassanamisco | small stones place |
| Hobbomock | evil spirit |
| Horseneck | a cave; cavern; rock shelter |

| | |
|---|---|
| Magunkaquog | place of the gift |
| Manchage | place of departure or marveling |
| Massachusetts | near the great hills |
| Mattakesit | black mud place |
| Merrimack | deep place |
| Monimoint | deep black mire ? |
| Nanepashemet | he walks the night (Moon Sachem) |
| Nashaway | between two river branches |
| Nashobah | between waters |
| Nashua | between streams |
| Natick | my home, my land (place where Massachusett language recorded by Indians and missionary John Eliot) |
| Nauset, Nawset | at the place between (Cape Cod Bay and Atlantic Ocean); on the point |
| Nonantum | I am glad, I rejoice |
| Nukkehkummees | small shelter |
| Okommakamesit | at the field other side |
| Ompaan, Umpame, Ampame | -- resting place ?<br>-- turn around or back (resurrect  this village?)<br>[first Plymouth Village of Pilgrims; an old Indian village called  Pautuxet; destroyed by epidemic. When English occupied,  called Ompaan  by Indians in King Philip's War (see B. Church, 1716)]) |
| Pakachoog | turning place? |
| Punkapog | shallow fresh water pond |
| Quabaug | beyond the pond |
| Quittacus | red rock; long brook |
| Saugus | the outlet; small outlet |
| Seekonk, Seaconke | black goose place; an outlet; mouth of the stream |

| | |
|---|---|
| Shawmut (Boston and surroundings & Wampanoag village) | -- at the neck (where we pull up our canoes) <br> -- canoe landing place |
| Somerset, Samerset | named after Samoset, a sagamore of Abenaki Indians who first greeted the Pilgrims in March, 1621 |
| Squannacook | --salmon place <br> --in the season of the gardens or green place |
| Squantum | a door or gate; angry god (place of ?) |
| Swampscott | at the red rock |
| Titicut (Tauton) | the principal river |
| Tittituck (Blackstone River) | the great or principal river |
| Wachuset | small mountain place |
| Waeuntug | good tidal stream ?; winding stream ? |
| Wamesit | there is room for all |
| Wannamoisett | at the good fishing place |
| Watchimoquet, Watchimoquit, Watchemoket | end of fishing place or cove |
| Watuppa | roots (for sewing); where we sit and talk |
| Wawayontat, Weweanteit (Wareham) | winding creek |
| Weetomoe | the wetu (lodge) keeper (name of famous Squaw Sachem of Pocassets) |
| Weshakim | surface of sea |
| Weweantic | crooked stream |
| Woronke | winding about place |
| Wunnashowatukqut (Blackstone R.) | where the river divides |

# Reservations and Settlements and Other Places

## Cape Cod

Some information taken from Gookin (1674). See also under Nations, Tribes, Villages.

| Name | Translation |
|------|-------------|
| Ashumet | pond at the spring |
| Ashimuit | at the spring |
| Assoowaamsoo , Assoowamset (part of Middleborough) | --the half-way place<br>--half-way to southwest<br>--other side of Sowams (south country) |
| Coatuit, Cotuit | --at the pine tree place<br>--at the long planting fields |
| Codtanmut | -- deserted place<br>-- trading place<br>-- where they sing |
| Comassakumkanit | at the rock which stands erect |
| Cotuhtikut, Titicut (part of Middleborough) | at the great tidal river |
| Hyannis | he [Sachem Iannough] wages war |
| Kitteaumut, Katamet (Sandwich or Buzzard's Bay) | principal fishing place |
| Manamoyik (Chatham) | carry or burden place |
| Mannamit (Sandwich, bottom of Buzzard's Bay) | where they carry burdens on their backs |
| Mashpee | land near the great cove; large pond |
| Matakees (Barnstable & Yarmouth harbors) | big meadow; little trees |
| Mattapoisett | little resting place |
| Meeshawn | -- a landing place<br>-- ferry (he goes by boat, place of)<br>-- great land neck |
| Monomoy Island | -- lookout place; deep water |

| Nantucket | -- place in the middle of the water<br>-- at far off sea-place<br>-- where it is, the sea gets broader<br>-- far off among the waves<br>-- point of land in the middle<br>-- narrow river |
|---|---|
| Nausett, Nawset (north part of Eastham) | at the place between (Cape Cod Bay and Atlantic Ocean); on the point |
| Nobsquassit (N. East part of Yarmouth) | at the rock ledge cliff |
| Pawpoesit (within Town of Mashpee) | -- snipe (or partridge) country<br>-- at the little place |
| Pispogutt | at the miry pond |
| Popponesset | --at the frost fish or tomcod fishing place<br>--place of obstructed outlet<br>--lookout place |
| Potanumaquut (S. East Eastham) | foaming island place |
| Punonakanit | -- out of the way beach<br>-- distant enclosure |
| Quashnet | at the small cove |
| Saconeset, Sokones (Falmouth) | dark earth |
| Satuit | -- cold brook<br>-- salt (or cold) stream |
| Sawkattukett (West part of Harwich) | at the outlet of the tidal creek |
| Setucket | at the mouth of the tidal river |
| Shumuit | at the spring of good water |
| Sokones | dark earth |
| Wakoquet, Waquoit (within Town of Mashpee) | house place |
| Waquoit | at the end (of the bay) |
| Wawayontat, Wewewanteit (Wareham) |  |
| Weequakut, Chechwacket | place at the end |
| Weesquobs | shining rocks |

# Reservations and Settlements and Other Places

## The Islands

(Block Island, Martha's (Martin's) Vineyard, Elizabeth Islands, Chappaquidick Island)

See also under Nations, Tribes, Villages.

| Name | Translation |
|---|---|
| Aquinnah (Gay Head) | peace camp |
| Capowak | --enclosed pond or harbor<br>-- land of fog, clouds |
| Chappaquiddick | at the separated island |
| Manisses, Manissean (Block Island) | --little island<br>--little god (place of?) |
| Nantucket | -- place in the middle of the water<br>-- at far off sea-place<br>-- where it is, the sea gets broader<br>-- far off among the waves<br>-- point of land in the middle<br>-- narrow river |
| Nashuakemmiuk | middle of dark land |
| Nope (Martin's or Martha's Vineyard) | menhaden fish place |
| Nunnepoag | fresh or narrow pond |
| Oggawame, Agawam | -- low land<br>-- overflowed by water<br>-- an unloading place |
| Ohkatomka | top of the rock |
| Pacamkik | --abode of codfish (Haddock?)<br>--dark land (well fertilized)<br>--open land |
| Peschameeset | --where we catch & split small fish<br>--blue place ? |
| Seconchqut | at the summer place |

| | |
|---|---|
| Sengekontakit | at cold, long creek |
| Squatesit | red place or brook |
| Talhanio | low meadow |
| Toikiming (Christiantown) | at the mill or rushing spring |
| Wammasquid | at the plain |

# Reservations and Settlements and Other Places

## State of Connecticut

See also under Nations, Tribes, Villages.

| Name | Translation |
|---|---|
| Connecticut | place of long tidal river |
| Housatonic | beyond the mountain |
| Maanexit | path; gathering |
| Mashantucket | well-forested place |
| Mohegan | wolf people |
| Mystic | great tidal river |
| Naugatuck | one tree |
| Paucatuck, Pawcatuck | clear divided tidal stream |
| Pequot | destroyers |
| Quantisset | long brook |
| Quinebaug | long pond |
| Schaghticoke, Scaticook | where the river branches |
| Shantok | midway up the river |
| Sicaog (Hartford) | dark earth; muddy place |
| Wabquissit | west of the Quinebaug River |

# SOURCES & REFERENCES

Afable, Patricia O. & Madison S. Beeler. "Place Names". Pp. 185-199 in Ives Goddard (ed.), *Handbook of North American Indians* (vol. 17). Washington, DC: Smithsonian Institution, 1996.

Arnold, James N. *Vital Records of Rhode Island 1636-1850*, 21 vols. (Providence, 1891-1912)

Arnold, Samuel Greene. *History of The State of Rhode and Providence Plantations By Samuel Greene Arnold, Vol. I, 1636-1700*. New York: D. Appleton & Company, 346 & 348 Broadway, London: 16 Little Britain, 1859. http://www.hti.umich.edu/cgi/t/text/text-idx?sid=e9bd3b8241673407d6fe41 99d943b0f7&c=moa&idno=AFJ7769.0001.001&view=toc

_____. *History of The State of Rhode Island and Providence Plantations From The Settlement of The State, 1636, to The Adoption of The Federal Constitution, 1790 By Samuel Greene Arnold In Two Volumes, Vol. II, 1700-1790*. New York: D. Appleton & Company, 443 & 445 Broadway, London: 16 Little Britain, 1860. http://www.hti.umich.edu/cgi/t/text/text-idx?sid=e9bd3 b8241673407d6fe4199d943b0f7&c=moa&idno=AFJ7769.0002.001&view=toc

Aubin, George. *A Historical Phonology of Narragansett*. Providence, RI: Brown University. (Ph.D. Dissertation), 1972.

_____. *A Proto-Algonquian Dictionary*. Ottawa : National Museums of Canada, 1975.

Bartlett. See Rhode Island (Colony). *Records of the Colony of Rhode Island and Providence Plantations, in New England (1636-1792)*.

Bicknell, Thomas W. *Sowams*. New Haven, CT: Associated Publishers of American Records, 1908.

_____. *The History of The State of Rhode Island and Providence Plantations by Thomas Williams Bicknell; Assisted By an Able Board of Advisors*. 5 Vols. New York: The American Historical Society, 1920.

Bliss, Leonard. *The History of Rehoboth, Bristol County, Massachusetts; Comprising a History of the Present Towns of Rehoboth, Seekonk, and Pawtucket, From Their Settlement to the Present Time; Together With Sketches of Attleborough, Cumberland, and a Part of Swansey And Barrington, to the Time That They Were Severally Separated From the Original Town*. Boston : Otis, Broaders, & Co., 1836.

Bloomfield, Leonard. "Algonquian." In *Linguistic Structures in Native America.* H. Hoijer (ed.). New York: Viking Fund Publications, 1946.

Bragdon, Kathleen J. *Native People of Southern New England*, 1500-1650. Norman, OK: University of Oklahoma Press, 1996.

Bright, William (ed.). *Native American Placenames of The United States.* Norman, Okla.: University of Oklahoma Press, 2004.

Brinley, Francis. "Francis Brinley's Briefe Narrative of the Nanhiganset Countrey". *Publications of the Rhode Island Historical Society,* 8(2):69-96. Providence, 1900.

Brodhead, John Romeyn. *Documents Relative to the Colonial History of the State of New York, Procured in Holland, England and France by John Romeyn Brodhead, Esq., Agent,* trans. Edmund B. O'Callaghan, Berthold Fernow, Albany: Weed Parsons, 15 vols, 1856-87.

Church, Benjamin. *Entertaining Passages Relating to King Philip's War, Which Began In the Month of June, 1675; as Also of Expeditions, More Lately Made Against the Common Enemy, and Indians Rebels, in the Eastern Part of New England.* Thomas Church, comp. Boston: B. Green, 1716.

Cotton, Josiah. "Vocabulary of the Massachusetts (Natick) Indian Language. " Cambridge, MA: *Massachusetts Historical Society Collection, Serial 3, Vol. II,* 1830.

Des Barres, Joseph F. W. (Joseph Frederick Wallet), 1722-1824. A chart of the harbour of Rhode Island and *Narraganset* Bay. Surveyed in pursuance of directions from the Lords of Trade to His Majesty's Surveyor General for the northern district of North America. Published at the request of The Right Honourable Lord Viscount Howe. [London] , map 104 x 75 cm., 1776.

Edney, Matthew H. "The Anglophone Toponyms Associated with John Smiths 'Description' and Map of New England". Names: *The Journal of Onomastics,* Vol. 57, No. 4, 2009, 189-207.

Eliot, John. *The Holy Bible: Containing the Old Testament and New Translated into the Indian Language by John Eliot.* Cambridge, MA: Samuel Green and Marmaduke Johnson. (Second edition, 1685.), 1663.

_____. *The Indian Grammar Begun; or, an Essay to Bring The Indian Language  into Rules for the Help of Such as Desire to Learn the Same for the Furtherance of the Gospel Among Them.* Cambridge, MA: Marmaduke Johnson, 1666. Reprinted (abridged) in *Old South Leaflets* 3(57), Boston, 1896; also reprinted in *Massachusetts Historical Society Collection, Serial 2, Volume IX,* Boston, MA, 1822 (with notes by P.S. Duponceau, and an introduction and supplementary observations by John Pickering).

Gahan, Lawrence K. "Methods of Translation of Indian Place Names." *Bulletin of the Massachusetts Archaeological Society* 21:41-47, October, 1959.

_____. "Gleanings from the Indian Languages". *Bulletin of the Massachusetts Archaeological Society* 22(3 & 4):65-66, 1961.

Goddard, Ives. "Indian Place Names in Connecticut by James Hammond Trumbull." *International Journal of American Linguisitcs*, vol. 43, no. 2, April, 1977.

_____. "Eastern Algonquian Languages". Pp. 70-77 in Handbook of North American Indians, Vol. 15 (Northeast). Bruce G. Trigger,Vol. ed. Washington, D.C.: Smithsonian Institution, 1978.

_____. "Massachusett Phonology: A Preliminary Look." *In Papers of the Twelfth Algonquian Conference*, ed. William Cowan. Ottawa: Carlton University, pp. 57-105, 1981.

_____. "Time to Retire an Indian Place-Name Hoax." Letter to the Editor, *New York Times*, Saturday, Sect. 1, page 22, September 29, 1990. http://www.nytimes.com/1990/09/29/opinion/l-time-to-retire-an-indian-place-name-hoax 571390.html?n=Top/Reference/Times%20Topics/Subjects/I/Indians,%20American

_____ (Volume Editor). *Handbook of North American Indians*, vol. 17. Washington, DC: Smithsonian Institution, 1996.

_____ . "Linguist Sheds Some Light on Roots of Word 'Aquidneck'". Letter to the Editor, *The Newport (R.I.) Daily News*, p. A7, July 6-7, 2002.

_____ ."Endangered Knowledge: What We Can Learn From Native American Languages." *Anthronotes, Museum Of Natural History Publication For Educators* . Vol. 25 No. 2, Fall 2004. Washington, DC: Smithsonian Institution, 2004. http://anthropology.si.edu/outreach/anthnote/anthronotes_2004fall.pdf

Goddard, Ives and Kathleen J. Bragdon. *Native Writings in Massachusett*. (*Parts* 1,2). Philadelphia: The American Philosophical Society, 1988.

Goddard, Ives and Thomas Love. "Oregon, the Beautiful." *Oregon Hist. Quarterly*, vol. 105, no 2, 2004. http://www.historycooperative.org/journals/ohq/105.2/goddard.html

Gookin, Daniel. *Historical Collections Of The Indians Of New England: Of Their Several Nations, Numbers, Customs, Manners, Religion, And Government, Before The English Planted There*, 1792. Reprinted

Edition, Arno Press, 1972.

Hagenau, Walter P. *A Morphological Study of Narragansett Indian Verbs in Roger Williams'* <u>A Key into the Language of America</u>. Providence, RI: Brown University (M.A. Thesis), 1962.

Harriot, Thomas. *A Breife and True Report of the New Found Land of Virginia: The Complete 1590 Theodor De Bry Edition* . New York: Dover, 1972. plate XVI.

Huden, John C. *Indian Place Names of New England.* New York: Museum of the American Indian (Heye Foundation), 1962.

Kennicutt, Lincoln N. *Indian Names of Places in Plymouth, Middleborough, Lakeville and Carver.* Worcester: Commonwealth Press, 1909. http://www.archive.org/details/indiannamesofpla00kinni.

_____. *Indian Names of Places in Worcester County, Massachusetts.* Worcester: Commonwealth Press, 1911. http://www.archive.org/details/indiannamesplace00kinn.

LaFantasie, Glenn W., ed. *The Correspondence of Roger Williams.* 2 vols. Providence, Rhode Island: Brown University Press, 1988.

Little, Elizabeth A. "Nantucket Indian Place Names." *Historic Nantucket,* Vol 46, No. 4 p. 9-16, Fall 1997.

Little doe Fermino, Jessie. *An Introduction to Wampanoag Grammar.* Cambridge, Mass.: Massachusetts Institute of Technology. (Unpublished Masters Thesis), 2000.

Masthay, Carl. "New England Indian Place Names." In R.G. Carlson (ed.), *Rooted Like the Ashes: New England Indians and the Land.* (Revised Edition). Naugatuck, CT: Eagle Wing Press, Inc., 1987

Mayhew, Experience. "Letter of Exp. Mayhew, 1722, on the Indian Language". *New England Historical and Genealogical Register,* Vol. 39, pp. 10-17, 1722/1855.

Moondancer [Francis J. O'Brien, Jr.] & Strong Woman [Julianne Jennings]. *Understanding Algonquian Indian Words (New England).* Newport, RI: Aquidneck Indian Council, 2001. http://www.docstoc.com/profile/waabu

_____ . *Indian Grammar Dictionary for N-Dialect: A Study of* <u>A Key into the Language of America</u> *by Roger Williams, 1643.* Newport, RI: Aquidneck Indian Council, 2001. http://www.docstoc.com/profile/waabu

_____ . *Introduction to the Narragansett Language: A Study of A Key into the Language of America by Roger Williams, 1643.* Newport, Rhode Island: Aquidneck Indian Council, 2001a. http://www.docstoc.com/profile/waabu

_____ . *Cultural History of The Native Peoples of Southern New England : Voices from Past and Present.* Boulder, CO: Baüu Institute Press, 2007.

Morton, Nathaniel. *New-Englands Memorial* [1669]. Pp. 1-224 in *Chronicles of the Pilgrim Fathers.* John Mansfield, ed. New York: E.P. Dutton, 1910.

Moses, King. *King's Pocket-book of Providence, R.I.* Cambridge, Mass: Tibbitts, Shaw & Co.: Providence, RI, 1882.

Nichols, Benjamin R. "Index to Cotton's Ms. Vocabulary of the Massachusetts (Indian) language." Boston, MA: Manuscript of the Massachusetts Historical Society, 1882.

O'Brien, Frank Waabu [Francis J. O'Brien, Jr.] *American Indian Place Names in Rhode Island: Past & Present,* 2003. http://www.docstoc.com/profile/waabu; http://www.rootsweb.ancestry.com/~rigenweb/IndianPlaceNames.html

_____. *Bibliography for Studies of American Indians in and Around Rhode Island, 16ᵗʰ -21ˢᵗ Centuries:* Newport, Rhode Island: Francis J. O'Brien, Jr., 2004
http://www.docstoc.com/profile/waabu
http://www.rootsweb.ancestry.com/~rigenweb/IndianBibliography.html.

_____. *American Indian Studies in the Extinct Languages of Southeastern New England.* Newport, RI: Aquidneck Indian Council, 2009. http://www.docstoc.com/profile/waabu

_____. *Grammatical Studies in the Narragansett Language.* 2nd ed. Newport, RI: Aquidneck Indian Council, 2005. http://www.docstoc.com/profile/waabu

Parsons, Usher. *Indian Names of Places in Rhode-Island: Collected by Usher Parsons, M.D. for the R.I. Historical Society.* Providence, RI: Knowles, Anthony & Co., Printers, 1861.
[http://www.hti.umich.edu/cgi/t/text/text-idx?c=moa;cc=moa;sid=f23b083a 37776c62c74395a43b76c87b;rgn=main;view=text;idno=ACK0689.0001.001].

Pilling, James C. *Bibliography of the Algonquian Languages. Bureau of American Ethnology Bulletin* 13, Washington, 1891.

Potter, Elisha R. *The Early History of Narragansett: With An Appendix of Original Documents, Many of Which are Now for the*

305

*First Time Published.* 2ed. 1886. Providence: Marshall, Brown and Company, 1835.

Prince, J. Dyneley and Frank G. Speck . "Glossary of the Mohegan-Pequot Language". *American Anthropologist,* N.S., Vol. 6, No. 1, pp. 18-45, 1904.

Rhode Island (Colony). *Records of the Colony of Rhode Island and Providence Plantations, in New England (1636-1792).* John R. Bartlett, ed. 10 vols. Providence: A. Crawford Greene and Brothers, 1856-1865.

Rhode Island (Colony). *Early Records of the Town of Providence.* 22 vols. Printed under the Authority of the Providence City Council and City Record Commissioners. n.d.

Rhode Island (Colony). *The Early Records of the Town of Portsmouth.* 1 vol. Librarian of the Rhode Island Historical Society, ed. Providence, Rhode Island: E. L. Freeman & Sons, Publishers, 1901.

Rhode Island (Colony). *The Early Records of the Town of Warwick.* 1 vol. Librarian of the Rhode Island Historical Society, ed. Providence, Rhode Island: E. A. Johnson & Co. Publishers, 1926.

Rhode Island (Colony). *Records of the Island of Rhode Island, 1637–1663.* 1 vol. Providence, Rhode Island: Office of the Secretary of State, Rhode Island State Archives. (Assession Number C#00206.), n.d.

Rhode Island (Colony). *Ancient Records of the Colony of Rhode d (Gyles Record), 1638–1670.* 1 vol. Providence, Rhode Island: Office of the Secretary of State, Rhode Island State Archives. (Assession Number C#00207.), n.d.

Rhode Island (Colony). *Portsmouth Town Records, 1638–1700; 1639–1697.* 2 vols. Portsmouth, Rhode Island: Portsmouth City Clerk, n.d.

Rhode Island (Colony). *Rhode Island Colony Records, 1646–1851.* 30 vols. Providence, Rhode Island: Office of the Secretary of State, Rhode Island State Archives. (Assession Number C#00209.), n.d.

Rhode Island (Colony). *Rhode Island Land and Public Notary Records, 1648–1776.* 10 vols. Providence, Rhode Island: Office of the Secretary of State, Rhode Island State Archives. (Assession Number C#00481.), n.d.

Rhode Island (Colony). *Proceedings of the General Assembly, 1649–1723.* 9 vols. Providence, Rhode Island: Office of the Secretary of State, Rhode Island State Archives. (Assession Number C#00260.), n.d.

Rhode Island (Colony). *Records of Deeds, Agreements & Orders: Prop. of Narragansett, 1651–1703 (Fones Record).* 1 vol. Providence, Rhode Island: Office of the Secretary of State, Rhode Island State Archives.

(Assession Number C#00209.), n.d.

Rhode Island (Colony). *Body of Laws of the Colony of Rhode Island, 1663–1705. Acts & Resolves* 1 vol. Providence, Rhode Island: Office of the Secretary of State, Rhode Island State Archives. (Assession Number C#00208.), n.d.

Rhode Island (Colony). *Governor & Council Records, 1667–1753.* 1 vol. Providence, Rhode Island: Office of the Secretary of State, Rhode Island State Archives. (Assession Number C#00558.), n.d.

Rhode Island (Colony). *Governor & Council Records, 1667–1802.* Providence, Rhode Island: Office of the Secretary of State, Rhode Island State Archives. (Assession Number C#01185.), n.d.

Rhode Island (Colony). *Narragansett Indians: Documents Relating, 1709–1842.* Providence, Rhode Island. Office of the Secretary of State, Rhode Island State Archives. (Assession Number C#00213.), n.d.

Rhode Island (Colony). *Public Laws of Rhode Island, 1719, 1730-36, 1744-52, 1767, 1772, 1798-1810.* Providence, Rhode Island: Office of the Secretary of State, Rhode Island State Archives. (Assession Number C#00612.), n.d.

Rhode Island (Colony). *Petitions to the General Assembly, 1725–1867.* 72 vols. Providence, Rhode Island: Office of the Secretary of State, Rhode Island State Archives. (Assession Number C#00165.), n.d.

Rhode Island (Colony). *Public Acts & Resolutions of the Rhode Island General Assembly, 1728– 1996.* Providence, Rhode Island: Office of the Secretary of State, Rhode Island State Archives. (Assession Number C#00210.), n.d.

Rhode Island (Colony). *Committee Reports to Rhode Island General Assembly, 1728–1860.* 14 vols. Providence, Rhode Island: Office of the Secretary of State, Rhode Island State Archives. (Assession Number C#00261.), n.d.

Rhode Island (Colony). *Colonial and State Census: 1774, 1777, 1865, 1875, 1885, 1905, 1915, 1925, 1925, 1935.* Providence, Rhode Island: Office of the Secretary of State, Rhode Island State Archives, n.d.

*Rhode Island. Commission on Narragansett Indians Narragansett Indians, Commission on, Minute Book, 1880–1883.* 1 vol. Providence, Rhode Island. Office of the Secretary of State, Rhode Island State Archives. (Assession Number C#00241.), n.d.

*Rhode Island Historical Society Rhode Island Court Records Abstracts.* 2 vols. Providence, Rhode Island: Rhode Island Historical Society, 1922.

Rhode Island Historical Society. *Rhode Island Land Evidences 1648-1696,* Volume 1 Providence: R.I. Historical Society, 1921, 1970.     307

Rider, Sidney S. *The Lands of Rhode Island as They Were Known to Caunounicus and Miatunnomu When Roger Williams Came in1636: An Indian Map of the Principal Locations Known to the Nahigansets, and Elaborate Historical Notes.* Providence, Rhode Island, 1904.

Smith, D.H. and K. S. Smith. *"Personal Names."* Pp 200-221 in Handbook of North American Indians, Vol. 17 (Languages). Washington, DC: Smithsonian Institution, 1996.

Staples, William R. *Annals of the Town of Providence, from its Settlement, to the Organization of the City Government, in June, 1832 .* Providence: Knowles and Vose, 1843.

Strong Woman & Moondancer. "Bringing back our lost language," *American Indian Culture & Research Journal*, 1998, 22(3): 215- 227

Swanton, John R. *The Indian Tribes of North America. Bureau of American Ethnology Bulletin* 145. Washington, D.C., 1952.

Trigger, Bruce G. (Volume Editor). *Handbook of North American Indians*, Vol. 15 (Northeast). Washington, DC: Smithsonian Institution, 1978.

Trumbull, James H. "The Composition of Indian Geographic Names Illustrated from the Algonkin Langauges". *Connecticut Historical Society Collections* 2:3-51. Hartford, Conn, 1870.

_____. "On the Best Method of Studying the North American Languages". By J. Hammond Trumbull. *Trans. Am. Phil. Assoc.*, 1869-70. Hartford, 8,  pp. 55-79, 1871.

_____. "The Indian Tongue and its Literature as Fashioned by Eliot and Others." In *The Memorial History of Boston, Including Suffolk County, Massachusetts, 1630-1880.* J. Winsor (ed.). Boston: James R. Osgood, 1880.

_____. *Indian Names of Places etc., in and on the Borders of Connecticut: with Interpretations of Some of Them.* Hartford, CT: Lockwood & Brainerd, 1881 (Reprinted 1974).

_____. *The Memorial History of Hartford County.* 2 vols. Boston, 1886.

_____. *Natick Dictionary.* Bureau of American Ethnology 25. Washington, D.C., 1903 [http://gallica.bnf.fr/scripts/ConsultationTout.exe?O=0027474]

Trumbull, James H. and Charles J. Hoadly (eds.). *Public Records of the Colony of Connecticut, 1636-1776.* 15 volumes. Hartford, Ct.: State of Connecticut, 1850-1890.

U.S. Geological Survey & U.S. Board on Geographic Names. Geographic Names Information System (GNIS), the Nation's Official Geographic Names Repository. Reston, Virginia: U.S. Geological Survey, National Headquarters, 2002. (http://geonames.usgs.gov/geonames/stategaz/RI_deci)

- "The database is maintained and updated continuously. The database was established in 1976, and designated by the U.S. Board on Geographic Names, which is responsible by law for standardizing geographic name usage for the Federal Government, in 1987 as the only source for official geographic names. No Federal agency may add or change a geographic name on a Federal product without the name's presence in GNIS. There is an electronic maintenance program (since 1987) whereby appropriate Federal Agencies submit additions, corrections, and enhancement to the database. This program will soon be extended to the States, and is presently being tested in Florida and Delaware (2002)." (e-mail 4 DEC 02 from gnis_manager@usgs.gov)

H. F. Walling, O. Harkness, J. Hanson, and Library of Congress [Newport County (R.I.) - 1850: LC G&M land ownership maps on microfiche]. [Washington, D.C.]: LC G&M Division, [1983?]. Geography and Map Division. 28.5 x 38 in. Scale 1:42,500. Originally published 1850. PC 9894 [**Microfiche 583, no. 827**]

H. F. Walling, G. C. Brown, and Library of Congress. [Providence County (R.I.) - 1851: LC G&M land ownership maps on microfiche]. [Washington, D.C.]: LC G&M Division, [1983?]. Geography and Map Division. 2 sheets, 38.5 x 25.5 in. and 38.5 x 26.5 in. Originally published 1851. PC 9904 [**Microfiche 583, no. 830**]

Williams, Roger. *A Key into the Language of America:, or, an Help to the Language of the Natives in that Part of America called New-England. Together, with Briefe Observations of the Customes, Manners and Worships, etc. of the Aforesaid Natives, in Peace and Warre, in Life and Death. On all which are added Spirituall Observations, General and Particular by the Author of chiefe and Special use (upon all occasions) to all the English Inhabiting those parts; yet pleasant and profitable to the view of all men.* London: Gregory Dexter, 1643. [Reprinted, Providence: Narragansett Club, 1866, J. H. Trumbull (Ed.); *RI Historical Society Collections*, Vol. 1, 1877].

Wood, William. "Nomenclator". In *New Englands Prospect. A True, Lively, And Experimentall Description of That Part of America, Commonly Called New England: Discovering the State of That Countrie, Both as it Stands to Our New-Come English Planters; And to the Old Native Inhabitants. Laying Down That Which May Both Enrich the Knowledge of The Mind-Travelling Reader, or Benefit the Future Voyager.* London: Tho. Cotes, 1634. [Reprinted Moondancer (Francis J. O'Brien, Jr.) & Strong Woman (Julianne Jennings). *Understanding Algonquian Indian Words (New England)*. Newport, RI: Aquidneck Indian Council, 2001. http://www.docstoc.com/profile/waabu].

**Frank Waabu O'Brien** (Dr. Francis Joseph O'Brien, Jr.), also known as Moondancer, earned his Ph.D. at Columbia University. He has authored several books and Internet websites on the history, culture and language of the American Indians of southern New England. Waabu is former President of the Aquidneck Indian Council, and a member of the Abenaki Tribe (Sokoki and St. Francis Bands), and The Rhode Island Indian Council. He is also a member of the National Museum of the American Indian, Rhode Island Historical Society, and American Names Society. He is a disabled veteran from The Vietnam War Era, and makes his living as a career civil servant mathematician for The Department of Defense.

His previous book was *A Cultural History of the Native Peoples of Southern New England: Voices From Past and Present* (with Strong Woman), published by Bäuu Press. Frank Waabu's website is http://www.docstoc.com/profile/waabu.

www.ingramcontent.com/pod-product-compliance
Lightning Source LLC
Chambersburg PA
CBHW070341090426
42733CB00009B/1247